Gilded Age and Progressive Era

Primary Sources

Gilded Age and Progressive Era

Primary Sources

Rebecca Valentine

Lawrence W. Baker, Project Editor

U.X.L
A part of Gale, Cengage Learning

GALE
CENGAGE Learning

Detroit • New York • San Francisco • New Haven, Conn • Waterville, Maine • London

GALE
CENGAGE Learning™

Gilded Age and Progressive Era: Primary Sources

Rebecca Valentine

Project Editor
Lawrence W. Baker

Rights and Acquisitions
Margaret Abendroth, Emma Hull, Jackie Jones

Imaging and Multimedia
Dean Dauphinais, Lezlie Light, Michael Logusz

Product Design
Pamela Galbreath, Jennifer Wahi

Composition
Evi Seoud

Manufacturing
Rita Wimberley

LIBRARY OF CONGRESS CATALOGING-IN-PUBLICATION DATA

Valentine, Rebecca.
  Gilded Age and Progressive Era reference library / Rebecca Valentine; Lawrence W. Baker, project editor.
    v. cm.
  Includes bibliographical references zand index.
  Contents: [1] Almanac -- [2] Biographies -- [3] Primary sources.
  ISBN-13: 978-1-4144-0193-5 (set : alk. paper) --
  ISBN-10: 1-4144-0193-0 (set : alk. paper) --
  ISBN-13: 978-1-4144-0194-2 (Almanac : alk. paper) --
  ISBN-10: 1-4144-0194-9 (Almanac : alk. paper) --
  [etc.]
  1. United States -- History -- 1865-1921 -- Juvenile literature. 2. United States -- History -- 1865-1921 -- Biography -- Juvenile literature. 3. United States -- History -- 1865-1921 -- Sources -- Juvenile literature. 4. Almanacs, American -- Juvenile literature. I. Baker, Lawrence W. II. Title.
  E661.V35 2006
  973.8 -- dc22   2006022839

ISBN-13:

978-1-4144-0193-5 (set)
978-1-4144-0194-2 (Almanac)
978-1-4144-0195-9
  (Biographies)

978-1-4144-0196-6
  (Primary Sources)
978-1-4144-0197-3
  (Cumulative Index)

ISBN-10:

1-4144-0193-0 (set)
1-4144-0194-9 (Almanac)
1-4144-0195-7
  (Biographies)

1-4144-0196-5
  (Primary Sources)
1-4144-0197-3
  (Cumulative Index)

This title is also available as an e-book.
ISBN-13: 978-1-4144-1046-3, ISBN-10: 1-4144-1046-8
Contact your Gale sales representative for ordering information.

Printed in the United States of America
4 5 6 7 14 13 12 11 10 09

Contents

Reader's Guide

The Gilded Age and Progressive Era in American history blended so seamlessly into one another that they can hardly be thought of separately. The Gilded Age was a major turning point in the nation, as it marked the rise of industrialism (an economy based on business and industry rather than agriculture) and the decline of an economy based on agriculture. Roughly 1877 to 1900, the Industrial Revolution made celebrities of robber barons such as oil magnate John D. Rockefeller and railroad tycoon Cornelius Vanderbilt. It encouraged the growth of a middle class as more and more Americans became members of the working class. It fostered competition in business even as it grew through the questionable practices of forming trusts and monopolies, and it made unimaginable wealth for a handful while sending millions of others into unrelenting poverty.

The Gilded Age was a time of great discontent as angry workers gave birth to the labor movement and muckraking journalists such as Ida M. Tarbell exposed big business for what it really was. The 1890s was a decade of economic depression for the entire nation; American farmers and laborers were so desperate that they took the radical measure of forming their own political party, the Populist Party. In no other era in history has America been led by so many presidents that time seems to have forgotten, and yet the Gilded Age led directly to the Progressive Era, which was ushered in by one of the most passionate, deliberate, incorrigible presidents: Theodore Roosevelt.

The Progressive Era, approximately 1900 to 1913, was a time of great reform in a nation that was just beginning to understand who it was, who it no longer could be, and who it just might become, given the right circumstances. The temperance movement eventually led to Prohibition (when the Eighteenth Amendment banned the manufacture and sale of alcohol). Labor laws gave rights to workers, and concerned citizens such as child labor photographer Lewis Hine and photojournalist Jacob Riis used their talents to secure improved living and working conditions for the urban poor and their children.

America in the Progressive Era was a melting pot that included millions of immigrants from around the world. As cities became overpopulated with people living in poverty, those who could moved to the outskirts of town, and suburban America was born. Those who could not escape the city led lives of intense hardship and heartache, but their underpaid and underappreciated labor kept America's economy going, even through the Panic of 1907. Reformers such as Jane Addams and Hannah Solomon dedicated their lives to helping where help was most needed: in urban slums.

Coverage and features

Gilded Age and Progressive Era: Primary Sources shows through eighteen documents and collections of illustrations just how transitional the Gilded Age and Progressive Era were in U.S. history. Readers are provided with a firsthand account from a survivor of the *Titanic,* the doomed luxury liner. Excerpts from important legislation, including the Dawes Severalty Act, the American Antiquities Act, and the Chinese Exclusion Act, drive home the concept that America was still trying to determine its priorities, even as it protected its natural resources yet prohibited immigrants from seeking a better life.

Readers may peruse pages from various issues of the Modern Home Sears Catalog from the 1900s, which gave Americans, for the first time, the opportunity to choose, buy, and build their own homes, even if they were not wealthy. Charles Dana Gibson's "Gibson Girl" was the nation's original supermodel, and readers will come to understand why she meant so much to so many.

Each document featured in the *Primary Sources* volume includes the following components:

An **introduction** places the document and its author in a historical context.

"Things to remember while reading . . . " provides readers important background information and directs them to central ideas in the document or gallery of images.

"What happened next..." provides an account of subsequent events related to the subject of the document.

"Did you know..." provides significant and interesting facts about the document, author, or events discussed.

"Consider the following..." poses questions or offers students and teachers research and activity ideas about the material to encourage critical thought beyond the immediate scope of the primary source.

"For More Information" lists sources for further information on the author, topic, or document.

Other features of *Gilded Age and Progressive Era: Primary Sources* include numerous sidebars containing interesting and related information about people and events of the time. Approximately ninety black-and-white photographs and illustrations complement the text. In addition, each document is accompanied by a glossary running alongside the margin that defines terms, people, and ideas. The volume begins with a timeline of important events and dates and a "Words to Know" section, and concludes with a general bibliography and subject index of people, places, and events discussed throughout *Gilded Age and Progressive Era: Primary Sources.*

U•X•L Gilded Age and Progressive Era Reference Library

Gilded Age and Progressive Era: Primary Sources is just one component of a three-volume U•X•L Gilded Age and Progressive Era Reference Library. The other titles in this set are:

Gilded Age and Progressive Era: Almanac gives comprehensive coverage of these decades by examining them from political, social, and cultural perspectives. Unlike other periods in history, these were not so directly informed by major wars or other political events (though war was certainly a contributor to the times), but by other more socially centered influences. The *Almanac* paints the Gilded Age and Progressive Era as they were: times of great sorrow and grand luxury. The eleven chapters begin with a brief review of Reconstruction, when the United States rebuilt itself following the Civil War (1861–65). In doing so, readers understand just how tumultuous a time in history the Gilded Age was. From there, students are given a tour of the business of doing business, including the struggles within the new labor movement. Immigration and its impact on the nation are detailed as it occurred, from sea to sea. The *Almanac* gives readers an understanding of the myth of the Wild West versus its reality as it concerned Native Americans. Students may also analyze the plight not only of the late nineteenth century farmer, but also of the African American in the South who was emancipated but not truly freed. Populism leads to Progressivism as readers see how a change in one aspect of life—whether business, social, cultural, or political—affects every other.

Gilded Age and Progressive Era: Biographies presents profiles of twenty-five people important to the development of the Gilded Age and Progressive Era. The volume covers such key figures as politicians Grover Cleveland and Theodore Roosevelt; writers Mark Twain and Upton Sinclair; activists Ida B. Wells-Barnett and Booker T. Washington; and sports great Ty Cobb and musician Scott Joplin.

A cumulative index of all three titles in this set is also available.

Acknowledgments

My deep gratitude goes to copyeditor Theresa Murray; proofreader Amy Marcaccio Keyzer; the indexers from Factiva, a Dow Jones & Reuters Company; and typesetter ITC/International Typesetting & Composition. I would be remiss if I failed to thank Larry Baker, project editor extraordinaire, and my family, who made do with less of my attention for longer than they would have liked.

Special thanks are due for the invaluable comments and suggestions provided by U•X•L's Gilded Age and Progressive Era Reference Library advisors and consultants:

- Sally Collins, Library Media Specialist, Highland Park Middle School, Dallas, Texas
- Nina Levine, Library Media Specialist, Blue Mountain Middle School, Cortlandt Manor, New York
- Bernadette Monette, Library Media Specialist, Sacopee Valley High School, Hiram, Maine

Comments and suggestions

We welcome your comments on *Gilded Age and Progressive Era: Primary Sources* and suggestions for other topics in history to consider. Please write: Editors, *Gilded Age and Progressive Era: Primary Sources,* U•X•L, 27500 Drake Road, Farmington Hills, MI 48331-3535; call toll-free 800-877-4253; fax to 248-699-8097; or send e-mail via gale.cengage.com.

Timeline of Events

1873 Mark Twain publishes his novel titled *The Gilded Age;* this term is used as the name of the era characterized by robber barons and their ostentatious displays of wealth.

1877 The Industrial Revolution begins, shifting America's economic focus from one of agriculture to industry.

January 4, 1877 The original robber baron, Cornelius Vanderbilt, dies with an estate worth $100 million.

July–August 1877 The Great Railroad Strike takes place across the nation, after the Baltimore & Ohio Railroad had cut wages for a second time in one year. The strike soon spread throughout the nation, and federal troops were called in. It is the first major strike of a newly industrialized nation. Forty-five days later, the strikes were put down.

1878 Thomas Edison founds the Edison Electric Light Company. It puts rival companies out of business and becomes General Electric.

January 10, 1878 The "Anthony Amendment," named after women's rights pioneer Susan B. Anthony, is introduced to Congress. It requests giving women the right to vote.

April 12, 1878 Politician William "Boss" Tweed, the corrupt leader of New York's Tammany Hall, dies in prison. Political cartoonist Thomas Nast was largely credited with Tweed's arrest.

1879 California passes a law forbidding the employment of Chinese laborers.

September 1879 Terence V. Powderly becomes grand master workman and leader of the Knights of Labor, a powerful labor union.

1880 The National Farmers' Alliance is formed. Farmers find themselves in tragic circumstances due to drought and flood, high interest rates on loans, and unfair railroad rates.

1880 The U.S. population reaches 50.1 million. More than 6 million are foreign born.

1880 The Arts & Crafts movement begins, hailing a return to furniture and interior decoration based on simplicity.

1880 The Alaska gold rush begins.

1880 Andrew Carnegie monopolizes the steel industry.

1881 President Rutherford B. Hayes forbids the sale of alcoholic beverages at military posts. His wife had already acquired the nickname "Lemonade Lucy" for her refusal to serve alcohol in the White House.

1881 Native American rights activist Helen Hunt Jackson publishes *A Century of Dishonor.*

1881 Booker T. Washington founds the Tuskegee Normal and Industrial Institute.

March 4, 1881 U.S. representative James A. Garfield of Ohio becomes president; New York politician Chester A. Arthur is vice president.

May 1881 Kansas becomes the first state to outlaw the sale of liquor.

July 2, 1881 President James Garfield is shot in a Washington, D.C., train station. He dies in September; Vice President Chester A. Arthur becomes president.

July 14, 1881 Famous criminal Billy the Kid is shot and killed.

1882 John D. Rockefeller organizes the Standard Oil Trust. The trust gets him around the laws of each state and becomes the model for future corporations.

1882 The first parade is held in New York City in observance of Labor Day, as ten thousand workers take the day off to march.

1882 The first commercial electric light system is installed on Pearl Street in New York City.

1882 Congress sets restrictions on immigration standards. Exceedingly poor people, convicts, and those declared insane are no longer welcome at Ellis Island.

1882 Canadian journalist James Creelman interviews Chief Sitting Bull, who discusses how his people would rather roam the land and risk starvation and hardship than be forced to live on reservations.

May 6, 1882 The Chinese Exclusion Act passes. Chinese immigrants are no longer welcome in the United States. The law would be repealed ten years later.

1883 The Brooklyn Bridge is completed. After taking fourteen years to build, New Yorkers consider it the eighth wonder of the world.

1883 Frances Willard founds the World Woman's Christian Temperance Union.

1883 Jewish poet Emma Lazarus writes the poem "The New Colossus," which is engraved on a plaque and hung at the base of the Statue of Liberty.

January 16, 1883 The Pendleton Act is passed, transforming the Civil Service to an agency of qualified employees who must pass tests in order to be hired.

1884 The Home Life Insurance building in Chicago, Illinois, is constructed. It is the world's first skyscraper. It is also the first building to have a steel frame upon which floors and walls are hung.

November 1884 New York governor Grover Cleveland is elected president.

1886 Riots against the Chinese occur in Washington. At least four hundred Chinese are forced from their homes. Federal troops intervene to restore order.

1886 Samuel Gompers organizes the American Federation of Labor.

May 4, 1886 The Haymarket Square Riot takes place in Chicago, Illinois. About fourteen hundred people gather to protest police brutality against workers on strike. Nearly two hundred police arrive to break up the crowd. A bomb is thrown into the midst of the police. The nation begins to equate workers on strike with violent anarchists.

October 28, 1886 President Grover Cleveland accepts the Statue of Liberty from France and delivers his dedication address.

February 4, 1887 The Interstate Commerce Act becomes law. A commission is created to ensure fair and reasonable rates for freight carriers.

February 8, 1887 Congress passes the Dawes Severalty Act. Every Native American family is to be given 100 acres of land to farm.

1888 Congress establishes a Department of Labor.

1888 Susan B. Anthony founds the National Council of Woman of the United States.

1888 Theodore Roosevelt publishes *Ranch Life and the Hunting-Trail,* a collection of essays concerning life on the American Frontier.

January 12, 1888 The Schoolchildren's Blizzard claims the lives of between 250 and 500 immigrants on the Dakota-Nebraska prairie; most of them are children.

November 1888 Former U.S. senator Benjamin Harrison of Indiana is elected president.

1889 North Dakota, South Dakota, Montana, and Washington become states.

1889 Jane Addams opens Hull-House in Chicago, Illinois, the first social services system.

1889 Land in Oklahoma that was given to the Native Americans is opened to white settlers, furthering antagonizing the relationship between Native Americans and whites.

May 31, 1889 The Johnstown flood claims the lives of more than two thousand Pennsylvanians.

June 1889 Andrew Carnegie publishes his famous philosophy, the "Gospel of Wealth."

1890 The American Women's Suffrage Association merges with the National Women's Suffrage Association, bringing solidarity to the suffrage movement.

1890 The McKinley Tariff Act is passed, establishing record-high tariffs on many imported goods.

1890 Photojournalist Jacob Riis publishes *How the Other Half Lives,* a book that provides a glimpse into the lives and hardships of America's urban poor and reveals the squalor of New York City's tenement homes. At the time, Theodore Roosevelt was the police commissioner of New York. He was moved by Riis's exposé and joined in the efforts to clean up the city.

January 25, 1890 Journalist Nellie Bly completes her trip around the world, which took her seventy-two days, six hours, and eleven minutes.

July 2, 1890 The Sherman Anti-Trust Act is passed, making it unlawful for businesses to form trusts that prohibit competition.

July 10, 1890 Wyoming becomes a state; later, it becomes the first state to give women the right to vote.

July 14, 1890 The Sherman Silver Purchase Act is signed by President Benjamin Harrison. The law increased the amount of money in circulation in the economy, but it also put a serious strain on the federal gold reserve.

October 1, 1890 Yosemite Park is created. Congress set aside 1,500 square miles of reserved forest lands.

December 15, 1890 Chief Sitting Bull is fatally wounded by one of his own men.

December 29, 1890 The Massacre at Wounded Knee officially closes the American frontier.

1891 Thomas Edison receives a patent for the first motion picture camera.

February 22, 1891 Women's rights activist Frances Willard delivers a speech at the National Council on Women of the United States; she acknowledges the ideological differences within the women's rights movement and calls for unification.

1892 Conservationist John Muir helps establish the Sierra Club. He remains its president until his death in 1914.

1892 Nearly 2 million acres of Crow Indian reservation in Montana are given to white settlers.

1892 Lizzie Borden is accused of murdering her father and stepmother with an axe. Though later found not guilty, her alleged crime remains one of the country's great unsolved mysteries.

January 1, 1892 Ellis Island opens to become the port of entry for all immigrants entering America via the Atlantic Ocean.

June 29, 1892 Carnegie Steel workers are locked out, an event that began the Homestead Steel Strike, one of the bloodiest work strikes in industrial history.

July 1892 The Populist Party is formed.

1893 Hannah Solomon establishes the National Council of Jewish Women.

1893 Frederick Jackson Turner delivers his lecture called "The Significance of the Frontier in American History."

1893 Ida B. Wells publishes a pamphlet on racism for distribution at the Chicago World's Fair. "The Reason Why the Colored American Is Not in the World's Columbian Exposition" was written by Wells, reformer Frederick Douglass, and other activists, and includes information on lynching, unfair legislation, and the convict lease system as well.

March 1893 Grover Cleveland is inaugurated to serve his second term as president of the United States. He is the first president to serve non-consecutive terms.

May 1, 1893 The World's Columbian Exposition, also known as the Chicago World's Fair, opens.

May 4, 1893 The New York Stock Exchange crashes, beginning the worst economic depression in American history to that point. The economy would not begin to recover until 1896.

May 24, 1893 The Anti-Saloon League is founded in Oberlin, Ohio.

June 1893 President Grover Cleveland successfully calls upon Congress to repeal the Sherman Silver Purchase Act.

June 20, 1893 Eugene V. Debs establishes the American Railway Union, the first industrial union in the United States.

1894 Congress officially declares the first Monday of every September to be Labor Day. This declaration is a sign of the growing importance of and concern given to American labor.

1894 Charles Dana Gibson's first illustration of the All-American Girl appears in print. His "Gibson Girl" was the symbol of America's modern woman through World War I (1914–18).

March 25, 1894 Jacob Coxey leads one hundred men from Ohio to Washington, D.C., in protest of the economic depression and with a demand that the government aid its citizens by creating jobs. "Coxey's Army" grew to include more than five hundred men by the time they reached Washington on April 30. Some of the men were arrested for trespassing on the lawn of the Capitol.

May 11, 1894 Fifty thousand Pullman Palace Car Company employees strike in Chicago, Illinois. The strike eventually included railroad workers across the nation, and President Grover Cleveland called upon federal troops to break up the event. Violence erupted and many strikers were killed and wounded.

1895 Lillian Wald opens Henry Street Settlement House on New York's East Side.

1895 George Eastman introduces the first pocket Kodak camera.

1895 Suffragist Elizabeth Cady Stanton publishes the controversial book *Woman's Bible*.

May 18, 1896 In *Plessy v. Ferguson,* the U.S. Supreme Court approves racial segregation by upholding the "separate but equal" doctrine. Justice Henry Billings Brown writes the majority opinion, while Justice John Marshall Harlan writes the dissenting opinion.

July 9, 1896 William Jennings Bryan delivers his rousing "Cross of Gold" speech.

November 1896 Ohio governor William McKinley defeats former U.S. representative William Jennings Bryan of Nebraska in the presidential election.

1897 The Dingley Tariff is passed, raising tariffs to a new high of an average of 50 percent.

November 1, 1897 The Library of Congress is housed in its own building for the first time.

February 15, 1898 The *U.S.S. Maine* explodes and sinks, killing 266 crew members. This event triggers the Spanish-American War, which lasts for one hundred days.

July 7, 1898 America annexes Hawaii.

1899 President William McKinley advocates an "Open Door" policy with China.

1899 Southern regionalist writer Kate Chopin publishes her scandalous novel, *The Awakening*.

February 4, 1899 The Philippine-American War breaks out. America had purchased the Philippine Islands after defeating the Spanish in Cuba. But the Philippines did not want to go from being ruled by one country to being ruled by another, so they rebelled. The bloody war lasted until July 4, 1902, when America won and did its best to modernize the Philippines. The islands gained their independence in 1946.

1900 The average American family has three or four children, compared to 1800, when it included seven or eight.

1900 Ragtime becomes the most popular genre of music in America. It has its roots in African American music and features fast tempos with syncopated rhythms.

May 25, 1900 Congress passes the Lacey Act, which protects particular animals and their habitats and outlaws the interstate shipment of wildlife that has been hunted illegally.

June 1900 The Boxer Rebellion takes place in China and lasts until August.

1901 Steel magnate Andrew Carnegie sells his steel mill to U.S. Steel and becomes the world's wealthiest man.

1901 J. P. Morgan incorporates the United States Steel Company, giving America its first billion-dollar company.

1901 The Tenement House Act is passed, improving the construction and safety of New York City's housing for the poor.

September 5, 1901 President William McKinley is shot by immigrant Leon Czolgosz. Nine days later, McKinley dies from his wounds and Vice President Theodore Roosevelt is sworn in as president.

1902 President Theodore Roosevelt dissolves the Beef trust and the Northern Securities Company (a railroad monopoly).

1902 Suffragist Carrie Chapman Catt organizes the National American Woman Suffrage Association.

1902 Muckraker Ida Tarbell publishes the first chapter of her exposé on the Standard Oil Company.

May 12, 1902 Anthracite coal miners walk off their jobs in Pennsylvania. The strike lasted 164 days and ended when President Theodore Roosevelt intervened and appointed J. P. Morgan to arbitrate the dispute.

1903 The Women's Trade Union League is formed.

1903 Reformer and activist W. E. B. Du Bois publishes his famous treatise, *The Souls of Black Folk,* in which he challenges the philosophy of Booker T. Washington and proposes his own "Talented Tenth" philosophy.

December 17, 1903 Wilbur and Orville Wright make history by becoming the first humans to ever fly. Their first flight lasted 12 seconds and went a distance of 120 feet (3.7 meters).

1904 The National Child Labor Committee forms and works tirelessly to campaign for child labor laws.

1904 President Theodore Roosevelt initiates the building of the Panama Canal. The project would take ten years and thirty thousand workers to be completed; the canal opened for business on August 15, 1914.

1904 Breaker boys (boys aged 7 to 13 who worked in the coal mining industry) earn 45 to 50 cents for a day's work. Each work day lasted ten to twelve hours. Author Peter Roberts writes *Anthracite Coal Communities,* which includes a chapter titled "The

Boys in the Breakers." It details the working conditions and general lifestyle of the breaker boys.

February 8, 1904 Japan attacks Port Arthur and conducts a quick series of victorious attacks on Russian naval fleets, marking the start of the Russo-Japanese War. The war ended in defeat for Russia in 1905.

October 27, 1904 The New York subway opens.

1905 The Victrola disc player is first sold on the market; by 1911, this early version of the record player could be found in millions of homes across America.

March 3, 1905 President Theodore Roosevelt gives the Bureau of Forestry a new name: the Forest Service; he appoints conservationist Gifford Pinchot as its director. Under Pinchot's leadership, the country's forests grew from 56 million acres to 172 million acres.

1906 Upton Sinclair publishes his muckraking novel *The Jungle*. It is an immediate best-seller and leads to federal reform in the food industry.

1906 The Meat Inspection Act is passed, providing hygiene standards in the meatpacking industry.

1906 The Pure Food and Drug Act is passed, requiring manufacturers to label their products with a list of ingredients.

April 18, 1906 San Francisco experiences one of the most significant earthquakes of all time. Resulting fires burned for more than three days. Hundreds of thousands of the city's residents were left homeless, and the death toll ranged between five hundred and three thousand.

December 10, 1906 President Theodore Roosevelt accepts the Nobel Peace Prize for his peacekeeping efforts in negotiating an agreement between Russia and Japan.

1907 Several large businesses and banking institutions file bankruptcy, causing an economic crisis known as the Panic of 1907. The crisis lasted just a few weeks because President Theodore Roosevelt worked with financier J. P. Morgan to provide assistance to needy firms so they could avoid bankruptcy.

1908 Henry Ford introduces the Model T automobile.

1908 Sears, Roebuck & Co. begins selling home-building kits through the mail.

June 8, 1908 The American Antiquities Act is passed, giving the president of the United States the authority to designate specific lands as historic monuments, thereby giving them federal protection for the purposes of preservation.

July 26, 1908 The Federal Bureau of Investigation (FBI) is established.

November 1908 Former U.S. secretary of war William Howard Taft is elected president of the United States.

December 26, 1908 Jack Johnson becomes the first African American boxer to win the heavyweight championship.

1909 The National Association for the Advancement of Colored People (NAACP) is established.

April 6, 1909 Explorer Robert Peary becomes the first human to reach the North Pole.

1910 Hannah Solomon founds the Chicago Women's City Club.

1911 Baseball is known as "America's favorite pastime."

March 25, 1911 The Triangle Shirtwaist Factory fire claims the lives of 146 immigrant workers, most of them young girls. It is the largest industrial accident to date in the country. Numerous newspaper accounts cover the horrors the Triangle workers faced as a result of the fire.

1912 The Progressive, or "Bull Moose," Party is established. Former president Theodore Roosevelt becomes that party's presidential candidate in the 1912 election after losing the Republican Party nomination to incumbent president William Howard Taft.

April 9, 1912 President William Howard Taft creates the Federal Children's Bureau, which provided much-needed money to help maintain the health and well-being of children throughout the nation.

April 15, 1912 The ocean liner *Titanic* sinks into the Atlantic Ocean, killing 705 passengers. Survivor Ruth Dodge tells her story in a newspaper account shortly thereafter.

November 1912 New Jersey governor Woodrow Wilson is elected the twenty-eighth president of the United States by defeating incumbent president William Howard Taft and former president Theodore Roosevelt.

1913 The Armory Show is presented in New York and attended by five thousand people. The exhibit featured art by the Ashcan School artists as well as Pablo Picasso and Marcel Duchamp. America was appalled by the new style of painting, but within a few years, the Modernist style would be all the rage.

1913 Miners in Ludlow, Colorado, go on strike. Events lead to the murder of the miners and their families at the hands of federal troops on April 20, 1914.

December 23, 1913 President Woodrow Wilson passes the Federal Reserve Act, which calls for banking and currency reform.

July 28, 1914 World War I, also known as the Great War, begins. America remains neutral until April 2, 1917, when President Woodrow Wilson declares war on Germany. The war ends on November 11, 1918.

Words to Know

abolitionists: People who worked to end slavery.

aeronautics: The study of flight and aircraft.

Ancient Order of Hibernians (AOH): A Catholic organization formed in America in 1836. Some of its members came from various organizations created centuries earlier in Ireland. The purpose of the AOH was to help Irish Catholic immigrants settle in America and to defend them from persecution. One way the AOH defended its members was to keep its meetings and actions secret.

anti-Semitism: Prejudice against Jewish people.

antitrust: Against the formation of monopolies or trusts.

bimetallism: A movement of the late nineteenth century aimed at expanding the amount of money in circulation by backing it with silver as well as gold. Also sometimes referred to as free silver.

boomtowns: Towns that were built quickly by gold-seekers.

capitalism: An economic system in which property and goods are privately owned, produced, and distributed.

civil service: The system in which civilians work for various government agencies and departments. Before civil service reform, people were appointed to positions depending on whom they knew in politics and business. After reform, people had to apply for a job and pass examinations in order to qualify.

conspicuous consumption: The buying of expensive and unnecessary items as a way of displaying one's wealth.

coolies: Unskilled Asian workers.

deflation: A decline in the prices of goods and services.

Democratic Party: One of the oldest political parties in the United States. Originally linked with the South and slavery, it transformed into one associated with urban voters and liberal policies.

depression: A long-term economic state characterized by high unemployment, minimal investment and spending, and low prices.

electoral votes: The votes a presidential candidate receives for having won a majority of a state's popular vote (citizens' votes). The candidate who receives the most popular votes in a particular state wins all of that state's electoral votes. Each state receives two electoral votes for its two U.S. senators and a figure for the number of U.S. representatives it has (which is determined by a state's population). A candidate must win a majority of electoral votes (over 50 percent) in order to win the presidency.

farm tenancy: An arrangement whereby farmers who no longer owned their own farm farmed someone else's land and were paid a share of the harvest.

Gilded Age: The period in history following the Civil War and Reconstruction (roughly the final twenty-three years of the nineteenth century), characterized by a ruthless pursuit of profit, an exterior of showiness and grandeur, and immeasurable political corruption.

grubstake: To advance money or supplies to miners in exchange for a percentage of profits from any discoveries.

horizontal integration: A business strategy in which one company buys out the competition; commonly known as a merger.

immigration: Leaving one's country to live in another.

imperialism: The practice of one country extending its control over the territory, political system, or economic system of another country.

Indian agents: Representatives of the U.S. government who worked with Native Americans. Their responsibility was to resolve conflicts and take the Native Americans' concerns to the government.

industrialism: An economy based on business and industry rather than agriculture.

inflation: A rise in the prices of goods and services.

Interstate Commerce Act: Passed in 1887, this law created the Interstate Commerce Commission (ICC), the first federal regulatory agency. It was designed to address railroad abuse and discrimination issues.

Ku Klux Klan: An organization of whites who believed in white superiority and who terrorized African Americans and their supporters in the South after the Civil War.

labor strike: A refusal of workers to work until management agrees to improvements in working conditions, wages, and/or benefits.

labor union: A formally organized association of workers that advances its members' views on wages, work hours, and labor conditions.

Molly Maguires: A secret society of workers established in Ireland in the 1840s whose mission was to fight discrimination. Some of its members immigrated to America later in the century. The Mollies were blamed for violence in the coal regions, though evidence against them was nonexistent.

monopoly: A condition created when one company dominates a sector of business, leaving the consumer no choices and other businesses no possibility of success.

mortgage: A loan of money to purchase property, such as a farm. The property is used as security for repayment of the loan; that is, if the borrower fails to pay, the property is seized.

muckrakers: Journalists who exposed scandal in Gilded Age society. These scandals usually involved public figures and established institutions and businesses, and focused on social issues such as child labor, political corruption, and corporate crime. The term "muckraking" was coined by President Theodore Roosevelt in 1906.

Mugwumps: A breakaway group of the Republican Party whose goal was to return Ulysses S. Grant to the White House.

naturalization: The process by which a person becomes a citizen of a country other than the one in which he or she was born.

P

patent: A grant by the government of the ownership of all rights of an invention to its creator.

patronage system: Also known as the spoils system. In patronage, someone donates large sums of money to help ensure the election of a candidate. That candidate repays the favor by making job appointments or by passing and proposing legislation that safeguards the interests of the business or person who donated the money.

philanthropy: Community service, financial donations, and volunteerism to promote human well-being.

political boss: A politically powerful—and often corrupt—person who can direct a group of voters to support a particular candidate.

popular vote: The result of the total number of individual votes in an election.

port: For an immigrant, the point of entry into a country.

poverty line: The least amount of income needed to secure the necessities of life. If someone lives below the poverty line, he or she cannot afford to purchase the basics needed to live, such as food, shelter, or medical care.

Progressive Era: A period in American history (approximately the first twenty years of the twentieth century) marked by reform and the development of a national cultural identity.

prospector: An explorer looking for minerals, such as gold.

reform: Change intended to improve a situation.

Republican Party: One of the oldest political parties in the United States. Founded as an antislavery party in the mid-1800s, it transformed into one associated with conservative fiscal and social policies.

reservations: Specific land allotted to the Native Americans by the U.S. government, as part of the solution to the "Indian Problem." The tribes did not own the land, but they managed it. These areas were the only places the Native Americans were allowed to live in the nineteenth century.

robber barons: The negative label given to powerful industrialists who amassed personal fortunes during the late nineteenth century, generally through corrupt and unethical business practices.

rustlers: Cattle thieves.

"Separate but Equal" doctrine: A policy enacted throughout the South that theoretically promoted the same treatment and services for African Americans as for whites, but which required the two races to use separate facilities.

settlement house: A center that provides community services to the poor and underprivileged in urban areas.

severalty: Individual ownership of land, as opposed to tribal ownership.

sluice: A wooden trough for washing gold. Soil is shoveled into a steady stream of water. Gold and other larger particles get caught in the bottom. Smaller sluices called rockers were often used during the gold rush. These sluices could be rocked back and forth to hasten the process of separating the gold from the soil.

Smithsonian Institution: A government institution with most of its grounds located in Washington, D.C. It includes 16 museums, 7 research centers, and 142 million items in its collections.

socialism: An economic system in which the government owns and operates business and production as well as controls the distribution of wealth.

sojourners: Immigrants who planned to stay in the United States temporarily; they usually stayed for a particular season or for a pre-determined number of years before returning to their homeland.

Spanish-American War: A war fought in 1898 in Cuba. Cuba wanted independence from Spanish rule. The United States fought on the side of Cuba and beat Spain within three months.

stampeders: Gold-seekers.

stock: A share of ownership in a business.

strike: A work stoppage by employees in protest of unfair treatment.

strikebreakers: Companies or individual employees who provide work during a strike; sometimes called scabs.

suffrage: The right to vote.

tariffs: Taxes imposed on goods imported from other countries.

temperance: A movement that campaigned for the public to refrain from drinking alcohol.

transcontinental railroad: The railroad system that traveled across the entire United States; this included five routes through the West. The last stake was driven into the railroad on May 10, 1869.

trust: The concept of several companies banding together to form an organization that limits competition by controlling the production and distribution of a product or service.

vertical integration: A business strategy in which one person or company is involved in more than one phase of production of a product or service, making the production process more efficient and, thereby, increasing the amount of production and level of profit.

wages system: An economic system in which people rely on other people to earn a living. Employees are paid money for their services.

Yukon: One of Canada's extreme northwest territories. It was the site of a gold rush in the 1880s. Sixty percent of the territory's population lives in its capital city, Whitehorse.

Gilded Age and Progressive Era

Primary Sources

U.S. Congress

Excerpt from the Chinese Exclusion Act; passed into law on May 6, 1882
Available at OurDocuments.gov *(Web site)*

"A disorderly Chinaman is rare, and a lazy one does not exist."

— Mark Twain, 1872

Chinese immigrants (people admitted to a foreign country to become legal citizens of that country) crossed the Pacific Ocean by the thousands in the mid-1800s. The event that sparked such massive migration was the 1849 California gold rush. Prior to that time, Chinese emigrated in smaller numbers, and they were favorably welcomed when they landed at Angel Island in San Francisco. Angel Island was the detention center for those immigrants coming to America's western shores. It was nicknamed the "Ellis Island of the west." (Ellis Island was the immigration processing center located in New York; see Chapter 3.)

The majority of the early Chinese immigrants were men. Most were successful businessmen. Those who were not businessmen brought with them other beneficial skills. These men were fishermen, artists, craftsmen, restaurant owners, or innkeepers. They quickly became known as dependable, hard-working citizens.

San Francisco was home to about twenty-five thousand Chinese by 1851; more than half the population of the United States was in that region. No longer primarily a skilled group of immigrants, the Chinese who came to the United States with the start of the gold rush were mostly unskilled laborers. They prospected for gold for themselves or sold their labor to other miners. Many Chinese were sojourners (people who came to another country temporarily to work and return home with money). A great number of them, however, discovered their chances for success were greater in San Francisco than they had been in their

Angel Island, located in San Francisco, was the West Coast immigration station of the United States from 1910 to 1940.
© CORBIS.

homeland. They opened businesses such as laundries and restaurants. During the gold rush years, they were guaranteed business. After the gold rush, many Chinese immigrants found work in railroad construction for the Central Pacific Railroad. The work was physically brutal and dangerous; hundreds of men died building the Transcontinental Railroad. Although ten thousand Chinese labored for the Central Pacific Railroad in the 1860s, they were never publicly recognized for their contribution. No Chinese workers appear in a famous group photo taken at Promontory Point in Utah, where the eastern track met with the western track.

Those who did not work for the railroad found low-paying industrial or agricultural jobs. These unskilled workers were referred to as "coolies" (derived from words from various languages that mean "hired laborers"), and American-born citizens came to resent their presence. They believed coolies were taking jobs from them, yet the jobs these Chinese immigrants took were those no native-born workers would accept, because they were dangerous, difficult, low-paying, or all three. Hatred of the Chinese intensified as American companies hired them while other workers were without jobs.

As anti-Chinese sentiment spread, violence toward the immigrants increased. In 1862, eighty-eight Chinese were reported murdered, a figure many historians say is inaccurately low. The Chinese did not want to further antagonize authorities, so they probably did not report every incident. When jobs became scarce even for skilled laborers, the immigrants organized the Chinese Consolidated Benevolent Association, a group of organizations better known as the Chinese Six Companies that acted as a clearinghouse where the Chinese would contract for work with American companies. Even with this organized labor activity, work became hard to find as Americans became more hateful. Many Chinese resorted to work as gardeners or domestic (household) servants.

American hatred was fueled by more than just resentment over jobs. As a society, America prided itself on its moral values. The Chinese immigrants had values and customs that differed from those of Americans. As a way of surviving in a foreign land without losing their cultural identity, the Chinese formed their own city-within-a-city, called Chinatown. Chinatowns were built all over the country, wherever a large Chinese population existed. These little cities operated completely independent of their surroundings. Everything the Chinese needed to survive and maintain their own traditions existed within the boundaries of Chinatown. Like other areas in cities, Chinatown offered activities of questionable morality, such as prostitution (selling sex) and gambling. Even as American-born citizens enjoyed these pastimes in Chinatown, they blamed the Chinese for being an immoral race.

In 1870, Congress passed the Naturalization Act. Naturalization is the process by which an immigrant becomes a legal citizen of a foreign country. During the early nineteenth century, immigrants from any country could become United States citizens. In a direct effort to cut down on the number of Chinese immigrants coming to America, the Naturalization Act restricted citizenship to "white persons and persons of African descent." No longer were Chinese immigrants eligible for legal citizenship.

That law was only the beginning of America's immigration restriction laws. On May 6, 1882, President Chester A. Arthur (1829–1886; served 1881–85) signed into law the Chinese Exclusion Act. This law forbid Chinese laborers from emigrating to the United States for ten years.

Mark Twain on Chinese Immigrants

December 16, 1885, Puck *magazine illustration shows humorist and writer Mark Twain (Samuel Clemens) speaking to an audience.* THE LIBRARY OF CONGRESS.

Mark Twain (Samuel Clemens, 1835–1910) was, above all others, the writer who exemplified the Gilded Age (roughly 1877–99). In fact, he was the one who coined the term "Gilded Age," when he titled his first novel-length work *The Gilded Age.* The Gilded Age was the period in history following the Civil War and Reconstruction (roughly the final twenty-three years of the nineteenth century), characterized by a ruthless pursuit of profit, an exterior of showiness and grandeur, and immeasurable political corruption.

Twain quickly became known for his sharp wit and social criticism. In 1872, he published a book titled *Roughing It,* in which he included comments about American sentiment toward Chinese immigrants. As was true in many cases, Twain was critical of America's behavior and attitude. What follows is an excerpt from *Roughing It:*

They are a harmless race when white men either let them alone or treat them no worse than dogs; in fact they are almost entirely harmless anyhow, for they seldom think of resenting the vilest insults or the cruelest injuries. They are quiet, peaceable, tractable [easily managed], free from drunkenness, and they are as industrious [productive] as the day is long. A disorderly Chinaman is rare, and a lazy one does not exist. So long as a Chinaman has strength to use his hands he needs no support from anybody; white men often complain of want of work, but a Chinaman offers no such complaint; he always manages to find something to do. He is a great convenience to everybody—even to the worst class of white men, for he bears the most of their sins, suffering fines for their petty thefts, imprisonment for their robberies, and death for their murders. Any white man can swear a Chinaman's life away in the courts, but no Chinaman can testify against a white man. Ours is the "land of the free"—nobody denies that—nobody challenges it. (Maybe it is because we won't let other people testify.) As I write, news comes that in broad daylight in San Francisco, some boys have stoned an inoffensive Chinaman to death, and that although a large crowd witnessed the shameful deed, no one interfered.

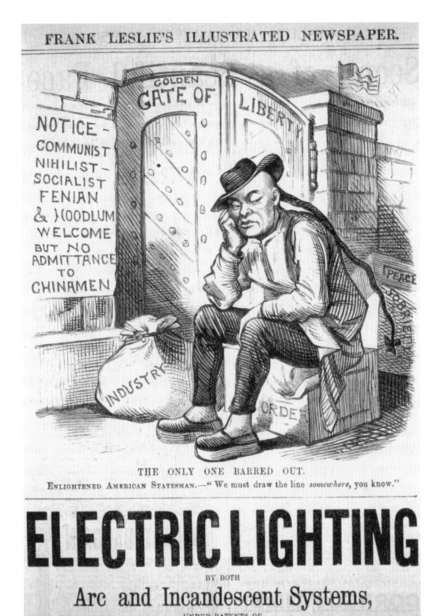

FRANK LESLIE'S ILLUSTRATED NEWSPAPER.

GOLDEN GATE OF LIBERTY

NOTICE —
COMMUNIST
NIHILIST —
SOCIALIST
FENIAN
& HOODLUM
WELCOME
BUT NO
ADMITTANCE
TO
CHINAMEN

PEACE TOBRAE

INDUSTRY

ORDER

THE ONLY ONE BARRED OUT.
ENLIGHTENED AMERICAN STATESMAN.—"We must draw the line *somewhere*, you know."

ELECTRIC LIGHTING

BY BOTH

Arc and Incandescent Systems,

UNDER PATENTS OF

WESTON, MAXIM, FARMER

Frank Leslie's Illustrated Newspaper *editorial cartoon criticizes the Chinese Exclusion Act. The cartoon caption is "The Only One Barred Out."* THE LIBRARY OF CONGRESS.

Things to remember while reading the excerpt from the Chinese Exclusion Act:

- Chinese immigrants already living in America at the time of passage of the act were allowed to remain in the country.

- Chinese businessmen and those in skilled trades were not barred from entering the United States under the Exclusion Act, but they could never become legal citizens. This meant they had no legal protection or the right to vote.
- The South was home to a large Chinese immigrant population, where laborers worked primarily in agriculture. The most violent opposition to the Chinese began in the South, where Americans historically believed themselves to be superior to any other race.

• • •

Excerpt from the Chinese Exclusion Act

An Act to execute certain treaty stipulations relating to Chinese.

Whereas in the opinion of the Government of the United States the coming of Chinese laborers to this country endangers the good order of certain **localities** within the territory thereof: Therefore,

Localities: Areas.

Be it enacted by the Senate and House of Representatives of the United States of America in Congress assembled, That from and after the expiration of ninety days next after the passage of this act, and until the expiration of ten years next after the passage of this act, the coming of Chinese laborers to the United States be, and the same is hereby, suspended; and during such suspension it shall not be lawful for any Chinese laborer to come, or having so come after the expiration of said ninety days to remain within the United States.

Master: Commander.

Vessel: Boat or ship.

Misdemeanor: Crime.

SEC. 2. That the **master** of any **vessel** who shall knowingly bring within the United States on such vessel, and land or permit to be landed, any Chinese laborer, from any foreign port or place, shall be deemed guilty of a **misdemeanor,** and on conviction thereof shall be punished by a fine of not more than five hundred dollars for each and every such Chinese laborer so brought, and may be also imprisoned for a term not exceeding one year.

Foregoing: Previously mentioned.

SEC. 3. That the two **foregoing** sections shall not apply to Chinese laborers who were in the United States on the seventeenth day of November, eighteen hundred and eighty, or who shall have come into the same before the expiration of ninety days next after the passage of this act, and who shall produce to such master before going on board such vessel, and shall produce to the collector of the port in the United States at which such vessel shall arrive, the evidence hereinafter in this act required of his being one of the laborers in this section mentioned; nor shall the two foregoing sections apply to the case of any master whose vessel, being bound to a port not within the United States, shall come within the jurisdiction of the United States by reason of being in distress or in stress of weather, or touching at any port of the United States on its voyage to any foreign port or place: Provided, That all Chinese laborers brought on such vessel shall depart with the vessel on leaving port.

SEC. 4. That for the purpose of properly identifying Chinese laborers who were in the United States on the seventeenth day of November eighteen hundred and eighty, or who shall have come into the same before the expiration of ninety days next after the passage of this act, and in order to furnish them with the proper evidence of their right to go from and come to the United States of their free will and accord, as provided by the **treaty** between the United States and China dated November seventeenth, eighteen hundred and eighty, the collector of **customs** of the district from which any such Chinese laborer shall depart from the United States shall, in person or by deputy, go on board each vessel having on board any such Chinese laborers and cleared or about to sail from his district for a foreign port, and on such vessel make a list of all such Chinese laborers, which shall be entered in registry-books to be kept for that purpose, in which shall be stated the name, age, occupation, last place of residence, physical marks of peculiarities, and all facts necessary for the identification of each of such Chinese laborers, which books shall be safely kept in the custom-house; and every such Chinese laborer so departing from the United States shall be entitled to, and shall receive, free of any charge or cost upon application therefore, from the collector or his deputy, at the time such list is taken, a certificate, signed by the collector or his deputy and attested by his seal of office, in such form as the Secretary of the Treasury shall **prescribe,** which certificate shall contain a statement of the name, age, occupation, last place of residence, personal description, and facts of identification of the Chinese laborer to whom the certificate is issued, corresponding with the said list and registry in all particulars. In case any Chinese laborer after having received such certificate shall leave such vessel before her departure he shall deliver his certificate to the master of the vessel, and if such Chinese laborer shall fail to return to such vessel before her departure from port the certificate shall be delivered by the master to the collector of customs for cancellation. The certificate herein provided for shall entitle the Chinese laborer to whom the same is issued to return to and re-enter the United States upon producing and delivering the same to the collector of customs of the district at which such Chinese laborer shall seek to re-enter; and upon delivery of such certificate by such Chinese laborer to the collector of customs at the time of re-entry in the United States said collector shall cause the same to be filed in the custom-house and duly canceled.

SEC. 5. That any Chinese laborer mentioned in section four of this act being in the United States, and desiring to depart from the United States by

Treaty: Agreement.

Customs: Money collected as taxes.

Prescribe: Recommend.

land, shall have the right to demand and receive, free of charge or cost, a certificate of identification similar to that provided for in section four of this act to be issued to such Chinese laborers as may desire to leave the United States by water; and it is hereby made the duty of the collector of customs of the district next adjoining the foreign country to which said Chinese laborer desires to go to issue such certificate, free of charge or cost, upon application by such Chinese laborer, and to enter the same upon registry-books to be kept by him for the purpose, as provided for in section four of this act.

Execution: Carrying out.

SEC. 6. That in order to the faithful **execution** of articles one and two of the treaty in this act before mentioned, every Chinese person other than a laborer who may be entitled by said treaty and this act to come within the United States, and who shall be about to come to the United States, shall be identified as so entitled by the Chinese Government in each case, such identity to be evidenced by a certificate issued under the authority of said government, which certificate shall be in the English language or (if not in the English language) accompanied by a translation into English, stating such right to come, and which certificate shall state the name, title or official rank, if any, the age, height, and all physical peculiarities, former and present occupation or profession, and place of residence in China of the person

Conformably: Similar.

to whom the certificate is issued and that such person is entitled, **conformably** to the treaty in this act mentioned to come within the United States.

Prima facie: Assumed to be true.

Such certificate shall be **prima-facie** evidence of the fact set forth therein, and shall be produced to the collector of customs, or his deputy, of the port in the district in the United States at which the person named therein shall arrive.

SEC. 7. That any person who shall knowingly and falsely alter or substitute any name for the name written in such certificate or forge any such

Utter: Put into circulation.

certificate, or knowingly **utter** any forged or fraudulent certificate, or falsely

Personate: Represent.

personate any person named in any such certificate, shall be deemed guilty of a misdemeanor; and upon conviction thereof shall be fined in a sum not exceeding one thousand dollars, and imprisoned in a penitentiary for a term of not more than five years.

SEC. 8. That the master of any vessel arriving in the United States from any foreign port or place shall, at the same time he delivers a **manifest** of

Manifest: List.

the cargo, and if there be no cargo, then at the time of making a report of the entry of the vessel pursuant to law, in addition to the other matter required to be reported, and before landing, or permitting to land, any Chinese passengers, deliver and report to the collector of customs of the district in which such vessels shall have arrived a separate list of all Chinese passengers taken on board his vessel at any foreign port or place, and all such passengers on board the vessel at that time. Such list shall show the names of such passengers (and if **accredited** officers of the Chinese Government traveling on the business of that government, or their servants, with a note of such facts), and the names and other particulars, as shown by their respective certificates; and such list shall be sworn to by the master in the manner required by law in relation to the manifest of the cargo. Any willful refusal or neglect of any such master to comply with the provisions of this section shall incur the same penalties and **forfeiture** as are provided for a refusal or neglect to report and deliver a manifest of the cargo.

SEC. 9. That before any Chinese passengers are landed from any such line vessel, the collector, or his deputy, shall proceed to examine such passenger, comparing the certificate with the list and with the passengers; and no passenger shall be allowed to land in the United States from such vessel in violation of law.

SEC. 10. That every vessel whose master shall knowingly violate any of the provisions of this act shall be deemed **forfeited** to the United States, and shall be liable to **seizure** and **condemnation** in any district of the United States into which such vessel may enter or in which she may be found.

SEC. 11. That any person who shall knowingly bring into or cause to be brought into the United States by land, or who shall knowingly aid or **abet** the same, or aid or abet the landing in the United States from any vessel of any Chinese person not lawfully entitled to enter the United States, shall be deemed guilty of a misdemeanor, and shall, on conviction thereof, be fined in a sum not exceeding one thousand dollars, and imprisoned for a term not exceeding one year.

SEC. 12. That no Chinese person shall be permitted to enter the United States by land without producing to the proper officer of customs the certificate in this act required of Chinese persons seeking to land from a vessel. And any Chinese person found unlawfully within the United States shall be caused to be removed therefrom to the country from **whence** he came, by direction of the President of the United States, and at the cost of the United States, after being brought before some justice, judge, or commissioner of a court of the United States and found to be one not lawfully entitled to be or remain in the United States.

SEC. 13. That this act shall not apply to diplomatic and other officers of the Chinese Government traveling upon the business of that government, whose credentials shall be taken as equivalent to the certificate in this act mentioned, and shall exempt them and their body and household servants from the provisions of this act as to other Chinese persons.

SEC. 14. That hereafter no State court or court of the United States shall admit Chinese to citizenship; and all laws in conflict with this act are hereby **repealed**.

Accredited: Given official approval.

Forfeiture: Fines.

Forfeited: Surrendered.

Seizure: Confiscation.

Condemnation: Disapproval.

Abet: Help.

Whence: Where.

Repealed: Abolished.

Construed: Understood.

SEC. 15. That the words "Chinese laborers", wherever used in this act shall be **construed** to mean both skilled and unskilled laborers and Chinese employed in mining.

• • •

What happened next...

The enforcement of the Chinese Exclusion Act sparked an illegal immigration movement that involved an Underground Railroad, similar to that used by African American slaves earlier in the century. Natural-born Americans and Chinese immigrants already in the United States worked together to smuggle Chinese across the border through Texas. Once in Texas, those illegal immigrants attended a secret school that taught them enough English to help them find work. As important as they were before 1882, Chinatowns took on an even more central role for immigrants, providing them with immediate and necessary shelter and work.

The act was renewed for another ten years in 1892, and it became permanent in 1904. Despite passage of the act, America's Chinese population continued to grow. It reached its peak in 1890, with approximately 107,488 Chinese living in America. China became America's ally in World War II (1939–45), and the ban was lifted in 1943. At that time, Chinese were subject to the same immigration laws as any other immigrant group. Most of the Chinese who came to the United States after the war were women, many of them wives of Chinese men already living in America.

Did you know...

- In 1890, the ratio of Chinese males to females was 27:1. Those immigrants lived in what is known as a bachelor (single male) society. The only reason the Chinese American population was sustained was through illegal immigration, which brought to the States thousands of Chinese women.
- A law known as the Scott Act was passed in 1888. The act, named after U.S. representative William Scott (1828–1891) of Pennsylvania, forbid any Chinese already living in the States to return to their homeland. As a result, thousands of Chinese families were permanently separated and would never see one another again.

- Chinatowns in the 1800s were often overcrowded, crime-ridden slums. Restoration led to a renewed interest in these cultural centers located in big cities, and they became profitable tourist destinations in the mid-1900s.

Consider the following...

- What are the similarities between illegal Chinese immigration of the late nineteenth century and the illegal immigration situation in current society? What are the differences?
- How could the federal government prevent the conflicts between Americans and Chinese immigrants?
- How did the preponderance of Chinese male immigrants contribute to the misconceptions Americans had of the immigrants and Chinese culture in general?

For More Information

BOOKS

Chang, Iris. *The Chinese in America: A Narrative History.* New York: Viking, 2003.

Daniels, Roger. *American Immigration: A Student Companion.* New York: Oxford University Press, 2001.

Gillenkirk, Jeff, and James Motlow. *Bitter Melon: Inside America's Last Rural Chinese Town.* Berkeley, CA: Heydey Books, 1993.

Lingen, Marissa K. *Chinese Immigration.* Philadelphia: Mason Crest Publishers, 2004.

McClain, Charles J. *In Search of Equality: The Chinese Struggle Against Discrimination in Nineteenth-Century America.* Berkeley: University of California Press, 1996.

Miscevic, Dusanka, and Peter Kwong. *Chinese Americans: The Immigrant Experience.* Westport, CT: Hugh Lauter Levin Associates, 2000.

Peffer, George Anthony. *If They Don't Bring Their Women Here: Chinese Female Immigration Before Exclusion.* Champaign: University of Illinois Press, 1999.

Yin. *Coolies.* New York: Philomel Books, 2001.

WEB SITES

"Chinese Exclusion Act." *Digital History.* http://www.digitalhistory.uh.edu/database/article_display.cfm?HHID=419 (accessed on July 14, 2006).

"Immigration, the Journey to America: The Chinese." *Thinkquest.org.* http://library.thinkquest.org/20619/Chinese.html (accessed on July 14, 2006).

Library of Congress. "Mark Twain's Observations About Chinese Immigrants in California." *American Memory: Rise of Industrial America, 1876–1900: Chinese*

Immigration to the United States, 1851–1900. http://memory.loc.gov/learn/features/timeline/riseind/chinimms/twain.html (accessed on July 14, 2006).

Lum, Lydia. "Angel Island: Journeys Remembered by Chinese Houstonians." *HoustonChronicle.com.* http://www.chron.com/content/chronicle/special/angelisland/intro.html (accessed on July 14, 2006).

"Transcript of Chinese Exclusion Act (1882)." *OurDocuments.gov.* http://www.ourdocuments.gov/doc.php?doc=47&page=transcript (accessed on August 9, 2006).

2

Sitting Bull

Remarks made to journalist James Creelman
  Originally published in On the Great Highway: The Wanderings and Adventures
    of a Special Correspondent, *1901*

"We have never dreamed of making white men live as we live."

Although conflicts between Native American tribes and white settlers had been common since the 1600s, the number and intensity of battles increased after the mid-1800s. The wars that occurred between 1866 and 1890 are known as the Plains Indian Wars and took place west of the Mississippi River.

Unlike some other tribes, Plains tribes (Native American tribes living in an area extending from the Mississippi River to the Rocky Mountains) were mostly peaceful. As increasingly large numbers of white settlers moved to tribal lands, Native Americans became angry. The settlers slaughtered once-plentiful buffalo herds into near extinction. This was a major threat to Plains tribes' way of life because they depended on the buffalo for food, clothing, and weapons. Historians have recorded fifty-two ways the tribes found to use the buffalo. The Plains Native Americans had built their existence around the mighty buffalo, which has been estimated to have been nearly sixty million strong before settlers arrived. By the end of the nineteenth century, there were fewer than one thousand.

The settlers caused other problems for the Native Americans as well. Railroads interfered with tribal hunting rituals and brought settlers to the West in larger numbers than the U.S. federal government had anticipated. With the completion of the Transcontinental Railroad in 1862, East now connected with West, and the traditional way of life enjoyed by Plains tribes was destroyed.

The federal government's method for dealing with the "Indian problem" was to sign treaties, or agreements. Most of these treaties were signed between 1850 and 1871. At that time, a law was passed forbidding the use of treaties with Native Americans. A total of 339 treaties were signed into law, but because of the unexpected number of settlers wanting to live in the West, the majority of those treaties were eventually broken by the government.

One of the Plains tribes was the Lakota, who arrived in the Black Hills of the Dakotas around 1775. This region of the Great Plains was considered sacred by many tribes and was off-limits to settlement according to the Fort Laramie Treaty of 1868. When gold was found in the Black Hills, miners and prospectors rushed by the thousands, hoping to strike it rich. The Lakota fought back in an effort to protect their lands. When they refused the federal government's offer to buy the Black Hills, the treaty was set aside. The commissioner of Indian Affairs decreed that any Lakota not settled on reservations (areas of land specified by the government for Native American settlement) by January 31, 1876, would be considered hostile.

Lakota chief Sitting Bull (1831–1890) and his people did not obey the government's orders to evacuate the Black Hills. Sitting Bull had a vision of soldiers dropping into the Lakota camp from the sky. Lakota war chief Crazy Horse (1849–1877) acted on his friend's vision and set out to battle the cavalry with five hundred warriors. Crazy Horse and his men were victorious, and to celebrate, the Lakota moved their camp to the valley of the Little Bighorn River. Here another three thousand Native Americans who left their reservations to follow Sitting Bull joined them. On June 25, General George Armstrong Custer (1839–1876) led the Seventh Cavalry in an attack on the Lakotas. The Battle of Little Bighorn resulted in the death of Custer and all 209 of his troops. The public was outraged.

The cavalry wanted revenge and spent the next couple years pursuing the Lakota, who had split up after the attack at Little Bighorn. Although many chiefs surrendered, Sitting Bull refused. As the years passed, the tribes suffered from starvation and disease. Many Native Americans died. On July 19, 1881, Sitting Bull surrendered. Because of the chief's ability to inspire his people, the government took the precautionary measure of keeping him a prisoner of war for two years at Fort Randall in South Dakota.

Sitting Bull continued to generate interest throughout the country. James Creelman (1859–1915) was a Canadian-born journalist whose

General George Custer fights in the middle of the Battle of Little Bighorn, also known as Custer's Last Stand. © CORBIS.

sense of adventure took him around the world. He and his family moved to New York in 1872, and it was there he became determined to be a writer. Creelman's willingness to take personal risks to get a good story led him to travel the globe covering wars and political conflicts. One of his most famous interviews was with Sitting Bull in 1882.

Things to remember while reading Sitting Bull's remarks:

- The job of any Native American chief is to protect his tribe and see that it remains healthy. Sitting Bull was completely unable to do his job, which must have been a great source of shame and regret.
- Sitting Bull's courage was legendary throughout the country. During a confrontation with soldiers in 1872, he led four fellow warriors into the middle of battle, sat down, and shared a pipe while bullets tore through the air around them. When they were done, the five men casually stood up and walked back to their battle lines.

- The dramatic events of the Battle of Little Bighorn brought General George Custer everlasting fame. Custer's "last stand" became the subject of songs, paintings, and stories. He was glorified in the minds of millions of Americans, and the fact that he died at the hands of "savages" only elevated his status more. For many Americans, Sitting Bull represented all Native Americans; he was as hated by them as Custer was loved.

• • •

Sitting Bull's remarks

I have lived a long time, and I have seen a great deal, and I have always had a reason for everything I have done. Every act of my life has had an object in view, and no man can say that I have neglected facts or failed to think.

I am one of the last chiefs of the independent Sioux nation, and the place I hold among my people was held by my ancestors before me. If I had no place in the world, I would not be here, and the fact of my existence entitles me to exercise any influence I possess. I am satisfied that I was brought into this life for a purpose; otherwise, why am I here?

This land belongs to us, for the Great Spirit gave it to us when he put us here. We were free to come and go, and to live in our own way. But white men, who belong to another land, have come upon us, and are forcing us to live according to their ideas. That is an injustice; we have never dreamed of making white men live as we live.

White men like to dig in the ground for their food. My people prefer to hunt the buffalo as their fathers did. White men like to stay in one place. My people want to move their tepees here and there to the different hunting grounds. The life of white men is slavery. They are prisoners in towns or farms. The life my people want is a life of freedom. I have seen nothing that a white man has, houses or railways or clothing or food, that is as good as the right to move in the open country, and live in our own **fashion.** Why has our blood been shed by your soldiers?

Fashion: Way.

There! Your soldiers made a mark like that in our country, and said that we must live there. They fed us well, and sent their doctors to heal our sick. They said that we should live without having to work. But they told us that we must go only so far in this direction, and only so far in that direction. They gave us meat, but they took away our liberty. The white men had many things that we wanted, but we could see that they did not have the one thing we liked best—freedom. I would rather live in a tepee and go without meat when game is scarce than give up my privileges as a free Indian, even though I could have all that white men have. We marched across the lines of our reservation, and the soldiers followed us.

They attacked our village, and we killed them all. What would you do if your home was attacked? You would stand up like a brave man and defend it. That is our story. I have spoken.

• • •

What happened next...

Sitting Bull lived for another eight years before he was accidentally shot in the head by a Lakota policeman. The remainder of the decade saw the birth of the Indian Rights movement. Well-meaning activists organized to take over where reservations had failed Native Americans. They believed education, U.S. citizenship, and a piece of land for each individual would help Native Americans assimilate into (adopt the lifestyle of and fit into) white American culture.

Lakota chief Sitting Bull.
© CORBIS.

The government continued to create programs designed to change the attitudes, experiences, beliefs, and lifestyle choices of Native Americans. Many of these experimental reforms were in education. Whites believed the best method for changing tribal members was to send young children away to school and prohibit them from seeing or spending time with their parents. In the minds of the government authorities, Native American parents were savages, unfit to raise their children. Native Americans, however, placed great value on their children: They were the center of tribal culture. With the reforms, Native American families were split apart at a time when they needed each other the most.

The educational reforms did little for young Native Americans, who, for the most part, returned to reservation life after completing school. There, they found little opportunity to use their newfound knowledge. They quickly reverted to their traditional lifestyle when it became clear there were few options. Those who did pursue a career were forced to take low-paying government jobs. Given that the purpose of the school reforms was to convert Native Americans into Christians and make them self-sufficient, the experiments could not be considered successful in any way.

The government passed the Dawes Severalty Act in 1887 (see Chapter 4), a law designed to give each Native American his own land, thereby

The Buffalo Nickel

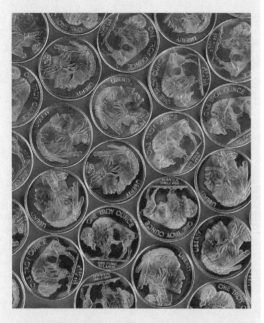

A collection of Buffalo nickels: on one side of the coin is a buffalo, on the other side is the head of a Native American. © ROYALTY-FREE/CORBIS.

The federal government had forced Native Americans off their land, herded them on to reservations, infringed upon their way of life, and slaughtered the respected buffalo. Ironically enough, it began printing a nickel in 1913 that featured a buffalo on one side and the head of a Native American on the other.

The nickel, known as the Buffalo nickel or the Indian Head nickel, was popular among the general public. It was designed by artist James Earle Fraser (1876–1953) and continued to be minted each year until 1938 (except during the years of 1922, 1932, and 1933), when it was replaced with a coin featuring the head of former president Thomas Jefferson (1743–1826; served 1801–9). More than one billion Buffalo nickels were coined.

destroying the power of tribal unity. The Dawes Act was a miserable failure. It gave each individual or family their own plot of land, but not the training necessary to learn to farm it. Without the skills or knowledge to make a life as an individual or family, and without dependence on the tribe, Native Americans had little chance of success. When the Act was finally overturned by Congress in 1934 because Native Americans as a group were no closer to becoming Americanized than they were nearly fifty years prior, Native American independence on the federal government had increased. They had lost their way of life, but nothing had replaced it. Their resistance to giving up their lifestyles to embrace values they did not share kept them from assimilating into white American society.

The Indian Wars ended with a brutal bloodbath known as the Wounded Knee Massacre. In the early morning hours of December 29, 1890, American troops attacked a peaceful camp of Lakotas in South Dakota. When the firearm of a warrior chief accidentally discharged, soldiers opened fire on the camp. Within the hour, more than three hundred Lakota tribal members had been slaughtered, most of them women and children. Their corpses were found as far as three miles from camp. Three officers and fifteen soldiers were awarded Medals of Honor for their actions in the Wounded Knee Massacre.

The government announced the closing of the frontier (wilderness areas open to settlers on a first come, first serve basis) that same year. The line between wilderness and settlement was no longer clear.

Did you know...

- Sitting Bull's Native American name was Tatanka-Iyotanka, which describes a buffalo sitting on its haunches, refusing to move.

- Just as he had experienced a vision telling him of Custer's defeat at Little Bighorn, so Sitting Bull had a vision of his own death. He knew he would be killed by his own people.
- In the twenty-first century, there are 304 federally recognized Native American reservations in the United States.

Consider the following...

- Imagine a completely unfamiliar group of people takes over the city or region where you live. They try to force you to adapt to their lifestyle in every way. How would you respond?
- What would be the hardest part of your lifestyle to give up: traditions such as celebrations, rituals, and holidays; general freedom to make choices; or ability to relocate and live where you please? Why?
- How is the discrimination against Native Americans in the late nineteenth and twentieth centuries similar to that against African Americans during the same time period? How is it different?

For More Information

BOOKS

Blaisdell, Bob, ed. *Great Speeches by Native Americans.* Mineola, NY: Dover Publications, 2000.

Creelman, James. *On the Great Highway: The Wanderings and Adventures of a Special Correspondent.* Boston: Lothrop, 1901.

Gibbon, Guy E. *The Sioux: The Dakota and Lakota Nations.* Boston: Blackwell Publishers, 2003.

Haugen, Brenda. *Geronimo: Apache Warrior.* Minneapolis: Compass Point Books, 2005.

Hermann, Spring. *Geronimo: Apache Freedom Fighter.* Springfield, NJ: Enslow, 1997.

Marrin, Albert. *Sitting Bull and His World.* New York: Dutton Children's Books, 2000.

Roop, Connie, and Peter Roop. *Sitting Bull.* New York: Scholastic Paperbacks, 2002.

WEB SITES

"Chief Sitting Bull." *The History Channel.* http://www.historychannel.com/exhibits/sioux/sittingbull.html (accessed on July 17, 2006).

"Chief Sitting Bull." *SittingBull.org.* http://www.sittingbull.org/ (accessed on August 9, 2006).

"Native Americans: Indian Wars Time Table." *U-S-History.com.* http://www.u-s-history.com/pages/h1008.html (accessed on July 17, 2006).

PBS. "Sitting Bull." *New Perspectives on the West.* http://www.pbs.org/weta/thewest/people/s_z/sittingbull.htm (accessed on July 17, 2006).

PBS. "Transcontinental Railroad: Native Americans." *American Experience.* http://www.pbs.org/wgbh/amex/tcrr/sfeature/sf_interview.html#c (accessed on July 17, 2006).

3

Emma Lazarus

"The New Colossus"

Available at The Academy of American Poets *(Web site); poem engraved at the base of the Statue of Liberty*

"Give me your tired, your poor, Your huddled masses yearning to breathe free..."

While attending a dinner party in France in 1865, French sculptor Frédéric Auguste Bartholdi (1834–1904) and his host, French scholar Édouard-René Lefebvre de Laboulaye (1811–1883), conceived the idea to give the United States a monument to commemorate the country's first centennial (one hundred years) as a free nation.

Construction of the monument began in 1875, and in 1877, America began fund-raising efforts to collect the money needed to build a pedestal (foundation) on which a 450,000-pound (204,300-kilogram) copper and steel statue would stand. American architect Richard Morris Hunt (1828–1885) was hired to design and build the pedestal. The cement foundation weighed 27,000 tons (24,489 metric tons).

Building of the statue was completed in Paris, France, in June 1884, but the pedestal was still a work in progress. Early in 1885, with the completion of the pedestal, "Liberty Enlightening the World" was dismantled and shipped to America in 350 pieces. The statue, which became known as Lady Liberty, arrived on Liberty Island in New York and was placed on Ellis Island, the primary immigration port for European immigrants. The pedestal and statue were assembled in 1886, ten years after the original target date. On October 28 of that year, President Grover Cleveland (1837–1908; served 1885–89 and 1893–97) accepted the Statue of Liberty and dedicated her in an official ceremony.

As part of America's fund-raising efforts, Jewish poet Emma Lazarus (1849–1887) composed a sonnet (a fourteen-line lyric poem,

Statue of Liberty Facts

An aerial view of the Statue of Liberty. © MICHAEL S. YAMASHITA/CORBIS.

- There are seven spikes in the crown, representative of the seven continents or the seven seas.

- At a windspeed of 50 miles (80.5 kilometers) per hour, the statue sways up to 3 inches (7.62 centimeters). The torch sways 5 inches (12.7 centimeters).

- If the statue was fitted for a pair of sandals, she would wear U.S. women's size 879.

- The Statue of Liberty measures 111 feet, 1 inch (33.86 meters) from her heel to the top of her head.

- The statue holds a tablet in her left hand. On that tablet is inscribed the date July 4, 1776, in Roman numerals, the day America declared its independence from Britain.

written using a distinct rhythm and rhyme) to be awarded to the highest bidder at an art auction. The poem, called "The New Colossus," reflected Lazarus's understanding of the role America played in the hopes of immigrants (people who move permanently to another country) in the late nineteenth century. Written in 1883, "The New Colossus" was engraved on a plaque and attached to the pedestal of the Statue of Liberty in 1903.

Lazarus herself was a fourth-generation member of a Jewish immigrant family. Although she was born into a family of wealth, her father was more concerned with integrating his family into Christian society than he was with honoring his Jewish ethnicity and religion. Although the Lazarus family associated with New York's elite (upper class), Emma sensed the hostility that lay underneath the seeming civility toward and tolerance of her family. According to the *Jewish Women's Archive*

Web site, in an 1883 letter to friend Philip Cowen, Lazarus wrote, "I am perfectly conscious that this contempt and hatred underlies the general tone of the community toward us...." She knew from experience what it felt like to be an outsider in America.

Immigration began in great numbers in the 1860s. People flocked to America from across the globe, but the largest immigrant populations came from Germany and Ireland. Immigrants left their homes for various reasons. Some were escaping intolerable levels of poverty; others wanted better jobs and the chance for brighter futures for themselves and their children. Still others were hoping to escape oppression (harsh treatment). Regardless of where they sailed from, the voyage to America was long. Europeans had to endure disgusting ship conditions for fourteen days in the late 1860s. For those who crossed the ocean forty years later, the voyages were reduced to five-and-a-half days.

Immigration was changing America forever. Urban areas became overpopulated, and crowded living conditions imposed serious risks from disease and crime on entire populations. Industrialization created more jobs than ever before, but the majority of them did not pay well. Poverty increased, despite the availability of jobs. As more immigrants arrived, wages decreased when employers realized there now was an abundance of labor willing to work for outrageously low wages. Immigrants were grateful to find work of any kind, and they were willing to do the dangerous and backbreaking jobs other Americans refused.

Many native-born Americans resented the presence of immigrants. They viewed them as simply foreigners who had no pride and stole jobs. Language was a barrier to communication, and nearly all immigrants brought with them habits, customs, and values not always in keeping with those of native-born Americans. Many Americans believed it was one thing to be forced to live among foreigners, quite another to have jobs—even those considered too shameful to accept—taken away.

Things to remember while reading "The New Colossus":

- Lazarus wrote the sonnet at the request of a friend who was organizing an art auction to raise money for a pedestal on which to mount the Statue of Liberty. The author had no intention of the poem being immortalized at the base of the monument. She

Emma Lazarus: A Portrait of Success

Emma Lazarus, author of "The New Colossus,"
engraved on the base of the Statue of Liberty.
©BETTMANN/CORBIS.

Most of Emma Lazarus's friends were Christian. Although she was accepted into high-class society, they never let her forget her roots. They referred to her as a "Jewess." Lazarus realized she would forever be an outsider.

Long before she penned "The New Colossus," Lazarus was writing poetry. In 1868, she sent a copy of her first book of poetry (which her father had published) to Ralph Waldo Emerson (1803–1882), one of the country's most famous essayists, poets, and philosophers. The two began a lifelong friendship. Lazarus visited Emerson at his home in Concord, Massachusetts, several times.

Lazarus's second book of poems was published in 1871 to much critical praise. Throughout the decade, she published many poems and essays in popular magazines. By 1882, more than fifty of her poems and translations of others' poems had been printed in these periodicals. Her best reviews came in 1881, upon publication of her translation of the works of German Jewish poet Heinrich Heine (1797–1856). Lazarus identified with Heine's expression of his Jewish identity. Both writers felt the effect of their Jewish backgrounds on their pursuit of artistic creativity.

Lazarus was a woman writer in an era when women writers were not celebrated or respected. Her struggle was made even more difficult because she was a Jewish woman. Despite the obstacles in her path, Lazarus used her writing to speak out on Jewish themes, especially from 1882 to 1883. The 1880s were years of harsh anti-Semitism (hatred of Jews) in Eastern Europe. Massive violent attacks against Russian Jews took place throughout the region, and thousands of men, women, and children were murdered. Others were left to starve to death. These attacks, called pogroms, lasted for more than three years and were supported at times by the authorities. In fact, the Jews themselves were blamed for the riots, and restrictions against them were intensified.

The pogroms caused many Russian Jews to flee to America. Lazarus acted as a spokesperson for these displaced refugees. She became an advocate for these frightened immigrants, and formed the Society for the Improvement and Colonization of East European Jews in 1883.

Lazarus died at the age of thirty-eight, from what twenty-first-century doctors believe was probably cancer. Her memory continues to inspire Jewish activists throughout the world.

was merely asked to write something that would be included in a portfolio of works by famous writers. She used her experience working with immigrants at a settlement house (an organization that offers aid to the needy) as inspiration for her poem.

- Lazarus died sixteen years before her poem was displayed on the Statue of Liberty pedestal.

- The engraved plaque initially hung on a second-floor inner wall of the building housing the pedestal. In 1945, the plaque was moved to the main entrance of the Statue of Liberty.

- Before the engraving, banker Samuel Ward Gray (1817–1907) wanted the phrase "wretched refuse" changed. The word "refuse" refers to something discarded as worthless. Gray, who was also a cofounder of New York's Metropolitan Museum of Art, felt the phrase was condescending (spoken as if immigrants were inferior). In the end, Lazarus's poem was left exactly as it had been written.

• • •

"The New Colossus"

Not like the **brazen giant of Greek fame,**
With **conquering limbs astride from land to land;**
Here at our sea-washed, sunset gates shall stand
A mighty woman with a torch, whose flame
Is the **imprisoned** lighting, and her name
Mother of **Exiles.** From her **beacon**-hand
Glows world-wide welcome; her mild eyes command
The **air-bridged harbor** that **twin cities** frame.
"Keep, ancient lands, your **storied pomp!**" cries she
With silent lips. "Give me your tired, your poor,
Your huddled masses **yearning** to breathe free,
The **wretched refuse** of your **teeming** shore.
Send these, the homeless, **tempest-tost** to me,
I lift my lamp beside the **golden door!**"

• • •

What happened next...

As Lazarus's sonnet gained notice, scholars began to explain it as a direct reflection of the author's own experiences. For example, rather than

Brazen giant of Greek fame: The Colossus of Rhodes, a gigantic bronze statue that stood at the entrance to the Greek island of Rhodes in 282 BCE.

Conquering limbs astride from land to land: A reference to the myth that the legs of the Colossus straddled both sides of the harbor.

Imprisoned: Interior.

Exiles: People who cannot return home.

Beacon: Guiding light.

Air-bridged harbor: East River with the Brooklyn Bridge spanning the banks.

Twin cities: Brooklyn and New York City.

Storied: Celebrated.

Pomp: Elegance.

Yearning: Longing.

Wretched refuse: Miserable waste.

Teeming: Overflowing (with people).

Tempest-tost: Storm-tossed.

Golden door: Opportunity.

Emma Lazarus's handwritten manuscript of "The New Colossus." © BETTMANN/ CORBIS.

judging the phrase "wretched refuse" as being insulting to immigrants, readers came to understand that Lazarus was not condescending, but rather, pointing out the prejudices native-born Americans would harbor against immigrants. This image, compared with the compassion Lazarus shows in the phrase "huddled masses yearning to breathe free," eventually came to be seen as an expression of the conflict of identity and ideals surrounding the phenomenon of immigration. The poem instilled in its readers an appreciation for the underlying tensions between freedom and oppression, speech and silence, ancient and modern. It came to be considered an appropriately powerful piece of literature.

Between 1900 and 1915, fifteen million immigrants sailed to America's shores, more than in the previous forty years combined. They accounted for nearly one-third of the country's population growth of that time. As feelings of nativism (anti-immigration) grew, more restrictions were placed on immigrants. The Immigration Act passed in 1907 increased the amount (called a head tax) paid per immigrant to $4. Prior to 1907, only immigrants with contagious diseases or who had been convicted of certain crimes were refused admission to America. The law of 1907 added more categories to the inadmissible list. Under the new restrictions, immigrants unable to enter America included those with physical or mental disabilities that would prohibit them from finding jobs; those considered imbeciles (persons who had moderate to severe mental disabilities); unaccompanied children; anyone diagnosed with tuberculosis (a contagious lung disease); those considered feeble-minded (learning disabled); and women who intended to become prostitutes (sellers of sex).

In the Immigration Act of 1917, more restrictions would be passed, including a literacy test that required all immigrants age sixteen and older to be able to read and write in their native language, if not in English. Many immigrants never had the chance to learn to read or write before leaving home, and the U.S. federal government knew that. That same law prohibited nearly all Asians, not just the Chinese, from entering the United States. As the years passed, restrictions laws would become even more harsh. In 1965, the number of immigrants allowed from the Eastern hemisphere was 170,000, and from the Western hemisphere, 120,000. Although ceilings (maximum numbers of immigrants accepted) were eventually raised, by the late twentieth century, more restrictions were imposed in an effort to curb illegal immigration.

Did you know...

- In 1910, three-fourths of New York City's population were immigrants or first-generation Americans (sons and daughters of immigrants). In the twenty-first century, over 40 percent of the U.S. population are descendents of the 17 million immigrants that entered America through Ellis Island from 1892 to 1954.
- Lazarus's "The New Colossus" sold for $1,500 at the auction, more than any other piece of literature in the portfolio.
- The Statue of Liberty was declared a national monument in 1924.

Immigration authorities inspect female immigrants at Ellis Island. NATIONAL ARCHIVES AND RECORDS ADMINISTRATION.

- Ellis Island was shut down permanently as an immigration port in 1954. After extensive restoration, it reopened in 1990 as a museum and national monument.

Consider the following...

- In what ways would America be different today if immigrants had never arrived during the Gilded Age and the Progressive Era?
- Imagine you are the age you are now and have just arrived in America from Europe. What would be the five most difficult changes for you to adapt to?
- If you emigrated to a foreign country and were not able to read or write your own language, what stories about your family would

you orally pass down to your children so that they did not forget their history?

For More Information

BOOKS

Felder, Deborah G., and Diana Rosen. *Fifty Jewish Women Who Changed the World.* New York: Citadel Press, 2003.

Hollander, John, ed. *Emma Lazarus: Selected Poems.* New York: Library of America, 2005.

Merriam, Eve. *Emma Lazarus Rediscovered.* New York: Biblio Press, 1998.

Moore, H. S. *Liberty's Poet: Emma Lazarus.* Austin, TX: TurnKey Press, 2005.

Moreno, Barry. *The Statue of Liberty Encyclopedia.* New York: Simon & Schuster, 2000.

Sandler, Martin W. *Island of Hope: The Story of Ellis Island and the Journey to America.* New York: Scholastic, 2004.

WEB SITES

"The Agendas Behind the Monuments." *American Studies at the University of Virginia.* http://xroads.virginia.edu/~CAP/LIBERTY/politics.html (accessed on July 18, 2006).

Lazarus, Emma. "The New Colossus." *The Academy of American Poets.* http://www.poets.org/viewmedia.php/prmMID/16111 (accessed on August 9, 2006).

"The Light of Liberty." *National Geographic Kids.* http://www.nationalgeographic.com/ngkids/9907/liberty/liberty.html (accessed on July 18, 2006).

The Statue of Liberty–Ellis Island Foundation, Inc. http://www.ellisisland.org/ (accessed on July 18, 2006).

"Women of Valor: Emma Lazarus." *Jewish Women's Archive.* http://www.jwa.org/exhibits/wov/lazarus/el1.html (accessed on July 18, 2006).

4

U.S. Congress

Excerpt from the Dawes Severalty Act; passed into law on February 8, 1887
Available at University of Denver: Sturm College of Law *(Web site)*

"The Indian may now become a free man; free from the thralldom of the tribe; freed from the domination of the reservation system; free to enter into the body of our citizens. This bill may therefore be considered as the Magna Carta of the Indians of our country."

— Alice Fletcher, leader of the "Friends of the Indian"

Conflict between various Native American tribes and white settlers had been ongoing since the 1600s. The American Revolution (1775–83) gave America a new government after the colonies battled to achieve independence from Great Britain. That federal government had to address how to convince tribes in the Northwest to leave their homeland so white settlers could move in.

Several years and many battles later, the Treaty of Greenville (1795) was signed. This treaty established a boundary dividing Native American land from white settlement land. According to the agreement, in exchange for necessities such as blankets, cooking utensils, and animals used for food, Native Americans gave up their land in eastern and southern Ohio as well as portions in Indiana, Michigan, and Illinois. Almost immediately, settlers ignored the boundary and began settling on Native American land, and the U.S. government did nothing about the situation. In 1800, William Henry Harrison (1773–1841) became governor of Indiana and began aggressively pursuing claim to Native American land. In 1809, he secured more than 2.5 million acres (10,000 square kilometers) of Native American land in that territory, the particulars of which were outlined in the Treaty of Fort Wayne. Harrison managed to strike this deal between the Native Americans by agreeing to pay them two cents per acre.

The Treaty of Fort Wayne was in direct conflict with the Treaty of Greenville. Angered by this breach of contract, the Native Americans formed a confederacy (a group made of members from various tribes). Its leader was Shawnee chief Tecumseh (c. 1768–1813), who later was killed in the War of 1812 (1812–14). Tecumseh called upon Harrison to void the new treaty, but Harrison stood firm. While Tecumseh was in the south scouting for more tribes to join and support the confederacy in 1811, Harrison marched against the confederacy and beat them in the Battle of Tippecanoe. Among those defeated was Tecumseh's brother, Tenskwatawa (c. 1768–1837).

Tecumseh sought revenge by joining the side of the British in the War of 1812. Unfortunately for him and his tribes, the great warrior's death in battle allowed the government to develop a policy for removing Native Americans from what little land they had left. By 1860, most had been relocated across the Mississippi River. They were forced onto reservations, land set aside by the federal government for Native Americans to inhabit.

Few of the tribes went willingly or peacefully, and the Great Plains region was the location of hundreds of skirmishes and battles that together became known as the Plains Indian Wars (1866–90). Never before had American troops faced such persistent and skilled opponents. The government underestimated the strength and determination of the Native Americans, and the process of assimilating them (integrating them into a foreign or different culture) proved more challenging than had been imagined.

The 1880s were years of Native American reform. Whereas the government was content to force tribes onto reservations and let them figure out a new way of life on their own, many American citizens were not. These citizens organized into associations and rights groups and worked together toward two goals. The first was to persuade the government to pass legislation that would protect and help Native Americans assimilate. The second was to pick up where the government's efforts left off.

By 1871, it had become clear to everyone that sending tribes to live on reservations was not a successful solution to the government's dilemma. Some Native Americans realized immediately that their traditional way of life was no longer an option. They did what they could

A Navajo boy named Tom Torlino is shown in his native dress as he entered Carlisle Indian School (left) and after the "assimilation" process began following the passage of the Dawes Severalty Act in 1887. NATIONAL ANTHROPOLOGICAL ARCHIVES, SMITHSONIAN INSTITUTION.

to make the most of their situation by learning to farm. Some found work on the reservations as police or judges; others worked beyond the reservations in logging camps, railroads, and mines. These families converted to Christianity and sent their children to school. They did their best to assimilate.

Many Native Americans, however, refused to accept what the government was handing them. They would not give up their spiritual beliefs. They refused to learn to farm, and they had no desire to become "civilized." To most members of white society, Native Americans were considered primitive, or uncivilized, because they did not share society's values and norms. For example, settlers were Christian; Native Americans were not. Settlers walked around fully clothed in public; Native Americans sometimes did, but not always. Settlers lived in log homes; Native Americans lived in teepees that could be easily disassembled to move on when weather and food required it of them. Eating habits, spiritual rituals, customs and celebrations—all of these were very different between the two cultures. Among those who held onto their traditions were the older warriors who had fought the government and lost. Bitter and resentful, these once-honored fighters and chiefs found reservation life lonely and miserable. Clearly, the government understood that reservations were not the path to Native American independence.

Most rights activists had good intentions; they truly wanted to help "Americanize" these primitive "savages." In addition to being considered uncivilized, Native Americans were portrayed in white society as savages. This stereotype was upheld by the leading adventure writers of the day, such as James Fenimore Cooper (1789–1851), who wrote the novel *The Last of the Mohicans*. In that novel, he called Native Americans "savages," as well as "murderers" who drank the blood of their "victims." Add to that eyewitness accounts from soldiers who had battled the Native Americans, and it is clear why activists believed someone needed to save the souls of this culture. The best way to achieve their goals, they believed, was to convert the Native Americans to Christianity, give them U.S. citizenship, and allow them to own their own land rather than to live on reservations as a group.

Despite their intentions, these activists failed to take into consideration that tribes had never known anything *but* communal (group) living. Everything they did—every ritual, ceremony, routine—was done as a group. To separate families from their support system would surely serve only to undermine their cultural values. It would remove from them any sense of independence they had as a race.

The activists may have overlooked this aspect of their plan, but government officials did not. They were completely aware that the separation of tribes would mean a decrease in the amount of power they held. Less power for the Native Americans meant more power for the federal government in its efforts to encourage assimilation. When it became clear that the reservation system was not working as planned, officials knew they had to come up with another program.

The answer came to them via U.S. senator Henry L. Dawes (1816–1903), a Republican from Massachusetts, who sponsored a bill called the Dawes Severalty Act. (Severalty means individual ownership.) Also known as the General Allotment Act (allotment refers to land set aside for a specific purpose), this law would guarantee each Native American a plot of land and full U.S. citizenship. But in order to get the land, tribe members would be required to give up their legal standing as a tribe. Citizenship would not be granted for twenty-five years, so for that quarter of a decade, they would have no individual legal protection, nor would they have protection through tribal ties.

The Dawes Severalty Act was passed on February 8, 1887.

Things to remember while reading excerpts from the Dawes Severalty Act:

- The land the government "gave" to the Native Americans was not the government's to give. It is the same land it took from the tribes.

- Reformers supported the act, but so did railroads and other businesses. Any surplus (leftover) reservation lands would be sold if the bill was passed into law. The lands could be bought for little money and turned into immediate profit for businesses.

- Many people genuinely believed they were doing the Native Americans a favor by forcing them to abandon the only way of life they had ever known. It never occurred to them that their new way of life was not best for everyone.

- One of the advantages for Native Americans under the Dawes Act was full citizenship. But Native Americans had lived in America longer than any of the settlers who were forcing them off the land.

U.S. senator Henry L. Dawes of Massachusetts, author of the Dawes Severalty Act of 1887. © BETTMANN/CORBIS.

• • •

Excerpt from the Dawes Severalty Act

An Act to provide for the **allotment** of lands in **severalty** to Indians on the various reservations, and to extend the protection of the laws of the United States and the Territories over the Indians, and for other purposes.

Be it enacted by the Senate and House of Representatives of the United States of America in Congress assembled, That in all cases where any tribe or band of Indians has been, or shall hereafter be, located upon any reservation created for their use, either by treaty **stipulation** or by virtue of an act of Congress or executive order setting apart the same for their use,

Allotment: Distribution.

Severalty: Individual ownership.

Stipulation: Agreement.

Surveyed: Examined and measured.

One-quarter of a section: 160 acres.

One-eighth of a section: 80 acres.

Embraced: Included.

One-sixteenth of a section: 40 acres.

Patents: Ownership rights.

Allottees: Native Americans.

Trust: Property held by one party for another party.

Decease: Death.

Heirs: People who inherit the belongings of another.

Aforesaid: Mentioned before.

Discharged: Freed.

Incumbrance: Mortgage against a property, which prevents owner from legally owning it.

Reside: Live.

Jurisdiction: Legal authority.

Civilized life: A life that includes the values and accepted behaviors of white society.

Immunities: Legal protections.

the President of the United States be, and he hereby is, authorized, whenever in his opinion any reservation or any part thereof of such Indians is advantageous for agricultural and grazing purposes, to cause said reservation, or any part thereof, to be **surveyed,** or resurveyed if necessary, and to allot the lands in said reservation in severalty to any Indian located thereon in quantities as follows:

To each head of a family, **one-quarter of a section;**

To each single person over eighteen years of age, **one-eighth of a section;**

To each orphan child under eighteen years of age, one-eighth of a section; and

To each other single person under eighteen years now living, or who may be born prior to the date of the order of the President directing an allotment of the lands **embraced** in any reservation, **one-sixteenth of a section...**

Sec. 5. That upon the approval of the allotments provided for in this act by the Secretary of the Interior, he shall cause **patents** to issue therefore in the name of the **allottees,** which patents shall be of the legal effect, and declare that the United States does and will hold the land thus allotted, for the period of twenty-five years, in **trust** for the sole use and benefit of the Indian to whom such allotment shall have been made, or, in case of his **decease,** of his **heirs** according to the laws of the State or Territory where such land is located, and that at the expiration of said period the United States will convey the same by patent to said Indian, or his heirs as **aforesaid,** in fee, **discharged** of said trust and free of all charge or **incumbrance** whatsoever:

Sec. 6. That upon the completion of said allotments and the patenting of the lands to said allottees, each and every member of the respective bands or tribes of Indians to whom allotments have been made shall have the benefit of and be subject to the laws, both civil and criminal, of the State or Territory in which they may **reside;** and no Territory shall pass or enforce any law denying any such Indian within its **jurisdiction** the equal protection of the law. And every Indian born within the territorial limits of the United States to whom allotments shall have been made under the provisions of this act, or under any law or treaty, and every Indian born within the territorial limits of the United States who has voluntarily taken up, within said limits, his residence separate and apart from any tribe of Indians therein, and has adopted the habits of **civilized life** is hereby declared to be a citizen of the United States, and is entitled to all the rights, privileges, and **immunities** of such citizens, whether said Indian has been or not, by birth or otherwise, a member of any tribe of Indians within the territorial limits of the United States without in any manner affecting the right of any such Indian to tribal or other property....

Sec. 8. That the provisions of this act shall not extend to the territory occupied by the Cherokees, Creeks, Choctaws, Chickasaws, Seminoles, and Osage, Miamies and Peorias, and Sacs and Foxes, in the Indian Territory, nor to any of the reservations of the Seneca Nation of New York Indians in the State of New York, nor to that strip of territory in the State of Nebraska adjoining the Sioux Nation on the south added by executive order. . . .

• • •

What happened next...

The Dawes Act was enforced gradually; reservations did not disappear completely. And although some specific tribes were excluded from the law, the provisions under the Dawes Act eventually included them as well beginning in 1893.

The Dawes Act was a disaster. Native Americans were not equipped to live life in individual family groups. From the beginning of time, they lived as a community and depended upon the various strengths and abilities of each tribe member to survive and grow. White settlers would have been thrilled to be given 160 acres of land, but the allotment meant nothing but heartache and difficulty for most Native Americans. Many of them, unable to farm, sold their allotment to white neighbors.

Those who did make an effort to learn to farm often failed because they had no formal training and no money or credit to buy the machinery necessary to run a farm. They were not allowed to use their land as collateral (something of value pledged to assure payment of debt), and the government had set aside only $30,000 for machinery, livestock, seed, and other farming necessities. The Dawes Act had neither the financial backing nor the personnel available to train the Native Americans, so success would have been surprising.

In addition to the increased obstacles to assimilation, Native Americans lost much of their land under the Dawes Act. When it was passed in 1886, tribes owned about 138 million acres of land. By 1900, they owned just 78 million acres; the total would dwindle to 48 million by 1934. The surplus land was sold to the highest bidder at astoundingly low prices. Despite its obvious problems, the Dawes Act remained in effect until 1934, when it was repealed by the government.

In an effort to repair the damages done by the Dawes Act, the Indian Reorganization Act (also known as the Wheeler-Howard Act or

The Merriam Report

In 1926, the federal government requested that the Institute for Government Research conduct a thorough investigation into the economic and social conditions of the Native Americans. Director Lewis Merriam and his staff presented officials with a detailed report on their findings. The Merriam Report found that, overall, Native Americans lived in poverty. They were disease ridden and lived in unsanitary conditions. Because they had no understanding of money management, they had no concept of the value of money or land. Their lack of knowledge bred in them an attitude of apathy (not caring one way or the other), and there was no evidence that they were adjusting to their new economic or social conditions. Finally, the report stated that the Native Americans were suffering in their new lifestyles and were very dissatisfied.

Although the Dawes Act was not wholly responsible for the conditions and circumstances reported, it was given as one of the main causes. The Merriam Report indicated that giving the Native Americans land without instruction or training on how to use it did nothing to decrease their economic independence on the federal government. It did, in fact, increase it.

The report recommended improved living and working conditions, better recordkeeping, bicultural and bilingual (multilanguage) education. The general message was that the root of the problem lay in imposing white cultural values on the Native American race.

the Indian New Deal) was passed in 1934. Under the new law, the allotment program was discontinued, and Native Americans were encouraged to re-form their tribes. They were given the right to form their own governments and rule themselves, and they were allowed to form tribal corporations. In addition, the federal government set aside money to be used as loans for college or career-training expenses for qualifying Native Americans.

The Reorganization Act helped Native Americans become more self-sufficient. Although they would never be able to return completely to their traditional way of life, with assistance from the government, social programs, and concerned citizens, they were able to make the new law work for them.

Did you know...

- Under the initial proposal for the Indian Reorganization Act, Native Americans would have had the opportunity to buy back some of the surplus land that had been taken from them in the Dawes Act. That clause was deleted from the bill before it was passed, and severe restrictions were placed on tribes' ability to buy back their land. This was just one more way the U.S. government could maintain control of Native Americans.

- Under the Dawes Act, surplus land in Colorado sold for $7.27 per acre in 1910, the least expensive price of any land available in the United States. The most expensive land sold that year was in the state of Washington, where it sold for $41.87 an acre.

- Some tribes became landless as individual Native Americans sold their allotted land to white settlers. By 1954, sixty-one tribes had been dismantled by the federal government.

Consider the following...

- On whom do you think the Dawes Act was hardest in Native American tribes: men, women, or children? Why?
- Predict what might have happened to the Native Americans had the Merriam Report never been published.
- What provisions could have been added to the Dawes Act to make it more effective?

For More Information

BOOKS

Andrist, Ralph K. *The Long Death: The Last Days of the Plains Indians.* New York: Macmillan, 1964. Reprint, Norman: University of Oklahoma Press, 2001.

Cooper, James Fenimore. *The Last of the Mohicans.* Philadelphia: H. C. Carey & I. Lea, 1826. Multiple reprints.

Hansen, Emma I. *Memory and Vision: Arts, Culture, and Lives of the Plains Peoples.* Seattle: University of Washington Press, 2006.

O'Neill, Terry, ed. *The Indian Reservation System.* San Diego: Greenhaven Press, 2002.

WEB SITES

"The Dawes Act." *NebraskaStudies.org.* http://www.nebraskastudies.org/0600/ frameset_reset.html?http://www.nebraskastudies.org/0600/stories/ 0601_0200.html (accessed on July 20, 2006).

"Dawes Severalty Act." *University of Denver: Sturm College of Law* http://www.law. du.edu/russell/lh/alh/docs/dawesact.html (accessed on August 11, 2006).

Harmon, Alexandra. "American Indians and Land Monopolies in the Gilded Age." *The Journal of American History.* http://www.historycooperative.org/cgi-bin/ justtop.cgi?act=justtop&url=http://www.historycooperative.org/journals/ jah/90.1/harmon.html (accessed on July 20, 2006).

"History of Allotment, Part 2." *Indian Land Tenure Foundation.* http://www. indianlandtenure.org/ILTFallotment/introduction/introII.htm (accessed on July 20, 2006).

Library of Congress. "Immigration: Native Americans." *American Memory.* http:// memory.loc.gov/learn/features/immig/native_american.html (accessed on July 20, 2006).

5

Theodore Roosevelt

Excerpt from *Ranch Life and the Hunting-Trail*
Originally published in 1888; available at Bartleby.com *(Web site)*

"The hunter is the arch-type of freedom. His well-being rests in no man's hands save his own. He chops down and hews out the logs for his hut, or perhaps makes merely a rude dug-out in the side of a hill, with a skin roof, and skin flaps for the door. He buys a little flour and salt, and in times of plenty also sugar and tea; but not much, for it must all be carried hundreds of miles on the backs of his shaggy pack-ponies."

For those Americans living in the Gilded Age, the western territories of the country were mysterious, dangerous, intriguing. The Wild West was the stage for the Plains Indian Wars (1866–90), and those more urbanized populations in the East and even in the South considered the frontier (the far edge of the wilderness, characterized by some settlement) a boundary. Cross that imaginary dividing line between civilization and wilderness (vast acreage of unsettled land) and there was no telling what could happen. And women—"proper" single women—dared not travel in the frontier.

For as long as it has existed, America's wilderness frontier has been the birthplace of myths and legends. The adventures of men such as explorer Daniel Boone (1734–1820), outlaw Jesse James (1847–1882), and gunfighter Wild Bill Hickok (1837–1876) were told and retold until their stories were more fiction than fact. Mountain men, those who lived high in the mountains and survived by their own skills of hunting and trapping, were the subjects of many novels and short stories. To live on the frontier meant dealing with outlaws and other men of questionable

Theodore Roosevelt dressed in his hunting clothes on his Dakota Territory ranch in 1885.
© CORBIS.

and rough character; women of the era were believed to be delicate in nature, not able to take care of themselves. Having been raised to appreciate good manners, the security of home, and the safety provided by a well-bred husband, most women could not imagine life in the wilderness frontier.

Even before becoming president of the United States, Theodore Roosevelt (1858–1919) profoundly influenced the history of the American West. Although often ill as a child, he increased his physical endurance through exercise. In doing so, he developed a love of the outdoors.

Roosevelt first headed West from New York in 1883. Having heard reports that the buffalo herds of the Dakota Territory were all but extinct (gone forever), the outdoorsman wanted to shoot himself a buffalo to add to his trophy collection. While in the West, he developed a great appreciation and affection for not only the land but also its people. He bought two ranches in the Dakota Badlands before heading home. Throughout his life, those ranches would be his escape from city and political life.

Roosevelt began publishing books about his experiences in the West. His engaging writing style and sense of humor made these books popular among readers not only in America but also throughout the world. One of these books was titled *Ranch Life and the Hunting-Trail* and was published in book form in 1888. Before that, the stories were published in *Century Magazine* over the course of many months.

Things to remember while reading an excerpt from *Ranch Life and the Hunting-Trail:*

- Most of the readers of Roosevelt's work lived in the eastern regions of the United States. They had never been West, and so their perception of what the frontier was like was formed by what they read.
- Roosevelt's account of the West was romantic; it focused on portraying Americans there as strong, determined, and able-bodied.

His stories gave America a version of itself it wanted to believe, one rooted, perhaps, more in storytelling than in accuracy.

- Roosevelt was a biased (judgmental) writer. Although he discussed the course of events as the frontier was settled and how they affected both sides, there was never a doubt which side he was on. Without hesitation, he favored the pioneers and settlers over Native Americans.

- The following excerpt is from a chapter entitled "Frontier Types."

• • •

Excerpt from *Ranch Life and the Hunting-Trail*

The old race of Rocky Mountain hunters and trappers, of reckless, **dauntless** Indian fighters, is now fast dying out. Yet here and there these restless wanderers of the **untrodden** wilderness still linger, in wooded **fastnesses** so **inaccessible** that the miners have not yet explored them, in mountain valleys so far off that no ranchman has yet driven his herds **thither**. To this day many of them wear the fringed **tunic** or hunting-shirt, made of buckskin or homespun, and belted in at the waist—the most picturesque and distinctively national dress ever worn in America. It was the dress in which [explorer] Daniel Boone was clad when he first passed through the **trackless** forests of the Alleghanies [sic] and penetrated into the heart of Kentucky, to enjoy such hunting as no man of his race had ever had before; it was the dress worn by grim old [frontiersman] Davy Crockett when he fell at the Alamo. The wild **soldiery** of the backwoods wore it when they marched to victory over [British major Patrick] Ferguson and [British general Edward] Pakenham, at **King's Mountain** and **New Orleans;** when they conquered the French towns of the Illinois; and when they won at the cost of [Native American leader] Red Eagle's warriors the bloody triumph of the **Horseshoe Bend.**

These old-time hunters have been the forerunners of the white advance throughout all our Western land. Soon after the beginning of the present century they boldly struck out beyond the Mississippi, steered their way across the flat and endless seas of grass, or pushed up the valleys of the great lonely rivers, crossed the passes that wound among the towering peaks of the Rockies, toiled over the melancholy wastes of sage brush and alkali, and at last, breaking through the gloomy woodland that belts the coast, they looked out on the heaving waves of the greatest of all the oceans. They lived for months, often for years, among the Indians, now as friends, now as foes, warring, hunting, and marrying with them; they acted as guides for exploring parties, as scouts for the soldiers who from

Dauntless: Fearless.

Untrodden: Roadless.

Fastnesses: Areas.

Inaccessible: Unreachable.

Thither: There.

Tunic: A loose fitting robe-like garment.

Trackless: Pathless.

Soldiery: Soldiers.

King's Mountain: South Carolina site of an American Revolution battle.

New Orleans: Louisiana site of a War of 1812 battle.

Horseshoe Bend: Alabama site of a Creek War battle in the War of 1812.

Frederic Remington: Painter of the Wild Frontier

"The Bronco Buster," one of the most famous works of Frederic Remington. The artist's illustrations were included in Theodore Roosevelt's Ranch Life and the Hunting-Trail. THE LIBRARY OF CONGRESS.

No artist is more connected with the American West than Frederic Remington (1861–1908). Like many young men of his day, Remington heeded the call to "Go West" and left his home in New York for the adventure of a lifetime. His travels gave him time to sketch the people of and places on the frontier. In 1886, he solidified his reputation as an artist of the West when he began selling his work to the major magazines of the time.

Remington worked primarily in charcoal, but quickly established himself as a painter. Most of his illustrations were of sweeping landscapes, Western heroes, and moments of danger that captured America's perception of the wild frontier. Nearly all his works revolve around the theme of the struggles of the individual against overwhelming odds.

Remington focused his efforts on sculpture beginning in the mid-1890s, and he quickly became a master of the art. His bronze sculptures were popular for the energy the artist was able to capture within them. One of his most famous pieces was the "Bronco Buster."

By the time of his death in 1908, Remington had produced more than three thousand drawings and paintings, twenty-two sculptures, over one hundred articles and stories, a novel, and a Broadway play. He worked with Theodore Roosevelt on the memoir *Ranch Life and the Hunting-Trail,* enhancing the text with colorful illustrations.

Although Remington's talent cannot be denied, it was his understanding of America's need to see itself as tough, independent, and optimistic that gave the artist a lasting place in American art history. Remington gave his country a vision of itself that it wanted to see; in return, he became a permanent part of the American West.

Intervals: Periods of time.

Coarse: Rough.

time to time were sent against the different hostile tribes. At long **intervals** they came into some frontier settlement or some fur company's fort, posted in the heart of the wilderness, to dispose of their bales of furs, or to replenish their stock of ammunition and purchase a scanty supply of **coarse** food and clothing.

From that day to this they have not changed their way of life. But there are not many of them left now. The basin of the Upper Missouri was their last stronghold, being the last great hunting-ground of the Indians, with whom the white trappers were always fighting and bickering, but who nevertheless by their presence protected the game that gave the trappers their livelihood. My cattle were among the very first to come into the land, at a time when the buffalo and beaver still abounded, and then the old hunters were common. Many a time I have hunted with them, spent the night in their smoky cabins, or had them as guests at my ranch. But in a couple of years after the inrush of the cattlemen the last herds of the buffalo were destroyed, and the beaver were trapped out of all the plains' streams. Then the hunters vanished likewise, save that here and there one or two still remain in some **nook** or out-of-the-way corner. The others wandered off restlessly over the land—some to join their **brethren** in the **Coeur d'Alene** or the northern Rockies, others to the coast ranges or to far-away Alaska. Moreover, their ranks were soon thinned by death, and the places of the dead were no longer taken by new recruits. They led hard lives, and the unending strain of their **toilsome** and dangerous existence shattered even such iron frames as theirs. They were killed in drunken brawls, or in nameless fights with roving Indians; they died by one of the thousand accidents **incident to** the business of their lives—by flood or quicksand, by cold or starvation, by the stumble of a horse or a footslip on the edge of a cliff; they perished by diseases brought on by terrible **privation,** and [diseases] aggravated by the **savage orgies with which it was varied.**

Yet there was not only much that was attractive in their wild, free, reckless lives, but there was also very much good about the men themselves. They were—and such of them as are left still are—**frank,** bold, and self-reliant to a degree. They fear neither man, brute, nor **element.** They are generous and hospitable; they stand loyally by their friends, and pursue their enemies with bitter and **vindictive** hatred. For the rest, they differ among themselves in their good and bad points even more markedly than do men in civilized life, for out on the border virtue and wickedness alike take on very pronounced colors. A man who in civilization would be merely a **backbiter** becomes a murderer on the frontier; and, on the other hand, he who in the city would do nothing more than bid you a cheery good-morning, shares his last bit of **sun jerked** venison with you when threatened by starvation in the wilderness. One hunter may be a dark-browed, evil-eyed **ruffian,** ready to kill cattle or run off horses without hesitation, who if game fails will at once, in Western phrase, "take to the road,"—that is, become a **highwayman.** The next is perhaps a quiet, kindly, simple-hearted man, law-abiding, modestly unconscious of the worth of his

Nook: Secluded place.

Brethren: Brothers; fellow human beings.

Coeur d'Alene: Northern area of Idaho.

Toilsome: Characterized by hard work.

Incident to: Regularly occurring in.

Privation: Hardship.

Savage orgies with which it was varied.: Opposite of privation; excessive indulgence in food and alcohol, for example.

Frank: Honest and direct.

Element: Weather, usually severe.

Vindictive: Vengeful.

Backbiter: One who makes mean or spiteful comments about another person.

Sun jerked: Sun-dried.

Ruffian: Bully.

Highwayman: Thief who preys on travelers.

Chivalric: Honor.

Arch-type: Perfect symbol.

Hews: Cuts.

own fearless courage and iron endurance, always faithful to his friends, and full of **chivalric** and tender loyalty to women.

The hunter is the **arch-type** of freedom. His well-being rests in no man's hands save his own. He chops down and **hews** out the logs for his hut, or perhaps makes merely a rude dug-out in the side of a hill, with a skin roof, and skin flaps for the door. He buys a little flour and salt, and in times of plenty also sugar and tea; but not much, for it must all be carried hundreds of miles on the backs of his shaggy pack-ponies. In one corner of the hut, a bunk covered with deer-skins forms his bed; a kettle and a frying-pan may be all his cooking-utensils. When he can get no fresh meat he falls back on his stock of jerked venison, dried in long strips over the fire or in the sun.

Queer: Strange, odd.

Doleful: Sad.

Contemptuously: Scornfully.

Peltries: Furs.

Most of the trappers are Americans, but they also include some Frenchmen and half-breeds. Both of the last, if on the plains, occasionally make use of **queer** wooden carts, very rude in shape, with stout wheels that make a most **doleful** squeaking. In old times they all had Indian wives; but nowadays those who live among and intermarry with the Indians are looked down upon by the other frontiersmen, who **contemptuously** term them "squaw men." All of them depend upon their rifles only for food and for self-defense, and make their living by trapping, **peltries** being very valuable and yet not bulky. They are good game shots, especially the pure Americans; although, of course, they are very boastful, and generally stretch the truth tremendously in telling about their own marksmanship. Still they often do very remarkable shooting, both for speed and accuracy. One of their feats, that I never could learn to copy, is to make excellent shooting after nightfall. Of course all this applies only to the regular hunters; not to the numerous pretenders who hang around the outskirts of the

Unwary: Unsuspecting.

towns to try to persuade **unwary** strangers to take them for guides.

• • •

What happened next...

With vivid detail and humorous stories about the ranching life, Roosevelt's writing prompted many wealthy easterners to visit the Dakota Territory. Tourists came in such great numbers that many ranchers opened up their ranches to them. These operations, which became known as dude ranches, welcomed city dwellers to stay and get a taste of the ranching life. Visitors wore Western clothing, helped with chores around the ranch, learned to herd cattle.

In addition to helping establish a new tourist industry, Roosevelt's stories directly affected the way the general public perceived the Wild

West. By giving the impression that westerners were self-reliant, honorable, and hard-working, Roosevelt made the frontier a challenge for all Americans. If they could make it there, they could survive anywhere.

The frontier wilderness closed two years after the publication of Roosevelt's memoirs. In 1890, U.S. Cavalry slaughtered more than three hundred Lakota Indians at Wounded Knee, South Dakota. Known as the Wounded Knee Massacre, that bloody conflict marked the end of the Plains Indian Wars as well as the frontier. From that point on, it was no longer considered wilderness area, as thousands of settlers migrated West.

Roosevelt saw firsthand what could happen to natural resources if left in the hands of the greedy, the ignorant, and the selfish. He witnessed the overgrazing of land, the clear-cutting of forests, battles for water rights, and the over-hunting of many animal species, the buffalo in particular. A common activity among men during the era was to shoot buffalo from passing trains. Nothing was done with the dead and wounded animals; the point of the shooting was just to be able to do it. Roosevelt's already-developed sense of connection to the outdoors was only intensified during his years in the Dakota Territory.

When he became president in 1901, Roosevelt took it upon himself to use his power and authority to conserve, or save, what he saw as America's most valuable resources. As was true of anything else Roosevelt believed, he was not afraid to speak his mind, and he made

TR's Opinion of Women on the Frontier

Theodore Roosevelt admired frontier women, as evidenced by this excerpt from *Ranch Life and the Hunting-Trail:*

> There is an old and true border saying that "the frontier is hard on women and cattle." There are some striking exceptions; but, as a rule, the grinding toil and hardship of a life passed in the wilderness, or on its outskirts, drive the beauty and bloom from a woman's face long before her youth has left her. By the time she is a mother she is sinewy and angular, with thin, compressed lips and furrowed, sallow [pale] brow. But she has a hundred qualities that atone for the grace she lacks. She is a good mother and a hard-working housewife, always putting things to rights, washing and cooking for her stalwart spouse and offspring. She is faithful to her husband, and, like the true American that she is, exacts faithfulness in return. Peril cannot daunt her, nor hardship and poverty appall her. Whether on the mountains in a log hut chinked with moss, in a sod or adobe hovel on the desolate prairie, or in a mere temporary camp, where the white-topped wagons have been drawn up in a protection-giving circle near some spring, she is equally at home. Clad in a dingy gown and a hideous sun-bonnet she goes bravely about her work, resolute, silent, uncomplaining.

no apologies when some people perceived him as the "bully" president. Afire with commitment to his beliefs, Roosevelt often spoke with the enthusiasm and intention of converting his audience, much like that of a preacher at his pulpit. Roosevelt himself referred to the White House as being a bully pulpit, a splendid place from which to pursue an agenda. He also established himself as the conservation president; while in office, many conservation and environmental laws were passed.

As president, Roosevelt was concerned with the long-term well-being of the nation. He considered the land an economic resource that must be conserved, managed, and protected. Among the conservation legislation passed throughout Roosevelt's presidency were the Alaska Game Act (1902; a law protecting certain game animals); the National Reclamation Act (1902; an act requiring the money from the sale and disposal of public lands in certain states and territories to be spent on the construction of irrigation works for dry lands, making them livable); and the Antiquities Act (1906; a law that allowed the president to designate federally protected national monuments for the sake of historic and scientific preservation; see Chapter 13).

Did you know...

- Roosevelt established 150 national forests, 51 bird preserves, 5 national parks, and 18 national monuments during his time as president.
- Most of the early cowboys in the 1870s and 1880s were Irish and Welsh immigrants from Ireland and Great Britain.
- One of the many jobs of children on the frontier was the gathering of buffalo chips (dried buffalo waste). These were used for fuel in the fireplace.
- Wanting a rest after completing his presidency in 1909, Roosevelt and his son Kermit went on a safari in Africa. They killed thousands of animals, including elephants, rhinos, and lions.
- Many cowboy words come from Mexican culture. Among them are "lariat," "chaps," "buckaroo," and "rodeo." Although largely considered the epitome of western wear, the cowboy hat also has its roots in Mexican culture and is a version of the sombrero.

Consider the following...

- How are the conservation concerns during the early twentieth century similar to those today? How are they different?
- How has Hollywood influenced America's perception of the cowboy?
- How might the life of a woman on the frontier differ from the life of a woman living in an eastern city?

Former president Theodore Roosevelt stands by the rhinoceros he just killed during a hunt on his African expedition in 1909. © CORBIS.

For More Information

BOOKS

Hafen, LeRoy R., ed. *Mountain Men and Fur Traders of the Far West.* Lincoln: University of Nebraska Press, 1982.

Kraft, Betsy Harvey. *Theodore Roosevelt: Champion of the American Spirit.* New York: Clarion Books, 2003.

Roosevelt, Theodore. *Ranch Life and the Hunting-Trail.* New York: The Century Co., 1888. Multiple reprints.

West, Elliott. *Growing Up with the Country: Childhood on the Far-Western Frontier.* Albuquerque: University of New Mexico Press, 1989.

WEB SITES

PBS. "Frederic Remington." *American Masters.* http://www.pbs.org/wnet/ americanmasters/database/remington_f.html (accessed on July 25, 2006).

PBS. "Theodore Roosevelt." *New Perspectives on the West.* http://www.pbs.org/ weta/thewest/people/i_r/roosevelt.htm (accessed on July 25, 2006).

"Ranch Life and the Hunting-Trail." *Bartleby.com.* http://www.bartelby.com/54/ (accessed on July 20, 2006).

Zimmerman, Emily. "The Mountain Men: Pathfinders of the West, 1810–1860." *American Studies at the University of Virginia.* http://xroads.virginia.edu/ ~hyper/HNS/Mtmen/home.html (accessed on July 25, 2006).

6

Andrew Carnegie

Excerpt from "The Gospel of Wealth"
  Originally published in the North American Review, *June 1889; available at* American Studies
    at the University of Virginia *(Web site)*

> "In bestowing charity, the main consideration should be to help those who will help themselves; to provide part of the means by which those who desire to improve may do so; to give those who desire to rise the aids by which they may rise; to assist, but rarely or never to do all."

More than any other time in American history, the Gilded Age (approximately 1877–99) was characterized by the phenomenal wealth and far-reaching power of a handful of men. Known as robber barons, these men ruled the business world by taking complete control of the industrialization (a transition to an economy based on business and industry rather than agriculture) of the country, also known as the Industrial Revolution. Generally speaking, they accumulated billions of dollars by exploiting (using to their advantage) the working-class poor. They underpaid and overworked the labor that made their factories and businesses run. Robber barons were not known for their honesty or integrity in the way they conducted business.

It would be incorrect to say that the robber barons set the standards for the industrialization of America. They did not. The Industrial Revolution happened because of the determination and perseverance of small-business owners who relied on proven business strategies to keep their companies alive. And that is where the robber barons differed greatly from other industrialists: They took risks by experimenting with strategies that no one had ever used before in business. Those strategies, supplemented by the barons' greed and desire for power, gave them wealth but a bad reputation as well.

Industrialist, robber baron, and philanthropist Andrew Carnegie. © CORBIS.

Among the most notable robber barons were John D. Rockefeller (1839–1937), owner of the Standard Oil Company, which at its peak controlled 90 percent of America's oil industry; Cornelius Vanderbilt (1794–1877), a railroad tycoon (exceptionally wealthy industrialist) considered by many to be the first true robber baron; Jay Gould (1836–1892), a railroad financier (one who deals with large amounts of money in finance and investment businesses) who often competed with Vanderbilt; and J. P. Morgan (1837–1913), the most famous banker and financier of his day. Unlike his peers, Morgan had a reputation as a man of his word who valued honesty more than money.

Another famous robber baron was Andrew Carnegie (1835–1919), owner of Carnegie Steel. Unlike his fellow industrialists, Carnegie was an immigrant. Born in Scotland, he moved to the United States at the age of twelve. Although born into poverty, Carnegie's intelligence and resourcefulness turned misfortune to fortune. By the age of thirty-three, the Scotsman was worth $400,000 (approximately $5 million in twenty-first-century money).

Like the other robber barons, Carnegie overworked and underpaid his employees. In doing so, he kept his operating costs as low as possible, which allowed him to provide steel to buyers at a price lower than his competitors.

Carnegie was in the right business at the right time. The industrialization of America made steel the number-one selling product. Steel was used in the construction and maintenance of railroads as well as nearly every other industry of the day. He sold his company to U.S. Steel (owned by robber baron J. P. Morgan) in 1901 for $250 million ($4.5 billion in twenty-first-century money) and became the wealthiest man in the world.

Carnegie's wealth troubled him. He had known poverty and despair in his younger years, so he understood firsthand the struggles and suffering of the poor. Although he reigned as king of the steel industry for thirty years, he privately longed to change his focus from making money to doing good for those less fortunate than himself. In this respect, Carnegie set himself apart from his robber baron colleagues.

In 1889, Carnegie published an essay in a political magazine. In the essay, he explained his philosophy on wealth and how to distribute it after death. The essay attracted much attention because its author claimed that the wealthy have a responsibility to give back to society and work for its greater good. This attitude was not popular among America's upper class, who had been living for decades with the idea that hard work was all that was needed to succeed. The general attitude was that the poor were poor because God made them that way and that they deserved their status in society.

Carnegie developed his ideas while reading the work of a philosopher he greatly admired, Herbert Spencer (1820–1903). Spencer's philosophy was based on the evolutionary theory of Charles Darwin (1809–1882), which said the strong survive while the weak die. Spencer applied that biological theory to society and promoted the idea that competition was natural and that those most fit to live in society would rise to the top. It was Spencer who coined the phrase "survival of the fittest." Carnegie found in Spencer's philosophy the permission to succeed in business, even as he struggled internally with his high-society position and life of privilege.

Things to remember while reading the excerpt from "The Gospel of Wealth":

- Carnegie was highly respected in American society. His opinions mattered. His was a true rags-to-riches story. Carnegie was considered a perfect example of a poor man who achieved the American Dream.

- Carnegie's life was one of paradox (contradictions). As the richest man in the world, he spoke out against privilege. He championed the working man, even as he crushed labor unions and cut his employees' wages.

- Before the Industrial Revolution, the gap between the upper classes and the lower classes was not so large. There had always been people who had money and people who did not, but industrialism allowed people in the right circumstances to make more money than was ever possible before. Without the working class, robber barons could not have elevated themselves to the highest positions in American society.

A Different Kind of Gospel

The industrialization of America was looked upon by some as progress. Others considered it a phenomenon that caused more harm than good. There were those who believed that industrialization gave birth to overcrowded slums and a greatly increased poor population that lived in despair and hopelessness.

There was nothing anyone could do to stop industrialization. But churches and religious organizations were determined to do what they could to improve the situation for the working-class poor. The result was what religious leaders from different faiths called the Social Gospel. The concept was based on the idea that through reform laws and religion, a fair and just society was attainable.

The Social Gospel sought reform on every level: child labor, work conditions, housing, education, and more. In some ways, the idea was the opposite of the "survival of the fittest" beliefs of men like Andrew Carnegie and John D. Rockefeller. They believed the powerful and wealthy had the right to their lives of privilege, even while others suffered. But in other ways, the philosophies were similar. Both Carnegie and Rockefeller were famous for their philanthropy (charitable donations). Between the two of them, hundreds of millions of dollars were given to help those in need.

The major difference between the Social Gospel movement and the philanthropy of Carnegie and Rockefeller was that the activists sought to change the law and offer protective measures to the poor. The robber barons did not want the laws changed; the laws already in place worked in their favor and allowed them to run their businesses in such a way that they made millions off the cheap labor of the working class.

Social Gospel faded away as an active movement, but its efforts influenced the reforms of the Progressive Era (approximately 1900–17). The philosophy of the Social Gospel movement stands as the foundation for religious charities throughout the world.

• • •

Excerpt from "The Gospel of Wealth"

Administering: Distributing.

Competence: Money used for the basics in life.

Surplus: Extra.

Decedents: Dead.

Bequeathed: Given.

What is the proper mode of **administering** wealth after the laws upon which civilization is founded have thrown it into the hands of the few? And it is of this great question that I believe I offer the true solution. It will be understood that fortunes are here spoken of, not moderate sums saved by many years of effort, the returns from which are required for the comfortable maintenance and education of families. This is not wealth but only **competence,** which it should be the aim of all to acquire.

There are but three modes in which **surplus** wealth can be disposed of. It can be left to the families of the **decedents;** or it can be **bequeathed** for public purposes; or, finally, it can be administered during their lives by its possessors. Under the first and second modes most of the wealth of the world that has reached the few has hitherto been applied. Let us in turn consider each of these modes.

The first is the most **injudicious.** In **monarchical countries,** the estates and the greatest portion of the wealth are left to the first son [so] that the **vanity** of the parent may be gratified by the thought that his name and title are to descend to succeeding generations unimpaired. Why should men leave great fortunes to their children? If this is done from affection, is it not misguided affection? Observation teaches that, generally speaking, it is not well for the children that they should be so burdened. Neither is it well for the state. Beyond providing for the wife and daughters moderate sources of income, and very moderate allowances indeed, if any, for the sons, men may well hesitate, for it is no longer questionable that great sums bequeathed oftener work more for the injury than for the good of the recipients. Wise men will soon conclude that, for the best interests of the members of their families and of the state, such bequests are an improper use of their **means.**

As to the second mode, that of leaving wealth at death for public uses, it may be said that this is only a means for the disposal of wealth, provided a man is content to wait until he is dead before it becomes of much good in the world. Knowledge of the results of **legacies** bequeathed is not calculated to inspire the brightest hopes of much **posthumous** good being accomplished. The cases are not few in which the real object sought by the **testator** is not attained, nor are they few in which his real wishes are **thwarted.** In many cases the bequests are so used as to become only monuments of his **folly.**

There remains, then, only one mode of using great fortunes; but in this we have the true **antidote** for the temporary unequal distribution of wealth, the reconciliation of the rich and the poor—a reign of harmony—another ideal, differing, indeed, from that of the Communist in requiring only the further evolution of existing conditions, not the total overthrow of our civilization. It is founded upon the present most intense individualism, and the race is prepared to put it in practice by degrees whenever it pleases. Under its **sway** we shall have an ideal state in which the surplus wealth of the few will become, in the best sense, the property of the many, because [it will be] administered for the common good; and this wealth, passing through the hands of the few, can be made a much more potent force for the elevation of our race than if it had been distributed in small sums to the people themselves. Even the poorest can be made to see this and to agree that great sums gathered by some of their fellow citizens and spent for public purposes, from which the masses reap the **principal** benefit, are more valuable to them than if scattered among them through the course of many years in **trifling** amounts.

This, then, is held to be the duty of the man of wealth: first, to set an example of modest, **unostentatious** living, shunning display or **extravagance;**

Injudicious: Unwise.

Monarchical countries: Nations ruled by kings or queens who inherited their positions.

Vanity: Excessive pride.

Means: Wealth.

Legacies: Gifts.

Posthumous: After death.

Testator: Person who leaves behind a will distributing his property and wealth.

Thwarted: Prevented.

Folly: Foolish ideas.

Antidote: Cure.

Sway: Controlling influence.

Principal: Main.

Trifling: Small, of little importance.

Unostentatious: Simple.

Extravagance: Luxury.

Brethren: Brothers; fellow human beings.

to provide moderately for the legitimate wants of those dependent upon him; and after doing so to consider all surplus revenues which come to him simply as trust funds which he is called upon to administer, and strictly bound as a matter of duty to administer in the manner which, in his judgment, is best calculated to produce the most beneficial results for the community—the man of wealth thus becoming the mere agent and trustee for his poorer **brethren,** bringing to their service his superior wisdom, experience, and ability to administer, doing for them better than they would or could do for themselves. . . .

Bestowing: Giving away to.

In **bestowing** charity, the main consideration should be to help those who will help themselves; to provide part of the means by which those who desire to improve may do so; to give those who desire to rise the aids by which they may rise; to assist, but rarely or never to do all. Neither the individual nor the race is improved by **almsgiving.** Those worthy of assistance, except in rare cases, seldom require assistance.

Almsgiving: Giving to the poor.

Such, in my opinion, is the true gospel concerning wealth, obedience to which is destined some day to solve the problem of the rich and the poor, and to bring "Peace on earth, among men goodwill."

• • •

What happened next . . .

For all their greed and corruption, many robber barons defied the label given them and established the model for the basis of American philanthropy. Carnegie himself refused to simply give money to the poor, but in his lifetime, his wealth established nearly three thousand public libraries throughout the world, numerous universities and educational foundations, several music halls (including the famous Carnegie Hall in New York City), and other self-improvement and scientific initiatives.

Carnegie founded the Carnegie Corporation of New York. Its mission was to "promote the advancement and spread of knowledge and understanding." This charitable organization remains active in the twenty-first century and regularly donates to institutions that provide educational grants, universities, colleges, and companies focused on education. The popular children's television show *Sesame Street,* for example, is funded in part by the Carnegie Corporation.

Other robber barons became philanthropists as well. J. P. Morgan left one of the most extensive art collections ever put together upon his death, and he donated sizeable sums of money to art museums and collections throughout his life. Rockefeller and Carnegie were in

Carnegie Hall on the day of its opening, May 5, 1891. © CORBIS.

direct competition with each other's level of giving throughout their later years. Newspapers even kept score of who donated more money to charity. For instance, in 1904, the *Times of London* reported Carnegie's total at $21 million and Rockefeller's at $10 million; in 1910, the *New York American* said Carnegie was up to $179.3 million and Rockefeller over $134.2 million; and in 1913, the *New York Herald* noted that Carnegie's sum had increased to $332 million and Rockefeller's $175 million.

The age of the robber baron and his philanthropy ended with the presidency of Woodrow Wilson (1856–1924; served 1913–21), who passed legislation introducing the income tax (taxes paid on money earned) and estate tax (taxes paid on money left at the time of death). These taxes inhibited the quick growth of monetary fortune.

The New York Philharmonic performs at the renovated Carnegie Hall on December 15, 1986. © BETTMANN/CORBIS.

Did you know...

- Carnegie's sixty-four-room mansion was so big that it took two tons of coal to heat it on a typical winter day.
- Carnegie first worked as a bobbin boy setting up spools of thread in a cotton factory, where he earned $1.20 a week.
- By the time he died, Carnegie had given away $350 million. Per instructions left in his will, the remaining $30 million was given away to foundations and charities.

Consider the following...

- How does American society define "success"?
- Capitalism is based on the idea that every individual has an equal opportunity for success. Is this true in American society? Why or why not?
- Can a person be a ruthless businessman but still be a good person?

For More Information

BOOKS

Carnegie, Andrew, and David Nasaw. *The Gospel of Wealth and Other Writings.* New York: Penguin Classics, 2006.

Edge, Laura B. *Andrew Carnegie: Industrial Philanthropist.* Minneapolis: Lerner, 2004.

Rau, Dana Meachen. *Andrew Carnegie: Captain of Industry.* Minneapolis: Compass Point Books, 2006.

WEB SITES

Carnegie, Andrew. "The Gospel of Wealth." *North American Review.* June 1889. Reprinted at *American Studies at the University of Virginia.* http://xroads.virginia.edu/~DRBR/wealth.html (accessed on July 25, 2006).

Chernow, Rob. "Blessed Barons." *Time.com.* http://www.time.com/time/time100/builder/other/barons.html (accessed on July 25, 2006).

PBS. "Monkey Trial: People and Events: Fundamentalism and the Social Gospel." *American Experience.* http://www.pbs.org/wgbh/amex/monkeytrial/peopleevents/e_gospel.html (accessed on July 25, 2006).

PBS. "The Richest Man in the World: Andrew Carnegie." *American Experience.* http://www.pbs.org/wgbh/amex/carnegie/index.html (accessed on July 25, 2006).

7

Jacob Riis

Excerpt from *How the Other Half Lives*
Originally published in 1890; available at Yale University: American Studies Program *(Web site)*

"In the dog-days when the fierce heat and foul air of the tenements smother their babies by thousands, [abandoned babies] are found...on the doorsteps of the rich, with whose comfort in luxurious homes the wretched mother somehow connects her own misery. Perhaps, as the drowning man clutches at a straw, she hopes that these happier hearts may have love to spare even for her little one."

The Industrial Revolution (approximately 1877–1900) caused America to shift its economy from an agricultural base (one that depended upon the land) to an industrial one. As time passed and technology advanced, skilled craftsmen were replaced with machinery. By 1900, one-third of the country's population was among the industrial workforce.

Those who owned businesses and factories made up the upper classes of American society. The middle class consisted largely of the men who filled executive positions and those who managed workers in those companies. Together with their families, these classes formed about half of American society.

This was the half who often read about themselves or their friends and coworkers in the newspapers, the half for whom magazine articles were written. When people thought of America, this was the half they imagined. Businessmen believed that anyone could succeed through hard work and that they were living proof of that philosophy.

The "other half" of society was the working class. One-third of these laborers were immigrants from other countries who had come to America

Writer and photographer Jacob Riis, who wrote How the Other Half Lives. © CORBIS.

in search of a better life. Many had sold everything they owned to cross the ocean. Life in America varied little from the lives they left behind, however. These people lived in overcrowded, unclean conditions. Disease was virtually inescapable.

The working class was not paid fairly for its efforts. Many of these laborers worked twelve-hour shifts in jobs no one else wanted, only to come home and work more. Yet 40 percent of them lived below the poverty line of $500 per year. (The poverty line is the minimum amount of money someone can make and still get by.)

Without the working class, the "other half" of American society could not have thrived. The rich got richer while the poor became poorer working for them. Although the upper and middle classes knew their laborers and employees lived in desperate conditions, most of them did little to help. They were more concerned with getting the most work out of them for the least amount of money.

Jacob Riis was born in Denmark in 1849 and immigrated to America in 1870. After months of little work and no luck finding a place to live, Riis fell into despair. Eventually, a friend tipped him off about a job, and Riis went to work as a writer for a news agency. While reporting for the agency, he bought himself a camera and taught himself the art of photography. By 1877, he was known throughout the city for his talent, and took a job as a police reporter for the *New York Tribune.* His job took him to police headquarters on Mulberry Street, which ran through the worst slum in the city.

Riis was shocked by the living conditions forced upon the working class. With camera in hand, he walked through the slums, capturing on film not only the cheap construction of the tenement (apartment) buildings found in the inner city but the desperation and hopelessness of its inhabitants as well. In 1888, the photojournalist took a job with the *Evening Sun* newspaper.

In 1890, Riis took his collection of photographs and wrote text to accompany them. The final product was a groundbreaking book he called *How the Other Half Lives*. The book established Riis as a muckraker, or a journalist who used his reporting skills to uncover scandal and corruption. He used his book as a way to force New Yorkers to confront the intense poverty that affected thousands of the city's residents. He discussed the poor construction of the tenements, which were not only cheaply built but also dangerous to those who lived in them. His book included chapters on the high rent, the absentee (unavailable) landlords, the high rate of crime, and the dangerously filthy living conditions.

Things to remember while reading an excerpt from *How the Other Half Lives:*

- Riis's book was among the first of its kind to combine text with photographs to give a complete picture of the plight of America's working poor.

- The chapter the excerpt is taken from focuses on the orphaned and unwanted children of the city's slums.

- *How the Other Half Lives* was published at the beginning of an era of reform. People were just beginning to realize that the changes forced upon America by the Industrial Revolution were bringing about not only drastic change but also widespread social problems such as overcrowding, increased crime, and public sanitation issues.

- A few years before the publication of Riis's book, journalists Charles Loring Brace and James D. McCabe each had written books about urban poverty. Although they did not have the powerful effect of Riis's book, they did publicize the issues about which Riis was most concerned.

- Unlike most journalists of the time, Riis was not a sensationalist (someone who focuses on the emotional aspects, often with exaggeration). Instead, he used facts to bolster his arguments for reform. He backed up those facts with evidence, statistics, and firsthand accounts from the working class themselves. This approach earned his book a reputation for accuracy.

- The barriers Riis wrote about in the excerpt are those he believed charity had unknowingly set up. Riis and many others of his day believed charity in general did not help the poor. They thought that charitable giving did not offer solutions to the growing problem of poverty but only relieved some of the hardships.

• • •

Excerpt from *How the Other Half Lives*

Foundling Asylum: Children's orphanage.

Forlorn little waifs: Helpless, homeless orphans.

Arraignment: A request for help.

1. FIRST among these barriers is the **Foundling Asylum.** It stands at the very outset of the waste of life that goes on in a population of nearly two millions of people; powerless to prevent it, though it gather in the outcasts by night and by day. In a score of years an army of twenty-five thousand of these **forlorn little waifs** have cried out from the streets of New York in **arraignment** of a Christian civilization under the blessings of which the instinct of motherhood even was smothered by poverty and want. Only the poor abandon their children. The stories of richly-dressed foundlings that are dished up in the newspapers at intervals are pure fiction. Not one instance of even a well-dressed infant having been picked up in the streets is on record. They come in rags, a newspaper often the only wrap, semi-occasionally one in a clean slip with some evidence of loving care; a little slip of paper pinned on, perhaps, with some such message as this I once read, in a woman's trembling hand: "Take care of Johnny, for God's sake. I cannot." But even that is the rarest of all happenings.

Sisters of Charity: The religious order that ran the Foundling Asylum.

City's wards: Children in custody of the city.

Dog-days: Hottest days of summer.

Abodes: Homes.

Career: Lifetime experiences.

Mortality: Death rate.

2. The city divides with the **Sisters of Charity** the task of gathering them in. The real foundlings, the children of the gutter that are picked up by the police, are the **city's wards.** In midwinter, when the poor shiver in their homes, and in the **dog-days** when the fierce heat and foul air of the tenements smother their babies by thousands, they [abandoned babies] are found, sometimes three and four in a night, in hallways, in areas and on the doorsteps of the rich, with whose comfort in luxurious homes the wretched mother somehow connects her own misery. Perhaps, as the drowning man clutches at a straw, she hopes that these happier hearts may have love to spare even for her little one. In this she is mistaken. Unauthorized babies especially are not popular in the **abodes** of the wealthy. It never happens outside of the story-books that a baby so deserted finds home and friends at once. Its **career,** though rather more official, is less romantic, and generally brief. After a night spent at Police Headquarters it travels up to the Infants' Hospital on Randall's Island in the morning, fitted out with a number and a bottle, that seldom see much wear before they are laid aside for a fresh recruit. Few outcast babies survive their desertion long. Murder is the true name of the mother's crime in eight cases out of ten. Of 508 babies received at the Randall's Island Hospital last year 333 died, 65.55 per cent. But of the 508 only 170 were picked up in the streets, and among these the **mortality** was much greater, probably nearer ninety per cent, if the truth were told. The rest were born in the hospitals. The high mortality among the foundlings is not to be marvelled at. The wonder is, rather, that any survive. The stormier the night, the more certain is the police nursery to echo with the feeble cries of abandoned babes. Often

Homeless boys sleep on the streets of New York City in 1888. PHOTOGRAPH BY JACOB RIIS. LIBRARY OF CONGRESS.

they come half dead from **exposure.** One live baby came in a little pine coffin which a policeman found an inhuman wretch trying to bury in an uptown lot. But many do not live to be officially registered as a charge upon the county. Seventy-two dead babies were picked up in the streets last year. Some of them were doubtless put out by very poor parents to save funeral expenses. In hard times the number of dead and live foundlings always increases very noticeably. But whether travelling by way of the Morgue or the Infants' Hospital, the little army of waifs meets, reunited soon, in the trench in the **Potter's Field** where, if no medical student is in need of a subject, they are laid in squads of a dozen.

3. Most of the foundlings come from the East Side, where they are left by young mothers without wedding-rings or other name than their own to bestow upon the baby, returning from the island hospital to face an unpitying world with the evidence of their shame. Not infrequently they wear the **bed-tick regimentals** of the Public Charities, and thus their origin is easily

Exposure: Lack of protection from extreme weather.

Potter's Field: Graveyard for the city's poor and unwanted.

Bed-tick regimentals: Clothing made from the cheap, strong fabric made to cover mattresses.

Jacob Riis

Portal: Doorway.

Antecedents: Relatives.

Twelvemonth: Year.

Heinous: Wicked.

Exemplary fines: Fines serving as a warning.

Disreputable character: Bad reputation.

Illegitimate children: Children born out of wedlock.

Paregoric: A pain-relieving medicine containing opium.

Inanition: Lack of nourishment.

enough traced. Oftener no ray of light penetrates the gloom, and no effort is made to probe the mystery of sin and sorrow. This also is the policy pursued in the great Foundling Asylum of the Sisters of Charity in Sixty-eighth Street, known all over the world as Sister Irene's Asylum. Years ago the crib that now stands just inside the street door, under the great main **portal,** was placed outside at night; but it filled up too rapidly. The babies took to coming in little squads instead of in single file, and in self-defence the sisters were forced to take the cradle in. Now the mother must bring her child inside and put it in the crib where she is seen by the sister on guard. No effort is made to question her, or discover the child's **antecedents,** but she is asked to stay and nurse her own and another baby. If she refuses, she is allowed to depart unhindered. If willing, she enters at once into the great family of the good Sister who in twenty-one years has gathered as many thousand homeless babies into her fold. One was brought in when I was last in the asylum, in the middle of July, that received in its crib the number 20715. The death-rate is of course lowered a good deal where exposure of the child is prevented. Among the eleven hundred infants in the asylum it was something over nineteen per cent last year; but among those actually received in the **twelvemonth** nearer twice that figure.

5. An infinitely more fiendish, if to surface appearances less deliberate, plan of child-murder than desertion has flourished in New York for years under the title of baby-farming. The name, put into plain English, means starving babies to death. The law has fought this most **heinous** of crimes by compelling the registry of all baby-farms. As well might it require all persons intending murder to register their purpose with time and place of the deed under the penalty of **exemplary fines.** Murderers do not hang out a shingle. "Baby-farms," said Mr. Elbridge T. Gerry, the President of the [New York] Society [for the Prevention of Cruelty to Children, which was] charged with the execution of the law that was passed through his efforts, "are concerns by means of which persons, usually of **disreputable character,** eke out a living by taking two, or three, or four babies to board. They are the charges of outcasts, or **illegitimate children.** They feed them on sour milk, and give them **paregoric** to keep them quiet, until they die, when they get some young medical man without experience to sign a certificate to the Board of Health that the child died of **inanition,** and so the matter ends. The baby is dead, and there is no one to complain." A handful of baby-farms have been registered and licensed by the Board of Health with the approval of the Society for the Prevention of Cruelty to Children in the last five years, but none of this kind. The devil keeps the only complete register to be found anywhere. Their trace is found oftenest by the coroner or the police; sometimes they may be discovered hiding in the advertising columns of certain newspapers, under the guise of the

scarcely less heartless traffic in helpless children that is dignified with the pretense of adoption—for cash. An idea of how this scheme works was obtained through the disclosures in a celebrated divorce case, a year or two ago. The [S]ociety has among its records a very recent case of a baby a week old (Baby "Blue Eyes") that was offered for sale—adoption, the dealer called it—in a newspaper. The agent bought it after some haggling for a dollar, and arrested the woman slave-trader; but the law was powerless to punish her for her crime. Twelve unfortunate women **awaiting dishonored motherhood** were found in her house.

7. It is with a sense of glad relief that one turns from this misery to the brighter page of the helping hands stretched forth on every side to save the young and the helpless. New York is, I firmly believe, the most charitable city in the world. Nowhere is there so eager a readiness to help, when it is known that help is worthily wanted; nowhere are such armies of devoted workers, nowhere such abundance of means ready to the hand of those who know the need and how rightly to supply it. Its poverty, its slums, and its suffering are the result of unprecedented growth with the consequent disorder and crowding, and the common penalty of **metropolitan** greatness. If the **structure shows signs of being top-heavy,** evidences are not wanting—they are multiplying day by day—that patient **toilers** are at work among the **underpinnings.** The Day Nurseries, the numberless Kindergartens and charitable schools in the poor quarters, the Fresh Air Funds, the thousand and one charities that in one way or another reach the homes and the lives of the poor with sweetening touch, are proof that if much is yet to be done, if the need only grows with the effort, hearts and hands will be found to do it in ever-increasing measure. Black as the cloud is it has a silver lining, bright with promise. New York is to-day a hundredfold cleaner, better, purer, city than it was even ten years ago.

Awaiting dishonored motherhood: Pregnant out of wedlock.

Metropolitan: Urban.

Structure shows signs of being top-heavy: Poor population is increasing.

Toilers: Workers.

Underpinnings: Behind the scenes, at the bottom.

• • •

What happened next...

Riis's book was an immediate bestseller and sold well for the next five years. The book brought the plight of the city's poor into the spotlight where it could no longer be ignored.

The book was effective for many reasons. Riis had already developed a reputation as a reliable, honest investigative journalist. He brought those qualifications to his book, and readers felt they could believe what he was saying. The accompanying photographs illustrated the claims he was making. No one could see those photos without noticing

A tired worker sits in his living quarters in the cellar of a New York City tenement house in 1891. PHOTOGRAPH BY JACOB RIIS. © BETTMANN/CORBIS.

the hopeless expressions on the faces of the children, or the weary eyes in the adults.

Riis was the first social commentator to not only reveal the obvious and hidden problems of urban poverty but to present possible solutions as well. Rather than simply complain about the issues and very real hardships of poverty, he presented readers with thoughtful, realistic ways in which the war on poverty could be fought.

Riis knew his readers well. The middle and upper classes had a sense of Victorian values (the standards and morals of the age of Queen Victoria [1819–1901; reigned 1837–1901] in England). Family and home were of the utmost importance. By photographing the squalid

A group of people gather outside a tenement on New York City's Lower East Side in 1890. PHOTOGRAPH BY JACOB RIIS. © BETTMANN/CORBIS.

(filthy) living conditions of the poor, he challenged those values and made readers understand that what they took for granted—nicely furnished homes in safe buildings, privacy, the ability to stay clean, and money to buy food, clothing, and toys for the children—were not available to the average worker. Many of his photographs included mothers with their children, or children left to roam the streets alone or even sleep in the alleys. These photos did not match the common late-nineteenth-century ideals of how children should be raised.

Riis often photographed his subjects not as the focal point (the main object of focus, as in a portrait) but among their surroundings. These photos in particular gave readers a solid sense of the poverty that affected every part of working-class life.

As Americans gained a more thorough understanding of the issues surrounding poverty and urban slums, reforms were enacted that improved building safety and implemented sanitation standards. Riis

Working for Next to Nothing

Many of the home workers were young children. These children stayed home from school to help supplement the family's inadequate income. Some of these children rolled cigars; others did laundry for the wealthy. Still others did needlework and sewing. What follows is a list of just some of the sewing jobs children and their families would perform into the early morning hours, as well as the amount of additional weekly income brought in by such work.

- Finishing coats: 6 cents a piece ($2.40 to $3.00)
- Finishing pants: 6 to 10 cents a pair ($3.00 to $4.20)
- Making violets: 3 cents per 122 flowers ($2.75 to $3.50)
- Making little roses: 8 cents per 122 flowers ($2.75 to $4.00)
- Making large roses: 16 to 18 cents per 122 flowers ($3.00)
- Making baby dresses: 45 cents a dozen ($3.20 to $5.00). (Sewing up two sides, hemming the skirt, making sleeves and sewing them in, gathering and binding the neck into a band, sewing on one button, and making one button hole.)

WATSON, ELIZABETH C. "HOME WORK IN THE TENEMENTS." *SURVEY*, 1911, P. 772–81. AVAILABLE ONLINE AT *TENANT NET*. HTTP://TENANT.NET/COMMUNITY/LES/WATSON8.HTML (ACCESSED ON AUGUST 9, 2006).

had developed a lifelong friendship with the president of the Board of Police Commissioners, Theodore Roosevelt (1858–1919). After publication of *How the Other Half Lives,* the two men would walk the streets of the slums at midnight, with Riis pointing out the tenement workshops. These workshops were actually the homes of the laborers. Working twelve-hour days elsewhere was not bringing in enough money to pay the bills. The laborers would bring their work home so that they could work longer hours and make more money. They knew they were being exploited, but they were powerless to do anything about it.

Riis also took Roosevelt to see the police lodging houses (primitive housing where police brought drunks, the homeless, and petty criminals). The lodging houses were run-down, overcrowded, and disease-ridden. These midnight inspections led to Roosevelt shutting down the lodging houses in 1896 and closing about one hundred cigar-making tenement shops.

As a direct result of his book, Riis soon found himself taking public health officials on tours of the city. This firsthand education led to the destruction of many tenement buildings in 1896 and 1897 and improvements in lighting and ventilation in those left standing. The Tenement House Act of 1901 required tenement landlords to update their existing buildings to adhere to new safety codes. New tenements were to be built with more modern conveniences, including indoor toilets, running water, and windows in every room.

Settlement houses were urban centers that provided community services such as health care, kindergarten, and child care for free. Settlement houses had been in existence for two years before Riis's book was published, but his exposé helped America understand the importance of the work the settlement houses did. For example, poor women could take their young children to these settlements, which were located in the middle of the poorest slums. While the children were taken care of at no expense, or, if old enough, attended kindergarten, the mothers were taught valuable skills, such as cooking, sewing, reading, and writing. Since many of the urban poor were immigrants, very few knew how to write anything other than their names, and even fewer were able to read English. Riis's book encouraged the nation's wealthy to donate money to fund these settlement houses.

Did you know...

- Jacob Riis had a settlement house named after him in 1901. It is located in Long Island, New York.
- *How the Other Half Lives* is still considered a landmark in the field of photojournalism.
- Toilets in the early tenement buildings were built outside, usually one per building, and were not connected to sewage lines. Waste piled up, causing a foul smell and the spread of serious disease. Although landlords were supposed to remove the waste, most left that duty to the tenement dwellers.

Consider the following...

- Why do you think the middle and upper classes of America had such negative feelings toward the working class?
- Do slums still exist in the twenty-first century? What social and political factors contribute to their existence?
- How were children treated and valued differently in the late nineteenth century compared with children in the twenty-first century?

For More Information

BOOKS

Freedman, Russell. *Kids at Work: Lewis Hine and the Crusade Against Child Labor.* New York: Clarion, 1998.

Pascal, Janet. *Jacob Riis: Reporter and Reformer.* New York: Oxford University Press, 2005.

Riis, Jacob. *How the Other Half Lives: Studies among the Tenements of New York.* New York: Charles Scribner's Sons, 1890. Multiple reprints.

Riis, Jacob. *The Making of an American.* New York: Macmillan, 1901. Multiple reprints.

WEB SITES

Crozier, William, Clarke Chambers, Patrick Costello, Chad Gaffield, and Beverly Stadium, eds. "On the Lower East Side: Observations of Life in Lower Manhattan at the Turn of the Century." *Tenant Net.* http://tenant.net/Community/LES/contents.html (accessed on August 9, 2006).

Davis, Kay. "Documenting 'The Other Half': The Social Reform Photography of Jacob Riis & Lewis Hine." *University of Virginia.* http://xroads.virginia.edu/~MA01/Davis/photography/reform/reform.html (accessed on August 9, 2006).

Lower East Side Tenement Museum. http://www.tenement.org/ (accessed on August 9, 2006).

Riis, Jacob A. "How the Other Half Lives." *Yale University: American Studies Program.* http://www.yale.edu/amstud/inforev/riis/title.html (accessed on August 15, 2006).

8

Frances Willard

Excerpt from a speech delivered to the National Council of Women of the United States on February 22, 1891
Available at American Memory: Votes for Women *(Web site)*

"But God be thanked that we live in an age when men as a class have risen to such an appreciation of women as a class.... And this which is true now in large degree throughout the world will be a thousand times more true in a century from now."

Women had been fighting for their suffrage (right to vote) since the 1770s. In one of her many letters to her husband, Abigail Adams (1744–1818) reminded future U.S. president John Adams (1735–1826; served 1797–1801) to "remember the ladies" as he worked with the Continental Congress to develop new laws. Society was slow to progress, however, and women retained their status as second-class citizens well into the nineteenth century.

As second-class citizens, women were not allowed to own property, manage their own money, or even sign a contract. Education was considered dangerous because all strenuous physical or intellectual activity was considered a threat to the delicate female body and reproductive system. This view of woman as inferior to her husband was encouraged and upheld by organized religion, which reinforced the idea of woman as an object of beauty that belonged in the home, raising children and tending to her husband.

As the nineteenth century progressed, more and more women were refusing to accept the limitations imposed upon them by society. Many wanted more than the right to vote. They wanted the opportunity to go to college, build careers, and become active in public politics. They wanted their voices to be heard both within the home and outside it; they wanted lives that included, but did not revolve around, their husbands and children.

Carrie Chapman Catt (center, in white garb) leads a women's suffrage march in New York in 1918. © AP/WIDE WORLD PHOTOS.

In 1848, the first women's rights convention was held in Seneca Falls, New York. Women's rights activist Elizabeth Cady Stanton (1815–1902) was one of several women residing over the convention. Stanton proposed the idea of suffrage at this convention.

The battle for voting rights was destined to be a long one. In 1868, the Fourteenth Amendment was ratified. This amendment stated that voters and citizens were male. Seen as a setback for all American women, Stanton and fellow activist Susan B. Anthony (1820–1906) formed the National Woman Suffrage Association (NWSA) that same year. The underlying philosophy of the NWSA was that women deserved the vote more than African American men, given that the men had only recently been freed from slavery.

At the same time, another women's rights group was established. The American Woman Suffrage Association (AWSA), led by activists Lucy Stone (1818–1893), Julia Ward Howe (1819–1910), and Henry Blackwell (1825–1909), was a more conservative rights group in several ways. First, its membership included men (the NWSA did not allow men into its ranks). Second, its members were in favor of suffrage for African Americans as well as for women, and it worked toward that goal. Lastly, the AWSA did not concern itself with other, more controversial issues, but focused only on suffrage.

Carrie Chapman Catt: Tireless Crusader

Women's rights crusader Carrie Chapman Catt. THE LIBRARY OF CONGRESS.

Carrie Chapman Catt (1859–1947) was another seemingly tireless women's rights activist. In 1886, she became San Francisco's first female newspaper reporter. The following year, she joined the Iowa Woman Suffrage Association and worked within the organization as a professional writer and lecturer.

Catt began working with the National American Woman Suffrage Association (NAWSA) in 1890, and ten years later took over as its president, a position she held until 1904. Those years were spent keeping the organization effective. Catt made speeches, organized women's groups, and planned campaigns. She gave the NAWSA a much-needed boost of energy, as it had been under the same leadership for years and the time for change was ripe.

In 1902, she organized the International Woman Suffrage Alliance. As the organization's president, Catt traveled throughout the world, promoting suffrage rights for women. Her presidency lasted nine years, after which she returned to America and the helm of the NAWSA. During her second presidency, the Nineteenth Amendment was passed, and women were granted the right to vote.

Catt left the NAWSA after winning suffrage and founded the League of Women Voters. She was the league's honorary president until her death in 1947. Catt published a valuable account of the women's suffrage movement in 1923. *Woman Suffrage and Politics: The Inner Story of the Suffrage Movement* gave an insider's view of a movement that was often divided among its ranks.

Catt spent the last years of her life working to end child labor. She also supported the League of Nations and founded the National Committee on the Cause and Cure of War. Catt died of heart failure at the age of eighty-eight.

Meanwhile, another women's movement was gaining momentum. This movement was known as the temperance (moderation) movement, and its goals were to encourage moderation in the consumption of alcohol, or—better yet—complete abstinence (self-restraint) from drinking these beverages. Women who had suffered at the hands of men with drinking problems led the movement. These women and their children had endured physical abuse and emotional distress from their husbands and fathers, and overconsumption of alcohol was blamed. In fact, the temperance movement cited alcohol as the cause of many of society's ills and evils.

The Woman's Christian Temperance Union (WCTU) was established in 1874; within five years, reformer and activist Frances Willard (1839–1898) became its president. Willard grew up with an alcoholic father and brothers; she believed alcohol was evil. Although Willard also believed that women belonged in the home as the keeper of the family's morality, she was in favor of education for women. A devout Christian, Willard embraced the concept that women were born to be mothers, that their needs and rights were secondary to those of their husbands and children. But she believed that an education would allow women to learn how to be better caretakers, which would lead to improvement in the quality of life for children.

One of the goals of the WCTU was to outlaw the selling of liquor. If such legislation was to pass, women would have to have the right to vote, as they were considered morally superior to men and would appreciate the value of such a drastic measure. Willard understood the importance of the female vote, so she began publicly promoting women's suffrage.

That stance led her to cooperate with the suffrage organizations. In 1890, the NWSA merged with the AWSA to form the National American Woman Suffrage Association (NAWSA). Elizabeth Cady Stanton was the organization's president, although she remained committed to her previous, more radical stance which insisted on the superiority of women over African Americans.

Once the temperance movement joined hands with the suffrage movement, the political power and influence of both drastically increased. Whereas once the temperance movement relied on morality to encourage Americans to abstain from (go without) drinking alcohol, it now wanted the federal government to legislate that morality and declare alcohol consumption illegal. And whereas organized religions had once frowned upon giving women suffrage, some of the more liberal members now recognized the importance in giving women a voice in politics.

In 1888, Susan B. Anthony founded the National Council of Women of the United States. The National Council was made up of national organizations concerned with women's issues in general. Willard was appointed president of the National Council.

Things to remember while reading an excerpt from Willard's speech:

- The "difference of opinion" Willard speaks of at the beginning of her address is the primary factor that divided the women's movement in the late nineteenth and early twentieth centuries: Some activists believed women were equal to men both morally and intellectually and should share equal opportunities. Other activists adhered more closely to the traditional belief that women were not equal to men and so should not have equal rights in all areas. They believed women should stay in the home, raising children. Willard was among these traditionalists.

Women's suffrage activist and National Council of Women of the United States president Frances Willard. THE LIBRARY OF CONGRESS.

- The fight for women's suffrage had to compete for attention and resources with America's focus on the rights of newly freed African Americans. There is no way to know if progress would have been made more quickly without that competing issue.

- America was just beginning to accept and understand the notion that empowering women could benefit all of society.

- Although there were no federal laws guaranteeing women suffrage, each state could enact laws giving its female residents the right to vote. The first states to do so were in the West, where the value of a woman was measured using different standards than those used in the East.

• • •

Excerpt from a speech delivered to the National Council of Women of the United States on February 22, 1891

Beloved Friends and **Comrades** in a Sacred Cause:

    "A difference of opinion on one question must not prevent us from working **unitedly** in those on which we can agree."

Comrades: Companions.

Unitedly: Together.

Frances Willard

Convened: Gathered together.

Annals: Historical archives.

From sexhood into humanhood: From solely being considered women to being considered human.

Dauntless: Unstoppable.

Golden Rule: "Do unto others as you would have others do unto you."

Propaganda: Information spread to further one's cause.

Auxiliaries: Supporters.

Organic unity: Essential bond of togetherness.

Particular: Instance.

Signally: Completely.

Vital powers: Healthy organs necessary for life, such as the liver or heart.

Prerequisite: Requirement.

These words from the opening address before the International Council **convened** in this auditorium three years ago were the key-note of a most tuneful chorus. The name of her who uttered words so harmonious is Elizabeth Cady Stanton, and it shall live forever in the **annals** of woman's heroic struggle up **from sexhood into humanhood.**

Our friends have said that, as President of the National American Woman Suffrage Association, Mrs. Stanton leads the largest army of women outside, and I the largest one inside, the realm of a conservative theology. However this may be, I rejoice to see the day when, with distinctly avowed loyalty to my Methodist faith, and as distinctly avowed respect for the sincerity with which she holds to views quite different, I can clasp hands in loyal comradeship with one whose **dauntless** voice rang out over the Nation for "woman's rights" when I was but a romping girl upon a prairie farm.

Could anything be broader than the basis laid for this great organization? Its Preamble declares:

"We, women of the United States, sincerely believing that the best good of our homes and nation will be advanced by our own greater unity of thought, sympathy and purpose, and that an organized movement of women will best conserve the highest good of the family and the State, do hereby band ourselves together in a confederation of workers committed to the overthrow of all forms of ignorance and injustice, and to the application of the **Golden Rule** to society, custom, and law.

Its "general policy" is stated in these words:

"This Council is organized in the interest of no one **propaganda,** and has no power over its **auxiliaries** beyond that of suggestion and sympathy: therefore, no society voting to become auxiliary to this Council shall thereby render itself liable to be interfered with in respect to its complete **organic unity,** independence, or methods of work, or be committed to any principle or method of any other society or to any utterance or act of the Council itself, beyond compliance with the terms of its Constitution."

It has been wisely remarked by one of our college-bred women, that in no **particular** has the average woman failed more **signally** than in keeping her own little ones alive. Four hundred thousand babies annually breathe their first and last in the United States—being either so poorly endowed with **vital powers** or so inadequately nourished and cared for that they can not longer survive. One-third of all the children born depart this life before they reach five years of age. In Oriental countries they swarm thick as flies, and the existence of woman (a being so impure that her husband begs pardon for referring to his wife at all) is tolerated only because she is a necessary **prerequisite** to the transformation of a man into a father of sons. It thus appears that exclusive devotion to **maternity** has not resulted in the best good of woman or the highest development of humanity. In those same Oriental countries, the **Anglo-Saxon** race has conquered the native and holds it **in subjection,** though outnumbered at the rate of twenty-five hundred to one. Possibly if fewer children were born, and of a better quality, it might be a blessing to all concerned. The fabled lioness which, on being **twitted of** her small family, replied proudly, eyeing her beautiful **whelp,** "It is true I have one only, but that one will grow up to be a lion," may, for **aught** we know, **prefigure** the woman of the future. It seems to be a law of nature that quantity decreases as quality improves. But, be this as it may, we are going to have, **ere** long, a **scientific motherhood.** Children will be born of set purpose and will **cut their teeth** according to a plan. The **empirical maxims** and old wive's fables of the nursery will give way to the hard-earned results of scientific investigation. The best work of the mother will be intelligently done, on the bases of heredity, **pre-natal** influence, and devout obedience to the laws of health. Doctors[,] diet and dress, ventilation, sleep and exercise will constitute her "council of physicians." Says Mrs. Frances Fisher Wood, a Vassar graduate and a successful mother:

Old-fashioned New England mothers are often **extolled** as an ideal type of motherhood, while college-bred women are the staple of popular newspaper jokes in their **alleged futile** attempts to care for their offspring. Yet statistics show that the mortality among native New England stock exceeds that of any other part in the United States, and the proportion of deaths to births is constantly increasing; while among the ridiculed college women nine-tenths of their children survive infancy, a record which I believe has never been equaled in any country or age since statistics furnished the data for such deductions. "I assert that a woman scientifically educated can in three hours be taught more about the care of infants than another, intellectually untrained, can learn from personal experience in a lifetime. In other occupations less exacting than a mother's, we allow experience alone to count for little." This college-bred mother supports her theory by offering for inspection "a healthy, happy specimen of scientific babyhood, who **rapturously** greets this scientific woman as 'ma-ma.' Happy child of a happy mother! In his twenty-two months of babyhood he has never known the torture of **colic,** goes to sleep at night and never wakens until morning, cuts his teeth with as little ceremony and suffering as a small kitten, contracts no infantile diseases, succumbs to no infantile disorders, and does not periodically upset the **equilibrium** of the entire family at intervals of two or three days by being mysteriously 'cross' after the manner of unscientific baby tyrants. The diet of this enviable baby consists now of water that has been boiled, milk that has been sterilized, oatmeal, baked apples, and **stock soup.**"

Maternity: Motherhood.

Anglo-Saxon: White.

In subjection: Under its rule.

Twitted of: Teased about.

Whelp: Baby.

Aught: All.

Prefigure: Foresee.

Ere: Before.

Scientific motherhood: Knowledge of motherhood based on proven fact and information rather than folklore and myth.

Cut their teeth: Develop.

Empirical maxims: Practical experience.

Pre-natal: Before birth.

Extolled: Celebrated.

Alleged futile: Supposedly useless.

Rapturously: Joyfully.

Colic: Abdominal pain that causes irritability and unending crying.

Equilibrium: Balance.

Stock soup: Broth.

What would you more:
What more could you expect?

Woman question: The discussion of the time about the value of women.

"Justified of her children": Necessary to help her children.

The aforementioned college-bred woman is a trustee of Barnard, a contributor of the press, a public speaker on various educational and scientific subjects, a woman of place in society, and, as has been declared already, a model homemaker. **What would you more?** The **woman question** has no higher, nobler outcome; and once again is wisdom **"justified of her children."**

• • •

What happened next...

The women's movement reached its peak in the 1890s and early 1900s. Stanton published *The Woman's Bible* in 1895, a controversial commentary on the role of and attitude toward women in the Bible. Stanton argued that throughout the New Testament, women were degraded. The activist also questioned the gender of God. Much of what she wrote became the basis for the modern feminist movement.

Willard died in 1898, Anthony and Stanton in the first decade of the twentieth century. Not one of them lived to see women granted suffrage. The battle was interrupted by World War I (1914–18), but with victory came a return to protesting, picketing, and public speaking by women's rights activists. In 1919, the Nineteenth Amendment passed Congress, and in 1920, women were given the right to vote. U.S. president Woodrow Wilson (1856–1924; served 1913–21) signed the law on August 26, 1920. Finally, women were considered first-class citizens of the United States of America.

The 150-Year Battle

Amendment XIX

1. The right of citizens of the United States to vote shall not be denied or abridged by the United States or by any State on account of sex.

2. Congress shall have power to enforce this Article by appropriate legislation.

Did you know...

• According to a Library of Congress Web site called *Women's Suffrage in the Progressive Era,* some people actually believed women would "grow beards" if given the right to vote.

• The Nineteenth Amendment is also known as the Susan B. Anthony Amendment.

• African American and poor white women were not included in the American ideal of true womanhood. They did not have

The Nineteenth Amendment goes to the states.

Harriet Taylor Upton, Maud Wood Park, Mary Garrett Hay and Helen Gardener with House and Senate leaders as Speaker Gillette signs the resolution

Speaker of the House Frederick Gillett signs a resolution on June 6, 1919, that would give women the right to vote; President Woodrow Wilson signed the bill into law on August 26, 1920, creating the Nineteenth Amendment. © CORBIS.

the luxury of staying inside the home, tending to their children, without taking part in the outside world. Daily life for women of these classes required that they be seen in public, going to and from work, scavenging for food, and selling goods in the marketplace.

- Most WCTU chapters (local branches) were segregated, forcing African American women to meet separately from white women.

Consider the following...

- You are an African American woman in the late nineteenth century. Which discrimination causes you the most hardship, racial or sexual?

- What are some of the threats men must have perceived in granting women suffrage?

- In what ways does society continue to discriminate against women?
- Compare the advantages and disadvantages of being a woman in the Wild West as opposed to the urbanized East.

For More Information

BOOKS

Bausum, Ann. *With Courage and Cloth: Winning the Fight for a Woman's Right to Vote.* Washington, DC: National Geographic Children's Books, 2004.

Frost-Knappman, Elizabeth, and Kathryn Cullen-Dupont. *Women's Suffrage in America.* Rev. ed. New York: Facts on File, 2005.

Hill, Jeff. *Women's Suffrage.* Detroit: Omnigraphics, 2006.

WEB SITES

Boydston, Jeanne. "Cult of True Womanhood." *PBS: Not For Ourselves Alone.* http://www.pbs.org/stantonanthony/resources/index.html?body=culthood.html (accessed on August 10, 2006).

"Exhibits." *History Channel: Woman's Suffrage.* http://www.historychannel.com/exhibits/woman/herstory.html (accessed on August 10, 2006).

Library of Congress. "Address of Frances E. Willard, President of the Woman's National Council of the United States . . . at its First Triennial Meeting, Albaugh's Opera House, Washington, D.C., February 22–25, 1891." *American Memory: Votes for Women.* http://lcweb2.loc.gov/cgi-bin/query/r?ammem/naw:@field(DOCID+@lit(rbnawsan4556div3)): (accessed on August 10, 2006).

Library of Congress. "Carrie Chapman Catt." *American Memory: Votes for Women.* http://memory.loc.gov/ammem/naw/cattbio.html (accessed on August 10, 2006).

Library of Congress. "Women's Suffrage in the Progressive Era." *American Memory.* http://memory.loc.gov/learn/features/timeline/progress/suffrage/suffrage.html (accessed on August 10, 2006).

"Links." *The Wisconsin Mosaic: People's Voices—Frances Willard.* http://www.scils.rutgers.edu/~dalbello/FLVA/voices/839/voices/willard/links.html (accessed on August 10, 2006).

Martin, Faith. "Frances Willard: America's Forgotten Feminist." *Spring Valley Press.* http://www.geocities.com/~svpress/articles/fwillard.html (accessed on August 10, 2006).

Ida B. Wells

Excerpt from "The Reason Why the Colored American Is Not in the World's Columbian Exposition"
Published in 1893; available at Digital Library *(Web site)*

"Our failure to be represented is not of our own working and we can only hope that the spirit of freedom and fair play of which some Americans so loudly boast, will so inspire the Nation that in another great National endeavor the Colored American shall not plead for a place in vain."

America in the last decade of the nineteenth century found itself in a whirlwind of change. The Industrial Revolution (approximately 1877–1900) changed nearly every aspect of American life: Skilled craftsmen were being replaced by machinery, and big business took over the country's booming economy. Cities were built to accommodate those people leaving the countryside in search of steady work. Immigrants sailed to America's shores in hopes of starting new and better lives. Americans applauded their nation's progress even as they feared their changing and uncertain circumstances.

The Chicago World's Fair, also known as the Columbian Exposition, was held from May 1 through October 31, 1893. Although the theme was the four hundredth anniversary of Christopher Columbus's (1436–1506) discovery of America, the real meaning of the fair was obvious: America was becoming an empire whose power and influence rivaled that of Europe. The fair was the perfect opportunity to show the rest of the world who America was—culturally, socially, and commercially.

Fair planners knew the event was going to be a success. From the planning process through the last day of its operation, newspapers and magazines covered the goings-on in great detail. Three thousand people each week paid twenty-five cents to sit and watch as fair buildings were

A poster advertising the World's Columbian Exposition in Chicago in 1893. © CORBIS.

constructed. The fair and its grounds took three years to plan and build, and all that time, the public's excitement was building as well. On opening day, one hundred thousand people walked through the main gates to enjoy a spectacle like they had never seen before. Sixty-five thousand display booths, a midway with carnival rides (including the first Ferris wheel), and its own railway system were just some of the attractions that made the Columbian Exposition the first fair of its kind.

Not everyone was thrilled with the fair, however. Although the event's planners wanted the fair to showcase America's diversity and goodwill, they refused active participation of one segment of its population: African Americans. Fair designers had an essential belief that society was shaped like a pyramid, with white Americans at the peak. Those who were not white were, according to the designers and much of society in general, born to serve.

In order to have exhibits at the fair, individuals, companies, and organizations first had to earn the acceptance of the selection committee. Nearly all African American exhibits were denied entrance. This outraged many in the African American community, but they had already been refused representation in the planning process. Not one of them was appointed to a position of authority on a commission or board in the planning and governance of the fair. According to historian Robert Rydell, as reported on the Web site *World's Columbian Exposition: A Vision of the Future, A Reflection of Its Present*, when some national leaders approached U.S. president Benjamin Harrison (1833–1901; served 1889–93) regarding this obvious act of racism, the president replied that to appoint an African American to a commission would "be distasteful to the majority of commissioners."

The only jobs for which African Americans were hired were waiters, train porters, and laborers. They were refused admittance to the police squad that protected the fairgrounds. Instead, they were given jobs as janitors and chair men (employees who rolled visitors around the ground in wheeled chairs).

Some African Americans accepted their lower status in the fair. Prominent African Americans who participated in the event included reformer Booker T. Washington (1856–1915) and writer Paul Lawrence Dunbar (1872–1906). African Americans with this attitude believed some exposure and representation in the fair was better than none at all. This group was led by abolitionist (antislavery activist) Frederick Douglass (1818–1895), who advised African Americans to take the opportunity to show how much progress their race had made since the outlaw of slavery after the Civil War (1861–65).

Other African Americans refused to attend the fair in protest of the racist treatment. One person who joined in the protests was Ida B. Wells (1862–1931). Wells had already gained notoriety as an activist with her tireless efforts to fight lynch laws, unwritten "laws" that led to hanging, primarily of African Americans. She was respected throughout the African American community, even by those who disagreed with her philosophical beliefs.

Ida B. Wells. HULTON ARCHIVE/GETTY IMAGES.

Wells herself reluctantly participated in the Columbian Exposition. She used her time there to speak out against lynching, to educate the public about the horrors and injustice of government-sanctioned murder of her fellow African Americans and their supporters. In addition, she found a way to silently reach millions of people—American and foreign—to make them aware of the unfair treatment of African Americans at the fair.

Wells, Douglass, and two other activists wrote a pamphlet that detailed the progress African Americans had made since the Civil War. The booklet also covered topics including lynch laws, legislation unfair to African Americans, and the convict lease system (see box). The pamphlet also criticized the planning commission of the fair—and society in general—for embracing racist policies.

Things to remember while reading an excerpt from "The Reason Why the Colored American Is Not in the World's Columbian Exposition":

- African Americans were divided into two main philosophical camps. One believed the race should take whatever opportunities were given them and make the best of each situation. The other believed African Americans should not have to settle for fewer or unequal rights than whites.

- The Chicago Exposition was not the first world's fair to be held in America, but it was given far more attention in the media and by planners because it was an opportunity for the nation to demonstrate its recent progress to the world. The first world's fair in America was held in 1829 in New York.

- Fairs were the single most culturally and socially influential events of the nineteenth century. By including demonstrations and information booths from manufacturers and companies as well as displays showcasing various cultures from around the world, fairs helped shape the modern world. To be left out of the Chicago Exposition was to miss a major opportunity to be seen—throughout the world—as an important participant in America's culture.

The Convict Lease System

The emancipation (freeing) of hundreds of thousands of African American slaves in the mid-1800s left whites in the South feeling uneasy. People they once owned and used to their advantage for labor now had rights. This was a direct threat to the concept of white supremacy (superiority), on which the South was built.

In addition to this problem, the emancipation of slaves left Southern whites in a serious business dilemma: How were they to find cheap labor to farm their fields, pick their cotton, and work the plantations now that slavery was illegal? The whole South was war-torn; rebuilding was necessary, but would be extremely costly if laborers had to be paid fair wages. The Southern economy was in serious danger.

The convict lease system solved this problem for the white South. Southern states enacted (or, in some cases, reinstated) Black Codes. These codes were actually laws that allowed whites to continue their rule over African Americans. Under the codes, African Americans could be thrown in prison for "crimes" such as standing on a sidewalk too long, or wandering around aimlessly, as if homeless.

The enforcement of the Black Codes caused prison populations to rise dramatically. In Mississippi, for example, the African American population in prison quadrupled between 1871 and 1879. In Alabama, it increased from 121 in 1870 to 1,302 in 1890. The prisons were not equipped to house so many people, so state governments had to find a resolution to the overcrowded conditions.

Under the convict lease system, convicts would be leased, or rented by the state government to private companies for hefty sums of money. These companies, in return, hired out the convicts to anyone who needed cheap labor. The South was rebuilt, the whites retained all the power, and African Americans lived in fear. It was a system that worked well for everyone except the prisoners, of whom two-thirds were African Americans.

The convict lease system eventually disappeared in the first half of the twentieth century, but not before thousands of African Americans, many of them innocent of any real crime, paid for the color of their skin with their lives.

• • •

Excerpt from "The Reason Why the Colored American Is Not in the World's Columbian Exposition"

To the seeker of the truth:

Columbia has bidden the civilized world to join with her in celebrating the four-hundredth anniversary of the discovery of America and the invitation has been accepted. At Jackson Park are displayed exhibits of her natural resources, and her progress in the arts and sciences, but that which would best illustrate her moral grandeur has been ignored.

The exhibit of the progress made by a race in 25 years of freedom as against 250 years of slavery, would have been the greatest tribute to the greatness and progressiveness of American institutions which could have been shown the world. The colored people of this great Republic number eight millions—more than one-tenth the whole population of the United States. They were among the earliest settlers of this continent, landing at Jamestown, Virginia in 1619 in a slave ship, before the Puritans, who landed at Plymouth in 1620. They have contributed a large share to American prosperity and civilization. The labor of one-half of this country, has always been, and is still being done by them. The first credit this country had in its commerce with foreign nations was created by productions resulting from their labor. The wealth created by their **industry** has **afforded to** the white people of this country the leisure essential to their great progress in education, art, science, industry and invention.

Those visitors to the World's Columbian Exposition who know these facts, especially foreigners will naturally ask: Why are not the colored people, who **constitute** so large an element of the American population, and who have contributed so large a share to American greatness,—more visibly present and better represented in this World's Exposition? Why are they not taking part in this glorious celebration of the four-hundredth anniversary of the discovery of their country? Are they so dull and stupid as to feel no interest in this great event? It is to answer these questions and supply as far as possible our lack of representation at the Exposition that the Afro-American has published this volume.

The Civil War of 1861–5 ended slavery. It left us free, but it also left us homeless, penniless, ignorant, name less [sic] and friendless. Life **is derived** from the earth, and the American Government is thought to be more humane than the Russian. Russia's **liberated serf** was given three acres of land and agricultural **implements** with which to begin his career of liberty and independence. But to us no foot of land nor implement was given. We were turned loose to starvation, **destitution** and death. So desperate was our condition that some of our statesmen declared it useless to try to save us by legislation as we were doomed to extinction.

"Lynch Law," says the [magazine] Virginia Lancet, "as known by that **appellation,** had its origin in 1780 in a combination of citizens of Pittsylvania County, Virginia, entered into for the purpose of suppressing a trained band of horse-thieves and counterfeiters whose well concocted schemes had **bidden defiance to** the ordinary laws of the land, and whose success encouraged and emboldened them in their outrages upon the community. Col. Wm. Lynch drafted the constitution for this combination of citizens, and hence 'Lynch Law' has ever since been the name given to the summary infliction of punishment by private and unauthorized citizens."

Industry: Work.

Afforded to: Allowed.

Constitute: Make up.

Is derived: Originates.

Liberated serf: Freed servant or slave.

Implements: Tools.

Destitution: Complete poverty.

"Lynch Law": Punishment of persons suspected of a crime without a fair trial.

Appellation: Name.

Bidden defiance to: Ignored.

This law continues in force today in some of the oldest states of the Union, where courts of justice have long been established, whose laws are **executed** by white Americans. It **flourishes** most largely in the states which foster the **convict lease system,** and is brought to bear mainly, against the Negro. The first fifteen years of his freedom he was murdered by masked mobs for trying to vote. Public opinion having made lynching for that cause unpopular, a new reason is given to justify the murders of the past 15 years. The Negro was first charged with attempting to rule white people, and hundreds were murdered on that pretended supposition. He is now charged with assaulting or attempting to assault white women. This charge, as false as it is foul, robs us of the sympathy of the world and is blasting the race's good name.

The men who make these charges encourage or lead the mobs which do the lynching. They belong to the race which holds Negro life cheap, which owns the telegraph wires, newspapers, and all other communication with the outside world. They write the reports which justify lynching by painting the Negro as black as possible, and those reports are accepted by the press associations and the world without question or investigation. The **mob spirit** had increased with alarming frequency and violence. Over a thousand black men, women and children have been thus sacrificed the past ten years. Masks have long since been thrown aside and the lynchings of the present day take place in broad daylight. The sheriffs, police, and state officials stand by and see the work done well. The coroner's jury is often formed among those who took part in the lynching and a verdict, "Death at the hands of parties unknown to the jury," is **rendered.** As the number of lynchings have increased, so has the cruelty and barbarism of the lynchers. Three human beings was burned alive in civilized America during the first six months of this year (1893). Over one hundred have been lynched in this half year. They were hanged, then cut, shot and burned.

The following table, showing the number of lynchings from 1882 to 1891, was published by the *Chicago Tribune* in January 1892.

Executed: Upheld.

Flourishes: Is widely upheld.

Convict lease system: A program based on Black Codes, which made illegal many innocent acts of African Americans beginning in the 1870s. Something as simple as standing on a street corner could put a man in jail, resulting in years of hard physical labor, done for free for the county, state, or private companies.

Mob spirit: Concept of thinking as a group, based on emotions, rather than thinking as an individual, based on fact.

Rendered: Decided upon.

Year	Negroes murdered by mobs
1882	52
1883	53
1884	39
1885	77
1886	73
1887	70
1888	72
1889	95
1890	100
1891	169

A man is lynched in 1884.
NATIONAL ARCHIVES AND
RECORDS ADMINISTRATION.

Inimical: Unfriendly.

Appropriation: Money
dedicated.

Recognizing that the spirit and purpose of the local management of the Exposition were **inimical** to the interests of the colored people, leaders of the race made effective appeals to Congress and asked that the general government reserve out of its **appropriation** to the Exposition a sum of money to be used in making a Statistical Exhibit which should show the moral, educational and financial growth of the American Negro since his **emancipation.** The colored people recognized that the discrimination which prevented their active participation in the Exposition work could not be **remedied,** but they hoped that the Nation would take enough interest in its former slaves to spend a few thousand dollars in making an exhibit which would tell to the world what they as freedmen had done.

But here they were disappointed again. Congress refused to act. One appropriation bill passed the Senate and at another time an appropriation was made by the House of Representatives, but at no time did both bodies agree upon the same measure. The help that was expected from Congress failed and having failed in every other quarter to secure some worthy place in this great National undertaking the Colored American recognized the inevitable and accepted with the best grace possible one of the severest disappointments which has fallen to **his lot.**

In consideration of the **color proof character** of the Exposition Management it was the refinement of irony to set aside August 25th to be observed as "Colored People's Day." In this wonderful hive of National industry, representing an outlay of thirty million dollars, and numbering its employes [sic] by the thousands, only two colored persons could be found whose occupations were of a higher grade than that of janitor, laborer and porter, and these two only clerkships. Only a **menial** is the Colored American to be seen—the Nation's deliberate and cowardly tribute to the Southern demand "to keep the Negro in his place." And yet in spite of this fact, the Colored Americans were expected to observe a designated day as their day—to rejoice and be exceeding glad. A few accepted the invitation, the majority did not. Those who were present, by the faultless character of their service showed the splendid talent which prejudice had led the Exposition to ignore; those who remained away **evinced** a spirit of manly independence which could but command respect. They saw no reason for rejoicing when they knew that America could find no representative place for a colored man, in all its work, and that it remained for the Republic of Hayti [Haiti] to give the only acceptable representation enjoyed by us in the Fair. That republic chose Frederick Douglass to represent it as Commissioner through which courtesy the Colored American received from a foreign power the place denied to him at home.

That we are not alone in the conviction that our country should have accorded an equal measure of recognition to one of its greatest citizens is evidenced by the following editorial in the Chicago *Herald* of Sunday, August 27th, 1893: "That a colored man, Douglass, Langston or Bruce, should have been named a National Commissioner, will be admitted by fair-minded Americans of all political parties. That President Harrison should have omitted to name one of them is apparently inexplicable. That the race has made extraordinary progress will also be **conceded."**

Emancipation: Freedom from slavery.

Remedied: Resolved.

His lot: In this instance, his race.

Color proof character: Unprejudiced attitude.

Menial: Unskilled worker.

Evinced: Upheld.

Conceded: Acknowledged.

An aerial view of the Columbian Exposition in Chicago, Illinois, in 1893. © BETTMANN/CORBIS.

Vindictiveness actuating:
Desire for revenge
motivating.

In vain: Without success.

The World's Columbian Exposition draws to a close and that which has been done is without remedy. The colored people have no **vindictiveness actuating** them in this presentation of their side of this question, our only desire being to tell the reason why we have no part nor lot in the Exposition. Our failure to be represented is not of our own working and we can only hope that the spirit of freedom and fair play of which some Americans so loudly boast, will so inspire the Nation that in another great National endeavor the Colored American shall not plead for a place **in vain.**

• • •

What happened next...

The Columbian Exposition was a phenomenal success, though it did not make a profit, despite bringing in $28 million. What it did do is cement America's place as a powerful society among the rest of the world.

The fair was meant to reflect reality, and even in its underlying racism, it met that goal. American society at that time believed in the separate-but-equal doctrine, which stated that African Americans could enjoy rights equal to those of white Americans, but still be kept separated. That same philosophy infiltrated the fair, evidenced by the decision of the planning commission to set aside one day, near the end of the six-month event, as "Negro Day."

At the same time, the planning commission had wanted the fair to represent America as an enlightened, progressive nation. In that regard, evidence of racism and prejudice prohibited them from achieving that goal. Seated at a table in Frederick Douglass's exhibit on Haitian culture, Wells silently handed out ten thousand copies of her pamphlet to Americans and foreigners alike. No one who read the arguments in that pamphlet, who understood the statistics that supported the African American community's claim of progress, could believe America's foundation was built on enlightened ideas. African Americans did not achieve a status of equality with whites at the 1893 Columbian Exposition, but Wells's effort spread the word that, emancipation aside, America was still a racist country.

Did you know...

- The Ferris wheel made its debut at the Columbian Exposition. U.S. engineer George Washington Gale Ferris (1859–1896) installed the ride, described by some as the exposition's answer to the Eiffel Tower in Paris, which had been built only four years earlier.
- The 1893 World's Fair was such a success that it became the model for all subsequent theme and amusement parks, including Disneyland.
- According to a report by Dr. Arthur Raper, which is discussed in an article on lynching on *Spartacus.schoolnet.co.uk,* 3,724 people, most of them men and more than four-fifths of them African American, were lynched in America between 1889 and 1930. The bodies were tortured, burned, mutilated, and dragged. Of the tens of thousands of lynchers and onlookers, only four were sentenced to a fine, a prison term, or both.
- Any statistics on lynchings are generally considered to be low. Many lynchings went unreported because African Americans feared further punishment if they spoke out.

- Wells became known as Ida Wells-Barnett after she married Chicago lawyer and newspaper publisher Ferdinand L. Barnett. The couple would have four children.

Consider the following...

- You are an African American at the time of the Columbian Exposition. You are fully aware of the racist attitude underlying the event, but there are many exciting spectacles to see. Would you go, and how do you justify your answer?
- If you could have appointed one African American to serve in a position of authority on the planning commission, what would his or her responsibilities have been?
- How has America's general attitude toward African Americans changed since 1893? How has it stayed the same?

For More Information

BOOKS

Bolotin, Norman, and Christine Laing. *The World's Columbian Exposition: The Chicago World's Fair of 1893*. Washington, DC: Preservation Press, 1992. Reprint, Champaign: University of Illinois Press, 2002.

Muccigrosso, Robert. *Celebrating the New World: Chicago's Columbian Exposition of 1893*. Chicago: Ivan R. Dee, 1993.

Royster, Jacqueline Jones, ed. *Southern Horrors and Other Writings: The Anti-Lynching Campaign of Ida B. Wells, 1892–1900*. Boston: Bedford Books, 1997.

Wells, Ida B., et al. *The Reason Why the Colored American Is Not in the World's Columbian Exposition*. Chicago, 1893. Reprint, Urbana: University of Illinois Press, 1999.

WEB SITES

"The Culture of Empire." *American Social History Project/Center for Media and Learning*. http://www.ashp.cuny.edu/video/acts6.html (accessed on August 11, 2006).

"Lynching." *Spartacus*. http://www.spartacus.schoolnet.co.uk/USAlynching.htm (accessed on August 11, 2006).

"Progress Made Visible: World's Columbian Exposition, Chicago, 1893." *University of Delaware Library*. http://www.lib.udel.edu/ud/spec/exhibits/fairs/colum.htm (accessed on August 11, 2006).

Sheldon, Randall G. "Slavery in the Third Millennium, Part II—Prisons and Convict Leasing Help Perpetuate Slavery." *The Black Commentator*. http://www.blackcommentator.com/142/142_slavery_2.html (accessed on August 11, 2006).

"The World's Columbian Exposition: Idea, Experience, Aftermath." *American Studies at the University of Virginia.* http://xroads.virginia.edu/~ma96/WCE/title.html (accessed on August 11, 2006).

World's Columbian Exposition: A Vision of the Future, A Reflection of Its Present. http://mason.gmu.edu/~ssaltzgi/Worlds_Fair/world_fair_essay.htm (accessed on August 11, 2006).

OTHER MEDIA

Wilder, Gene, narrator. *EXPO—Magic of the White City.* DVD. Mark Bussler, director. Pittsburgh: Inecom Entertainment Co., 2005.

10

U.S. Supreme Court

Excerpt from *Plessy v. Ferguson* trial of 1896

Opinions written by U.S. Supreme Court justices Henry Billings Brown (majority) and
John Marshall Harlan (dissent) on May 18, 1896; available at InfoUSA *(Web site)*

"Our Constitution is color-blind..."

— U.S. Supreme Court justice John Marshall Harlan

In January 1863, President Abraham Lincoln (1809–1865; served 1861–65) issued the Emancipation Proclamation, thereby freeing all African American slaves. That freedom was guaranteed when the Thirteenth Amendment was added to the U.S. Constitution in December 1865. The Thirteenth Amendment made slavery a crime and gave the federal government the authority to uphold freedom by law. The government took the law one step further in 1868 when it added the Fourteenth Amendment to the Constitution. Under this amendment, all persons born in the United States, including those who had once been enslaved, were considered citizens of the country. This citizenship gave everyone equal protection under the law. It would be another two years before the Fifteenth Amendment granted African American men the right to vote.

Despite the laws guaranteeing equality among all citizens, the reality of life for most African Americans during the late nineteenth century was a far cry from one of equality. African American men who dared to cast their vote in any elections ran the risk of being lynched (hanged) and tortured, especially in the South. White Southerners hated the fact that the race they once enslaved was now considered, by law, to be equal to themselves. Southern states began passing laws that revoked the civil rights granted to African Americans under the U.S. Constitution. These laws varied from state to state, but all of them had the same results: African Americans as a race were segregated (separated) from whites.

These discriminatory laws were known as Jim Crow laws, named after the character Jump Jim Crow found in minstrel programs (traveling musical shows). As an example of such laws, some states required African Americans to pass a literacy (reading and writing) test in order to vote. If they failed to pass, their right to vote was denied. Since most African Americans had never had formal schooling or much education of any kind, most failed the test. One common literacy test required African Americans to recite the entire U.S. Constitution and the Declaration of Independence from memory.

Because Jim Crow laws varied from state to state, it is impossible to say which law was the first to be enacted. Historians generally recognize the 1890 railroad segregation law of Louisiana as the initial Jim Crow legislation. The Separate Car law required African Americans traveling by train to sit in "blacks-only" cars.

Homer Plessy (1863–1925) was an American of African and European heritage. His skin was light enough that he often "passed" for white. In June 1892, Plessy bought a train ticket from New Orleans to Covington, Louisiana. His first-class ticket gave him the right to sit in a first-class (whites-only) railroad car. When Plessy told the train conductor that he was actually African American, he was told to move to the blacks-only car. He refused and was arrested and thrown into jail in New Orleans.

Plessy's arrest was not accidental. The Citizens' Committee, an organization of influential African American business and community leaders, chose Plessy to break the segregation law on purpose so that the issue could go before the U.S. Supreme Court. Although Plessy claimed the segregation law interfered with his rights under the Thirteenth and Fourteenth Amendments, state judge John H. Ferguson found him guilty. Plessy appealed, and in 1896, the U.S. Supreme Court accepted his case. The committee's strategy had worked.

Things to remember while reading excerpts from *Plessy v. Ferguson:*

- Plessy's lawyer argued that the state's railroad car law violated the Fourteenth Amendment because it denied Plessy equal protection under federal law.
- Ironically, each of the seven judges who voted against Plessy were from the North. The lone dissenting (disagreeing) vote came from

The Atlanta Compromise

Tuskegee University founder Booker T. Washington delivered an influential speech on September 18, 1895, that became known as the Atlanta Compromise. THE LIBRARY OF CONGRESS.

On September 18, 1895, educator and reformer Booker T. Washington gave a speech to a mostly white audience at an exposition (fair) in Atlanta, Georgia. Planners of the exposition took a risk by inviting an African American speaker, especially one of such importance as Washington, whose Tuskegee Institute was the first normal school (training for teachers) for African Americans.

Ultimately, planners decided that having an African American speaker would work in their favor by proving how much progress Southern African Americans had made since the Civil War (1861–65).

Washington's speech became known as the Atlanta Compromise, and it went down in history as one of the most influential speeches ever given. In it, Washington assured white Americans that his race would be satisfied with the rights awarded them, even if they were not equal to those of whites.

Toward the end of his speech, Washington said:

> The wisest among my race understand that the agitation of [worry caused by] questions of social equality is the extremest folly [silliness], and that progress in the enjoyment of all the privileges that will come to us must be the result of severe and constant struggle rather than of artificial forcing. No race that has anything to contribute to the markets of the world is long in any degree ostracized [ignored]. It is important and right that all privileges of the law be ours, but it is vastly more important that we be prepared for the exercise of these privileges. The opportunity to earn a dollar in a factory just now is worth infinitely more than the opportunity to spend a dollar in an opera-house.

Washington received a standing ovation for his speech. The reformer called his stance on the race issue "accommodationism," because it made room for the white laws without ever admitting to any inferiority. The speech also called upon whites to take responsibility for improving social and economic relations between African Americans and whites. Simplified, the Atlanta Compromise called for shared responsibility. Within moments of the close of the speech, Washington's words were telegraphed to every major newspaper throughout the nation.

Washington's accommodationist stance had its critics. The most outspoken of them was W. E. B. Du Bois (1868–1963), the Gilded Age's leading African American scholar. Although he initially accepted Washington's perspective, he eventually considered it to be an acceptance of the submission of African Americans by the white race.

U.S. Supreme Court justice Henry Billings Brown wrote the majority opinion in Plessy v. Ferguson. THE LIBRARY OF CONGRESS.

Underlying fallacy: Mistaken reasoning.

Plaintiff: Person who starts a lawsuit.

Inferiority: State of being less important.

Construction: Meaning.

Acquiesce: Agree.

Secured: Given.

Commingling: Mixing.

Affinities: Relationships.

Eradicate: Eliminate.

Accentuating: Emphasizing.

John Harlan (1833–1911), a white Southerner and former slave owner.

- Not all African Americans were angry about their second-class citizenship. Prominent African American Booker T. Washington (1856–1915) publicly encouraged his race to accept and make the best of what they were given (see box).

• • •

Excerpt from Justice Henry Billings Brown's majority opinion in *Plessy v. Ferguson*

We consider the **underlying fallacy** of the **plaintiff**'s argument to consist in the assumption that the enforced separation of the two races stamps the colored race with a badge of **inferiority**. If this be so, it is not by reason of anything found in the act, but solely because the colored race chooses to put that **construction** upon it. The argument necessarily assumes that if, as has been more than once the case, and is not unlikely to be so again, the colored race should become the dominant power in the state legislature, and should enact a law in precisely similar terms, it would thereby relegate the white race to an inferior position. We imagine that the white race, at least, would not **acquiesce** in this assumption. The argument also assumes that social prejudices may be overcome by legislation, and that equal rights cannot be **secured** to the negro except by an enforced **commingling** of the two races. We cannot accept this proposition. If the two races are to meet upon terms of social equality, it must be the result of natural **affinities,** a mutual appreciation of each other's merits, and a voluntary consent of individuals.

Legislation is powerless to **eradicate** racial instincts, or to abolish distinctions based upon physical differences, and the attempt to do so can only result in **accentuating** the difficulties of the present situation. If the civil and political rights of both races be equal, one cannot be inferior to the other civilly or politically. If one race be inferior to the other socially, the constitution of the United States cannot put them upon the same plane.

Excerpt from Justice John Marshall Harlan's dissenting opinion in *Plessy v. Ferguson:*

The white race deems itself to be the dominant race in this country. And so it is, in prestige, in achievements, in education, in wealth, and in power. So, I doubt not, it will continue to be for all time, if it remains true to its great heritage, and holds fast to the principles of constitutional **liberty.** But in view of the constitution, in the eye of the law, there is in this country no superior, dominant, ruling class of citizens. There is no **caste** here. Our constitution is color-blind, and neither knows nor tolerates classes among citizens. In respect of civil rights, all citizens are equal before the law. The humblest is the peer of the most powerful. The law regards man as man, and takes no account of his surroundings or of his color when his civil rights as guarantied [sic] by the supreme law of the land are involved. It is therefore to be regretted that this high **tribunal,** the final **expositor** of the fundamental law of the land, has reached the conclusion that it is competent for a state to regulate the enjoyment by citizens of their civil rights solely upon the basis of race.

There is a race so different from our own that we do not permit those belonging to it to become citizens of the United States. Persons belonging to it are, with few exceptions, absolutely excluded from our country. **I allude to the Chinese race.** But, by the statute in question, a Chinaman can ride in the same passenger coach with white citizens of the United States, while citizens of the black race in Louisiana, many of whom, perhaps, risked their lives for the preservation of the Union, who are entitled, by law, to participate in the political control of the state and nation, who are not excluded, by law or by reason of their race, from public **stations** of any kind, and who have all the legal rights that belong to white citizens, are yet declared to be criminals, liable to imprisonment, if they ride in a public coach occupied by citizens of the white race. It is scarcely just to say that a colored citizen should not object to occupying a public coach assigned to his own race. He does not object, nor, perhaps, would he object to separate coaches for his race if his rights under the law were recognized. But he does object, and he ought never to cease objecting, that citizens of the white and black races can be **adjudged** criminals because they sit, or claim the right to sit, in the same public coach on a public highway. The **arbitrary** separation of citizens, on the basis of race, while they are on a public highway, is a badge of **servitude** wholly inconsistent with the civil freedom and the equality before the law established by the constitution. It cannot be justified upon any legal grounds.

I am of opinion that the state of Louisiana is inconsistent with the personal liberty of citizens, white and black, in that state, and hostile to both

Liberty: Freedom.

Caste: Class system.

Tribunal: Court.

Expositor: One who explains.

I allude to the Chinese race: A reference to Chinese immigrants, who were banned from entering the United States under the Chinese Exclusion Act of 1892.

Stations: Positions.

Adjudged: Considered as.

Arbitrary: Random.

Servitude: Lack of liberty.

the spirit and letter of the Constitution of the United States. If laws of like character should be enacted in the several states of the Union, the effect would be in the highest degree mischievous. Slavery, as an institution tolerated by law, would, it is true, have disappeared from our country; but there would remain a power in the states, by sinister legislation, to interfere with the full enjoyment of the blessings of freedom, to regulate civil rights, common to all citizens, upon the basis of race, and to place in a condition of legal inferiority a large body of American citizens, now constituting a part of the political community, called the 'People of the United States,' for whom, and by whom through representatives, our government is **administered.**

For the reason stated, I am **constrained** to withhold my **assent** from the opinion and judgment of the majority.

• • •

U.S. Supreme Court justice John Marshall Harlan wrote the dissenting opinion in Plessy v. Ferguson. THE LIBRARY OF CONGRESS.

Administered: Run.

Constrained: Required.

Assent: Agreement.

What happened next...

Plessy was given the choice to pay a $25 fine or spend time in jail. In January 1897, he pled guilty and paid the fine. Life went on as normal for Homer Plessy.

The case itself had more far-reaching effect, as it served as the legal foundation for the doctrine that became known as "separate but equal." As long as African Americans were treated in the same way as their white counterparts, the law saw nothing wrong with keeping the populations separated. For almost sixty years, African Americans were forced to use separate public facilities such as bathrooms, entrances and exits, restaurants, parks, water fountains, buses and train cars, and even neighborhoods.

Nowhere else did the separate-but-equal doctrine have such a major impact as it did in public education. Not only were African Americans forced into segregated schools, they were severely underfunded. Because white voters controlled local and state governments, little money was set aside for African American pupils in comparison with that spent on their white peers. For example, in one Mississippi county in 1900, the school district spent $22.25 on each white pupil, but only $2 on each African American child.

In 1909, the National Association for the Advancement of Colored People (NAACP) was formed. This organization brought people of all races together to seek justice and equality for African Americans. The NAACP spent its first two decades fighting various Jim Crow laws with some success. But it was 1935 before the association took serious action against segregation in education.

In 1939, a young lawyer named Thurgood Marshall (1908–1993) became head of the NAACP Legal Defense Fund. Marshall got experience in the courtroom by successfully trying a number of important cases involving segregation. These cases helped set the stage for the most important federal case in the history of equality in education.

In the early 1950s, Linda Brown (1942–), a third-grade girl in Topeka, Kansas, had to walk one mile through a railroad switchyard (where trains switch tracks) to get to her all–African American elementary school. Just seven blocks from Brown's home was an all-white school. When the girl's father, Oliver Brown (1918–1961), tried to enroll her in that school, the principal refused her enrollment. Mr. Brown went to the NAACP and asked for help.

The NAACP eagerly agreed to represent the Brown family, and in 1951 *Brown v. Board of Education* was tried in the Kansas Supreme Court. The judges acknowledged that segregation had a negative impact on African American children because it encouraged the attitude that they were inferior to white children. However, the court was not ready to overturn the separate-but-equal doctrine and voted in favor of the school board.

The case headed to the U.S. Supreme Court in 1954, where the judges unanimously struck down the segregation laws upheld by *Plessy v. Ferguson*. They believed the separate-but-equal doctrine deprived African Americans of the equal protection guaranteed by the Fourteenth Amendment of the Constitution.

Although the ruling would not affect other public facilities and services, it declared unconstitutional the permissive and mandatory segregation laws that were in affect in twenty-one states at the time. The success of Marshall and his client was a major step in desegregating schools, though the process of desegregation would take many years.

Oliver Brown and his wife Leola and daughters Linda (left) and Terry Lynn. Oliver and Linda Brown were central figures in the 1954 Supreme Court case Brown v. Board of Education. CARL IWASAKI/TIME LIFE PICTURES/GETTY IMAGES.

Did you know...

- There were two U.S. Supreme Court justices named John Marshall Harlan. The elder justice (1833–1911) cast the lone dissenting vote in the *Plessy v. Ferguson* case. His grandson (1899–1971) was a Presbyterian minister who served on the Supreme Court from 1955 until 1971.
- NAACP lawyer Thurgood Marshall became the first African American justice to sit on the U.S. Supreme Court.

Consider the following...

- Do you think treating people equally means treating them the same? Why or why not?
- Educational institutions continue to segregate classes according to gender. What, if any, are the benefits of all-male or all-female education?
- *Plessy v. Ferguson* did not have the intended outcome for the Citizen's Committee. Still, it remains a prominent case in American history. How might race relations throughout the nation have differed had Plessy been found not guilty?

For More Information

BOOKS

Aaseng, Nathan. *Plessy v. Ferguson: Separate but Equal.* San Diego: Lucent Books, 2003.

"Brown v. Board of Education." In *West's Encyclopedia of American Law.* Detroit: Gale, 1998.

Fireside, Harvey. *Plessy v. Ferguson: Separate But Equal?* Springfield, NJ: Enslow Publishers, 1997.

Greenwood, Janette Thomas. "The New South." In *The Gilded Age: A History in Documents.* New York: Oxford University Press, 2000.

McNeese, Tim. *Plessy v. Ferguson.* New York: Chelsea House, 2006.

Schraff, Anne E. *Booker T. Washington: "Character Is Power."* Berkeley Heights, NJ: Enslow Publishers, 2005.

WEB SITES

Alridge, Derrick P. "Atlanta Compromise Speech." *The New Georgia Encyclopedia.* http://www.georgiaencyclopedia.org/nge/Article.jsp?id=h-2554 (accessed on August 14, 2006).

"Booker T. Washington Delivers the 1895 Atlanta Compromise Speech." *HistoryMatters.* http://historymatters.gmu.edu/d/39/ (accessed on August 14, 2006).

"Plessy v. Ferguson." *Landmark Supreme Court Cases.* http://www.landmarkcases. org/plessy/home.html (accessed on August 14, 2006).

Wormser, Richard. "Jim Crow Stories: The Fourteenth Amendment Ratified." *PBS: The Rise and Fall of Jim Crow Stories.* http://www.pbs.org/wnet/jimcrow/ stories_events_14th.html (accessed on August 14, 2006).

Wormser, Richard. "Jim Crow Stories: Plessy v. Ferguson." *PBS: The Rise and Fall of Jim Crow.* http://www.pbs.org/wnet/jimcrow/stories_events_plessy.html (accessed on August 14, 2006).

11

Charles Dana Gibson

Examples of images of the Gibson Girl

> Charles Dana Gibson "had a lot to reveal about the characters of his era and had more than a little to do with the shaping of it."
>
> — Illustrator Henry Pitz, 1969

Before the advent of television and movies, Americans got their fashion inspiration from magazines. Illustrators of the Gilded Age and Progressive Era (approximately 1878–1913) influenced popular fashions much as movie stars and celebrities do in the twenty-first century.

No illustrator had more influence at the turn of the century than Charles Dana Gibson (1867–1944). While Gibson endured a childhood illness that kept him bedridden, Gibson's father taught him how to make silhouettes (outlined shapes of an image, usually dark against a light background) of people and animals. Young Gibson became so skilled that he entered his silhouettes in an exhibition at age twelve and gained recognition as an artist.

Gibson spent his first two years of high school at the Art Students League in the Manhattan section of New York City. When tuition payments became impossible for Gibson's parents, the young student quit school and looked for work as an artist. Jobs were not easy to come by, and it took months before he sold his first drawing. Finally, he sold a sketch of a small dog, chained to his doghouse and howling at the moon, for $4 to *LIFE* magazine in 1886. It was the first sale of many to *LIFE;* Gibson maintained a professional relationship with the popular magazine for thirty years.

LIFE Magazine: A Cultural Icon

John Ames Mitchell (1845–1918) was a native New Yorker with a dream. An architect who dabbled in illustrating, Mitchell took his hobby—and a life savings of $10,000—and founded *LIFE* magazine, a forum for art, humor, and literature.

The first issue of *LIFE* appeared on newsstands in January 1883. Sales were somewhat slow initially, as the magazine was the first of its kind, and social values of the day did not allow "respectable" families to have joke books lying about the house. As word spread that the magazine had more to offer than humor, sales increased.

By 1894, it was clear that *LIFE* would continue to be published. Mitchell had an office building constructed in downtown New York. The building housed offices on the lower floor, apartments on the upper floors. Mitchell recognized the unpredictable work habits of his artistic staff and wanted to provide them with a

place where they could both work and live. Charles Dana Gibson's Gibson Girl illustrations were born in the offices of this building. The building still stands in the twenty-first century but is now the Herald Square Hotel.

In 1936, the popularity of the magazine prompted it to be published weekly, rather than monthly. This continued for the next thirty-six years. Mitchell hired some of the most famous artists of his day, including Norman Rockwell (1894–1978) and Maxfield Parrish (1870–1966). *LIFE* became the most popular magazine of the early twentieth century and is considered the standard for photojournalism periodicals.

Although it ceased production in 1972, *LIFE* returned in 1978 as a monthly publication, a schedule it adhered to until 2000. At that time, it became a weekend newsmagazine that was included in major newspapers throughout the United States.

Gibson was a contributing artist for all the major New York publications by 1890: *Harper's Monthly, The Century,* and *Weekly Bazaar.* The fashionable creation that was to become known as the Gibson Girl first appeared in print in the 1894 book titled *Drawings.* Soon, she graced the pages of *LIFE,* and her creator was instantly proclaimed a star. Gibson became the most eligible bachelor in town, thanks to the fame brought upon him by the Gibson Girl.

What made the Gibson Girl so attractive to the American public? Gibson called her "the American Girl to all the world." He intended her to represent the spirit of the New Woman, one who enjoyed the urban (city) life but who managed to maintain her class and self-confidence. She was independent, yet feminine; strong, yet soft. She dated, but was expected to marry; played sports, but did not sweat. By featuring the Gibson Girl in scenes depicting social situations involving money, love, and manners, the illustrator created an icon (symbol) that showed the courage of his era's women to move beyond traditional roles while at the same time safeguarded their morals and values. And always, he drew his Gibson Girl with a twinkle in her eye.

So that his Girl would not be lonely, Gibson created the Gibson Man to keep her company. Handsome, respectful, romantic, the Gibson Man was clearly in awe of his companion. Gibson the artist made it known, through his illustrations, that he considered women the superior sex, yet he did so without offending men. He used subtle facial expressions to convey his message, and the captions he wrote for his illustrations, though brief, created an entire story for each scene.

Gibson Girl illustrator Charles Dana Gibson. © CORBIS.

Things to remember while looking at the Gibson Girl images:

- The Gibson Girl was published in the most widely read magazines of the day. She embodied the spirit of the modern woman and was the first supermodel to gain international recognition. She was considered the ideal American woman.

- Gibson was born into a class of society that respected traditional values. His Gibson Girl creation, though spirited and independent, was nonthreatening because she did not offend the values of any of the social classes. She may have been employed outside the home, but she was not politically active. She may have participated in ladylike sports such as tennis, golf, or bicycling, but America never saw her break a sweat. She had manners, but was not particularly well educated. The Gibson Girl was a woman who could fit into any social class with ease.

- Gibson's illustrations were symbolic of the changing nature of class structure in America at the turn of the century. Initially, only working-class women wore the shirtwaist (button-down shirt with high collar and cuffs). With the help of the Gibson

Evelyn Nesbit: Model of a Tragedy

Model and actress Evelyn Nesbit in 1902. She was the inspiration for many Gibson Girl images drawn by Charles Dana Gibson. © A. S. CAMPBELL/GEORGE EASTMAN HOUSE/GETTY IMAGES.

Although not the original Gibson Girl, one Gibson Girl model is more famous than all the rest. Evelyn Nesbit (1885–1967) was sixteen years old when Charles Dana Gibson first saw her in photos. Soon, Nesbit was modeling for him. One of his most recognizable and famous illustrations, titled *The Question Mark,* used Nesbit as the model.

Nesbit was a beauty: thin, with long, thick hair and a wistful expression. Already well known through-out New York for her looks, the model's popularity only increased when she posed in 1901 for Gibson.

Architect Stanford White (1853–1906) was one of many to fall under Nesbit's spell. Nesbit and the more senior White—thirty years separated them—became sexually involved, despite the fact that White was married. White took the model to one of his many hideaways in the city, where he had a large swing for his pretty visitors. In time, Nesbit would become known throughout the world as "the girl in the red velvet swing."

The relationship with White lasted for about a year. During that time, Nesbit met Pittsburgh

Girl, who always wore the shirtwaist with a long, flowing skirt, the shirtwaist became stylish for upper-class women as well. This trend contrasted directly with the rigidity of class structure in England, where fashion trends were always dictated by the upper class.

- Gibson took a risk in creating his Girl. At a time when America was struggling to accept any ideas outside of traditional values and norms, the illustrator publicly admired women not only for their physical beauty (as was customary), but also for their intelligence, cunning, and ability to break out of the mold into which all women of the Gilded Age and early Progressive Era were born. Gibson's public admiration allowed other men to follow suit, millionaire Harry Kendall Thaw (1871–1947). Thaw was more than a decade older than Nesbit. He was determined to make the model his bride, and though she initially refused his advances and gifts, she must have realized her affair with White, as well as her low social standing as a model, would prevent her from receiving many choice marriage offers. Thaw and Nesbit married when she was twenty-one. She shared with her new husband stories of her relationship with White, painting the architect as a great seducer of her innocence. Thaw, a paranoid (irrationally distrustful) drug addict with a history of violence, believed White had forced his wife into a sexual relationship.

On June 25, 1906, Thaw and Nesbit were enjoying a rooftop performance of a musical comedy at Madison Square Garden. White and a companion were there as well. Just before the closing act, Thaw approached White's table and murdered him with a single shot between the eyes. The event immediately became known as "the murder of the century."

No murder had ever received more press. Many believed Thaw had every right to shoot White, whose morals did not match the standards of the day. The focus of the case, naturally, was on Nesbit. She painted White in an unfavorable light while proclaiming her husband to be the most gentle, caring man she had ever met. She neglected to tell them that Thaw had whipped her when she defied him, or that he had beat up hotel bellhops when they came to his room. At the request (and unfulfilled promise of $1 million) of Thaw's mother, Nesbit swore under oath that her husband was not a monster.

More than a year later, Thaw was found not guilty of murder by reason of insanity and sentenced to life in an asylum. He rode to his new home in a private train car filled with friends, fine food, and champagne. He soon escaped to Canada, only to be returned to an American jail. By that time, however, he was a sort of folk hero to many Americans and was eventually declared sane and set free. The first thing he did upon release was file for divorce from Nesbit. Thaw maintained a lavish lifestyle marked by fits of rage and died at the age of seventy-six. Nesbit bore a son during Thaw's confinement, but her husband refused to accept the child as his own. Forever seen as a major player in an immoral scandal, Nesbit died an alcoholic and a drug addict at the age of eighty-one.

and the Gibson Girl helped women break free of social expectations that had for centuries repressed them.

- By never naming his creation, Gibson assured her national appeal. She could be—and was—any woman.

• • •

Examples of the Gibson Girl images

Gibson Girl illustration titled "The Greatest Game in the World—His Move," by Charles Dana Gibson. By creating a partner for his Gibson Girl, the artist opened up a whole new world through which he could comment on life and love in the ever-changing Progressive Era.

Gibson Girl illustration titled "The Question Mark," by Charles Dana Gibson. Actress Evelyn Nesbit was the model for this image, the most famous of all Gibson Girl illustrations.

STUDIES IN EXPRESSION
When women are jurors.

Gibson Girl illustration titled "Studies in Expression—When Women Are Jurors," by Charles Dana Gibson. Using facial expressions and fashion styles, Gibson was able to portray the obvious as well as the subtle differences between the social classes.

Gibson Girl illustration titled "The Weaker Sex," by Charles Dana Gibson, from the July 4, 1903, issue of Collier's Weekly. *Gibson's understanding of the power of women over men is evident in this illustration, which plays on the idea of woman as the weaker sex. Under the magnifying glass and the close scrutiny of the women is a tiny man.* THE LIBRARY OF CONGRESS.

Gibson Girl drawing number 1 from Eighty Drawings Including the Weaker Sex: The Story of a Susceptible Bachelor, *by Charles Dana Gibson. Here again, Gibson's illustration depicts his own appreciation of women, and surely made male viewers smile in agreement as they recognized themselves in the confused and dazed bachelor. Times were changing, as were gender roles, and this illustration captures the tone of the era.* © CHARLES DANA GIBSON/MANSELL/TIME LIFE PICTURES/GETTY IMAGES.

Gibson Girl illustration titled "Picturesque America—Anywhere along the Coast," by Charles Dana Gibson. Gibson's girls are the true supermodels of the day, showcasing the latest beachwear.

Gibson Girl illustration titled "A Daughter of the South," by Charles Dana Gibson. Gibson captured the spirit of the Southern Belle in his pen-and-ink portrait. A captivating and classic beauty, this Gibson Girl's appeal lies in her mystery as she shies away from the viewer. THE LIBRARY OF CONGRESS.

Gibson Girl illustration titled "Not Worrying About Her Rights," by Charles Dana Gibson. This illustration was Gibson's idea of the Progressive Era woman: modern in dress and style, yet firmly holding on to the rights of whimsy afforded to young women of the day. Suffrage was a major issue in the early twentieth century, but this Gibson Girl couldn't care less about getting the right to vote.

Untitled Gibson Girl illustration by Charles Dana Gibson. This drawing was used on a U.S. postal stamp issued in 1998. The stamp was one of thirty in the "Celebrate the Century" program sponsored by the U.S. Post Office. Each stamp commemorated an important event or person who influenced society between 1900 and 1919. Other stamps featured Ellis Island, John Muir, the Teddy bear, the Grand Canyon, and Crayola Crayons, among other subjects.

I WANT YOU
FOR U.S.ARMY
NEAREST RECRUITING STATION

The famous 1916 U.S. military recruitment poster by James Montgomery Flagg shows Uncle Sam pointing and saying, "I want you for U.S. Army." LIBRARY OF CONGRESS.

• • •

What happened next...

The Gibson Girl brought her creator instant fame throughout the world. Charles Dana Gibson became the highest-paid illustrator of his time, and his Gibson Girl drawings set the standard for female beauty, fashion, and morality for the next twenty years.

The Gibson Girl became a popular cultural icon, and her image was reproduced on everything from wallpaper to ashtrays, umbrella stands to pillowcases to paper dolls. Americans ate off Gibson Girl plates atop Gibson Girl tablecloths. Millions of American women demanded Gibson Girl hairstyles at the beauty salon. Songs and plays were written, praising the virtues and beauty of the popular American idol.

Imitator illustrators at the turn of the century tried to get in on the American Girl theme, and Gibson Girl look-alikes began popping up throughout magazines across the country. James Montgomery Flagg (1877–1960) was the artist who most obviously copied Gibson's style. Flagg staked a claim in American history books for an illustration all his own in 1916 with a military recruiting poster featuring Uncle Sam that called all eligible men to battle in World War I (1914–18).

Gibson became the most sought-after illustrator of the era. Magazines competed to get him to contract with them and give them exclusive rights to the Gibson Girl. Gibson never severed his ties with *LIFE,* however. After World War I and *LIFE* founder John Mitchell's death, he took over as editor of the magazine. Now that he no longer had to worry about making enough money to pay the bills, Gibson had time to focus on a favorite hobby: oil painting. His paintings depicted his surroundings of family and home in Maine. Although they never enjoyed the popularity of the Gibson Girl, they were critically acclaimed. Gibson died in 1944.

By the time the war was over, a new image of the American woman appeared for a new cultural era, the Roaring Twenties (the third decade of the twentieth century). The Gibson Girl was no longer in fashion; the flapper embodied a new, daring female spirit, one focused on having fun. Long hair, flowing skirts, and an air of mystery gave way to bobbed hair, short dresses, and cigarettes. The flapper defied convention and spent

Four flappers dancing the Charleston during the Roaring Twenties. © BETTMANN/CORBIS.

her free time dancing, drinking and smoking, and turning her back on America's traditional social values.

The Gibson Girl remains, in the twenty-first century, a symbol for a period in history known as the Gay 90s, when hope and ideals of freedom kept America moving forward. She is memorialized in art museum collections and on postcards. A commemorative postage stamp featuring her image was issued in 1998.

Did you know...

- The Gibson Girl had an "hourglass" figure, so-called for its resemblance to a glass instrument used to tell time—narrow in the middle and wider at the ends. The hourglass style was achieved using a corset, which was a stiff undergarment that laced up the back. The tighter the corset was laced, the smaller a woman's waist would appear. The first corsets were made of steel. Corsets worn during the Gibson Girl era were somewhat slightly more flexible and allowed a woman to bend at the waist.

- Dana Charles Gibson's women were taller than any other women shown in magazine illustrations of the day. This gave them a more confident, proud look.

- Gibson's illustrations were in such high demand that he made as much as $50,000 for fifty-two pen-and-ink drawings at the turn of the century.

- In the early 1900s, it was understood that middle-class men should spend their time making money. Their wives were expected to appear more fashionable and sophisticated than women of the lower, working class. Styles and dress became direct reflections of conspicuous consumerism (spending more money for products than necessary because one had more to spend).

- Prior to the 1900s, all clothing was tailor-made to fit a person's unique body shape and measurements. There were no shopping malls, or even general stores, at which to purchase a dress or a shirt off a rack.

- In World War II (1939–45), the Gibson Girl emergency radio transmitter was placed in life rafts in the hope that downed airmen could use it to signal for help. The radio transmitted its signal along a wire connected to an antenna on a kite. The radio was shaped like an hourglass, just like the Gibson Girl's figure.

Consider the following...

- How did World War I influence America's shift in ideals and values as portrayed by the Gibson Girl and then the flapper?
- If you were to invent an "ideal woman" for the modern era, what would she look like? What values would she represent?
- How is social class and age reflected in women's clothing and style?

For More Information

BOOKS

Gibson, Charles Dana. *The Gibson Girl and Her America: The Best Drawings.* New York: Dover Publications, 1969.

WEB SITES

"A Charles Dana Gibson 'LIFE Magazine' Gallery." *The Herald Square Hotel.* http://www.heraldsquarehotel.com/CharlesDGibson_cvrs.htm (accessed on August 14, 2006).

"Drawing from Life." *Smithsonian Institution Libraries.* http://www.sil.si.edu/ondisplay/caricatures/author_drilldown.htm (accessed on August 14, 2006).

"The Gibson Girl: The Ideal Woman of the Early 1900s." *Eyewitness to History.* http://www.eyewitnesstohistory.com/gibson.htm (accessed on August 14, 2006).

Gibson-Girls. http://www.gibson-girls.com/ (accessed on August 14, 2006).

Library of Congress. *American Beauties: Drawings from the Golden Age of Illustration.* http://www.loc.gov/rr/print/swann/beauties/beauties-home.html (accessed on August 14, 2006).

LIFE. http://www.life.com/Life/ (accessed on August 14, 2006).

PBS. "Murder of the Century." *American Experience.* http://www.pbs.org/wgbh/amex/century/index.html (accessed on August 14, 2006).

12

Peter Roberts

Excerpt from "The Boys in the Breakers," a chapter in *Anthracite Coal Communities*
Originally published in 1904; available at eHistory.com *(Web site)*

"No industry in the State is so demoralizing and injurious to boys as the anthracite coal industry."

In the early twentieth century, there were few laws to protect children laborers in America. Child workers could be found in every industry imaginable, from agriculture to fabric mills, canneries to glass factories. Throughout the nation, young children were forced to sacrifice their childhoods in order to help put food on the table and a couple extra dollars in the family's change jar.

Most of the poorest families were immigrants. They came to America speaking little, if any, English, and understanding even less. Their desperate circumstances allowed dishonest managers and factory owners to exploit (take advantage of) them by paying adult laborers such low wages that families came to rely on their children to help supplement their income. Yet the income brought in by child laborers was very low; in most cases, the toll that working took on a child's health and well-being was far greater than the few dollars brought in.

The life of any child laborer was one of hardship. Forced to work, sometimes at the tender age of four or five years, these children never knew the simple joys of childhood. Sleeping in late, playing in the sunshine—such activities were not enjoyed by poor children in the Gilded Age and the Progressive Era. And no child's life was more dismal than that of a breaker boy. Breaker boys worked in a breaker, a large factory where coal was separated from debris, rock, and slate (a flat rock that splits into sharp pieces); cleaned; and processed for sale.

Anthracite coal mining was a major industry in Pennsylvania. Anthracite is a hard form of coal that burns cleanly. In 1902, the mining

What Did Child Laborers Do?

Factories: With the number of factories increasing throughout the Gilded Age and Progressive Era, companies needed to find cheap labor to perform the work. The labor need not be skilled; more important was an employee's ability to follow directions and obey the rules. Children worked in factories that manufactured products of all kinds, from boxes to glass. During busy times (such as around Christmas), young children were forced to work shifts as long as fifteen hours, often on their feet without a break. Most of these children were in their teens, although workers in candy factories were often as young as ten.

Agriculture: Children as young as five were expected to work in agriculture, usually picking or hauling berries. During the first decade of the 1900s, up to fifteen hundred children were employed to harvest one berry crop. The overseer of the field commonly charged the children $2 for an 8-cent bus ticket from their homes to the fields. Because most of these small immigrant children did not speak English, they did not know their boss was cheating them, just as they did not know he would regularly underpay

them for their work. Children working the fields missed four to five weeks of school every berry-picking season.

Tobacco: The tobacco industry was one of the largest employers of child labor in the Progressive Era. According to the book *Children in Bondage,* the U.S. population increased 50 percent from 1880 to 1900, but the population of boys ages ten to fifteen years working in the tobacco industry increased 100 percent, while girls of the same age increased 150 percent for the same time period. In 1901, twelve thousand children were working in the industry, either picking the fields or rolling cigars in factories and tenement shops (illegal shops set up in run-down tenement homes). Children worked in damp conditions, hunched over tables, and were paid 8 to 10 cents for every 100 cigars they rolled.

Canneries: Children as young as four years worked in shrimp and seafood canneries. The work was drudgery; workers had to pick the shrimp out of its shells for ten to twelve hours a day. A toxic chemical the shrimp released ate

region covered 488 square miles (785 square kilometers) of mountain land. More than 53.5 million tons (over 48.5 million metric tons) of coal had been mined there the previous year. Mining was dangerous, dirty, and difficult work. Most miners were Irish or from other immigrant groups.

Mining towns were little more than crude houses built along a dirt road. The families who lived there were traditionally large. Mining salaries were among the lowest of any industry, and boys as young as eight or nine were forced to work the mines with their fathers. While the adult men worked down in the mines, the boys labored in the breaker. Most miners began their careers as breaker boys. As they through the skin of their hands as well as the leather of their shoes. Oyster shucking was just as repetitive a task. Most of these young workers came from Maryland and Delaware.

Cotton mills: More children worked in the cotton mills (mostly in the South) than in any other industry in America. Conditions within the mills were unbearable. Dust, poor ventilation (air circulation) and light, and airborne lint (tiny cotton fibers) made breathing and seeing difficult. Children as young as twelve (though often, they were younger than the law permitted because no proof of age was required) awakened at 4:30 each morning and worked a twelve-hour shift. It was not uncommon for these young laborers to fall asleep at their loom at lunchtime, their unchewed food still in their mouths.

On the streets: Children worked many jobs on the streets of America's growing cities. Boys as young as eight years worked as newsies, or boys who sold newspapers. A 1905 analysis in New York showed that these eight-year-olds averaged forty cents for every three hours worked. The older teens earned even less: thirty-five cents for every three-and-one-half hours

worked. These children roamed the streets and alleys in search of buyers. Those who dared venture into saloons and hotels made more money, but they risked their lives doing so. In those days, children were considered property, not individuals. They did not belong on the streets and in public places, and if caught, their fate lay in the hands of those who caught them. Saloons and hotels were especially dangerous because they were often the scenes of violence. The other popular "street trade" was that of shoe shining, also called "bootblacking." These workers made anywhere from $2.50 to $6 every week.

Garment industry: Although the garment industry forbid anyone under the age of fourteen to work in the factories (though this law was commonly ignored), children of any age could perform the work in their homes. Families often took home "piece work" (small pieces of embroidering or sewing) to complete at night in their tenements. There, even the youngest children contributed to the work. A 1908 magazine article reported on a two-and-a-half-year-old girl: too young to go to school or the factory, the girl was expected to stay up late every night to help sew.

aged, they left the breaker for the mines. Years of toil in harsh conditions eventually sent the men back to the breaker, where the work was tedious but not as life-threatening. This pattern made for a common saying among the coal miners: Once a man, twice a boy.

Things to remember while reading the excerpt from "The Boys in the Breakers":

- The average age at death for an anthracite coal miner was 32.13 years. Insurance companies refused to cover them because their jobs were so dangerous.

Young girls take a break from rolling cigarettes outside the Danville, Virginia, Cigarette Factory in June 1911. THE LIBRARY OF CONGRESS.

- The fingers of breaker boys were often bloody, the flesh shredded, from spending long hours picking out sharp-edged slate from a moving conveyer belt. This condition was called red top.

- Between 1870 and 1900, a miner or laborer in the mines was killed every three days.

- Coal dust in the breaker was so thick that the breaker boys had to be taken to town to see the doctor every couple months to have their ears cleaned out.

- Approximately one-fourth of all mine employees were boys.

- Peter Roberts, the author of the excerpt, was an immigrant minister who had received his doctorate degree from Yale University in 1886. His motivation for writing about the Breaker Boys was nothing more than the horrifying devastation he witnessed resulting from the anthracite coal mining strikes of 1900 and 1902.

Child Laborers (Ages 10–15) in the United States, 1900

Age	Total number of children	Total number of children laborers	% of Children who work
Both Sexes			
10	1,740,628	142,105	8.2
11	1,583,131	158,778	10.0
12	1,637,509	221,313	13.5
13	1,550,402	268,427	17.3
14	1,568,564	406,701	25.9
15	1,533,018	552,854	36.1
Total	**9,613,252**	**1,750,178**	**18.2**
Males			
10	882,052	105,580	12.0
11	798,193	119,628	15.0
12	828,008	163,649	19.8
13	781,448	196,830	25.2
14	793,340	289,655	36.5
15	769,386	389,069	50.6
Total	**4,852,427**	**1,264,411**	**26.1**
Females			
10	858,576	36,525	4.3
11	784,938	39,150	5.0
12	809,501	57,664	7.1
13	768,954	71,597	9.3
14	775,224	117,046	15.1
15	763,632	163,785	21.4
Total	**4,760,825**	**485,767**	**10.2**

SOURCE: *Bulletin 69*, Department of Commerce and Labor, Bureau of the Census (Washington, D.C., January 1907).

• • •

Excerpt from "The Boys in the Breakers"

In the breakers of the **anthracite** coal industry there are nearly 18,000 persons employed as slate pickers. The majority of these are boys from the ages of 10 to 14 years. In an investigation conducted in an area where 4,131 persons wholly dependent on the mines lived, we found 64 children employed in and around the mines not 14 years of age. There were 24 boys employed in breakers before they were 12 years of age. In other sections of the coal fields the evil of employing children under age in **breakers** and mines is worse than in our limited area. But if the proportion above mentioned prevails in these coal fields, there are employed in the breakers about 2,400 boys under 12 years of age, and nearly 6,400 boys under 14 years of age working in and around the mines. The tabulated report of superintendents of public schools in Lackawanna [County, Pennsylvania] . . . shows how **prevalent** the evil of child labor is. Improved machinery for cleaning coal has displaced many boys, and it is hoped that a still further improvement and utilization of such machinery will render unnecessary the labor of boys hardly in their teens in these breakers. No industry demands the service

Anthracite: Hard.

Breakers: Factories where coal was processed.

Prevalent: Common.

Depreciating: Decreasing.

Displaced: Replaced.

of boys whose bone and muscle are not hardened and whose brain has not been developed for continuous and effective thinking. Muscle without intelligence is annually **depreciating**, being **displaced** by machinery which does nearly all the rough work. To stunt the body and dull the brains of boys in breakers is to rob them of the mental equipment which is essential to enhance their social worth and enable them to adjust themselves to the requirements of modern life.

Intricate: Detailed.

Statutes: Laws.

Jobbery: Corruption.

The laws of our State relative to child labor are an **intricate** mass of confusing **statutes**, which well illustrate the legislative **jobbery** of our representatives, who disregard both science and history in their eagerness to do something whereby their political prospects may be enhanced. The law requires every employer to keep a register of all boys employed under 16 years of age which may be seen by the inspectors. No employer does it. Certificates from the parents or guardians of the child, stating [the child's] age, are required before the child is employed. Employers secure these but they are not reliable. The employer is protected, the child sacrificed, and a premium is put on **perjury**.

Perjury: Lying.

No industry in the State is so demoralizing and injurious to boys as the anthracite coal industry. For the last half a century these breakers have been filled with boys who should have been in the public schools. They were put to work before they acquired the three "most essential parts of literary education, to read, write and **account**," and failing to acquire these to the degree in which it is necessary in order to derive pleasure and **utility** from them in daily life, they grow up in **illiteracy**, and by the time they are young men many of them cannot read or write their **mother tongue**. If society in anthracite communities is to be safeguarded against injuries which can be avoided only by increased intelligence, greater attention must be given to the public education of the children.

Account: Perform mathematical functions.

Utility: Usefulness.

Illiteracy: Inability to read and write.

Mother tongue: Native language.

Advocates: Supporters.

Necessity often accounts for the presence of boys in the breakers or mines. Many of the **advocates** of reform lose sight of this. There are many widows and poor families in these coal fields that need the wages earned by these children, and it would be well for kind-hearted people, who consider only the general desirability of fuller education of these boys, to remember this. On the other hand there are many parents who exploit their children. Of the 64 children employed as above referred to, 35 of the parents owned their own homes. Of the nationalities represented the **Sclavs** were in the lead, but the English, Irish and Welsh followed closely, while 12 of the parents were **native born**. These parents do not see that a liberal education to the boys is a better investment than to build a house. **Solon** made a law which **acquitted** children from maintaining their parents in old age who had neglected to instruct them in some profitable trade or business. Some such law is necessary to-day in anthracite communities to force parents, financially able, to keep their children in school until they graduate. . . .

Sclavs: One of a race of people from Eastern and Northern Europe.

Native born: Born in America.

Solon: A famous lawyer from Ancient Greece.

Acquitted: Excused.

A group of boys pick slate at an anthracite mine in a coal breaker in the early 1900s. © CORBIS.

The breaker, where most boys of mine employees begin their life as wage earners, is not favorable to the intellectual development of the lad, however bright his **parts** may be. Over the chute where the coal passes he stoops and with nimble fingers picks out the impurities. In breakers, where water is not used to wash the coal, the air is laden with coal dust;

Parts: Brain.

Quicken: Increase.

Aesthetic: Related to beauty and art.

Prominence: Importance.

"Ardor": High energy.

"Spats": Arguments.

Woe betide: Misery comes to.

"Mangled": Torn or crushed.

Cortege: Funeral procession.

in winter the little fingers get cold and chap, and at all times when the machinery is in motion the noise from revolving wheels, crushers, screens and the rushing coal is deafening. In such an environment there is nothing to **quicken** the talent or develop the **aesthetic** sense of a boy. All is depressing and the wonder is that so many boys who began life under such conditions have been able to rise to **prominence** in the various spheres of life.

The boy learns many things in the breakers and in the mines. The hard conditions do not dampen the **"ardor"** and crush the spirits of the average lad. Most of them are bright, cheerful and full of tricks. They have a good appetite and with dirty hands the contents of the dinner-pail generally disappears. They have their **"spats"** and fights, and **woe betide** the man who injures one of them. They are full of fun and frolic, but their curiosity sometimes leads them to injury and death. Many of them fall into the machinery and are **"mangled,"** or down the chutes and are smothered. Of all deaths in this risky business the death of one of these boys is the saddest. To witness a funeral procession of a boy hardly in his teens and the **cortege** made up of his companions in the breaker, is a sight sad enough to melt a heart of stone, and every humane soul asks: "Is this sacrifice of youth necessary for the prosperity of the mining industry?"

There are three things which boys learn in the breakers; they are chewing and smoking tobacco and swearing. Some indeed have learned these before they begin to work in the breaker. Old Abijah Smith [the man who introduced anthracite coal to the United States] said, in his reminiscences of the early days of anthracite mining, that no youth would think of using tobacco before he was 18 years of age. Times have changed in the Wyoming Valley and many lads now contract the habit before they are in their teens, while boys playing on the streets use **profane** language which horrifies the morally sensitive. Sclav boys when irritated swear shamelessly and **afford** considerable **mirth** to their seniors. Many boys trained in a religious home resist the temptations to obscenity and vicious practices so common in and around the mines, but it requires unusually strong moral qualities to develop moral character under conditions so unfavorable.

Profane: Foul.

Afford: Provide.

Mirth: Hilarity, usually accompanied by laughter.

One of the greatest enemies of these boys is the cigarette. In a mining town where this curse of boyhood was sold in three stores, the consumption was 1,200 boxes or 12,000 cigarettes a month. Miners who smoke use the pipe or a cigar, so that these cigarettes were sold to boys from 8 to 16 years. There were 480 youths of that age in the **borough,** so that the consumption per capita was 25 cigarettes, providing all of them smoked. If half the youths—many **novices** and some **veterans**—only indulged[,] the **per capita** consumption per month was double. This evil prevails extensively in mining towns. One of our public school principals was so convinced of the prevalence of the habit among his scholars, that he went to the stores selling

Borough: Government region, such as a county.

Novices: New workers.

Veterans: Experienced workers.

Per capita: Per person.

cigarettes and asked the traders not to **cut the boxes,** for many tots came to buy two cigarettes for a penny. The practice of cutting the boxes still goes on. Careful observation of the physical, mental and moral injury wrought by this habit upon boyhood ought to move every community to wage a war of extermination upon this foe which destroys so many boys. Anti-tobacco leagues are sadly needed here. But what hope is there of reforming the boys when the fathers are so addicted to the habit? A superintendent says: "Only one of our teachers uses tobacco; nearly all of the men in our town do use it, ministers, lawyers, doctors, **Sabbath** school superintendents, etc. Many of these men stand high in the community. . . . What chance has a poor female teacher that is not considered worth more than $28 per month with her children, who can go out and earn more picking slate than she?"

There are many other practices among these boys which **sap** their physical and moral powers. In Lackawanna county a practice known as the "knock down" prevails among the boys. They take regularly from their pay a certain amount before they give their wages to their parents. Some of the coal companies afford the boys an opportunity for this practice, by not issuing a statement of the wages earned by them. Few parents know the rate of wages paid the boys and the time worked by them. They can only find this out by asking the boss—a thing the average parent will not do. Fathers working in the same **colliery** as their children are so indifferent to the children's earnings, that they know not when the "knock-down" is practiced by the boys. The boys are exceedingly skillful at the business. Many of them live in the same neighborhood and know that their mothers

Cut the boxes: Open the boxes to sell cigarettes individually.

Sabbath: Sunday.

Sap: Weaken.

Colliery: Coal mine, outbuildings, and equipment.

Discrepancy: Difference.

Strike: Protest in which employees refuse to work.

Occasioned: Brought about.

"Bacca-box": Tobacco box.

Patronize: Use.

Zeal: Enthusiasm.

Main: Main fight.

Stealthily: Carefully.

Cunning: Deception.

Shrewdness: Business sense.

Vanity: Pride.

Follies: Foolishness.

Microcosm: Small system representative of a larger system.

"Flush": Rich.

On a par: Equal.

"Tick": Credit.

Hankers for: Desires.

A dissipation: Spending thoughtlessly.

compare notes at pay-day. In order to guard against detection which may arise from a **discrepancy** in the pays of boys rated alike, they meet and agree to take out the same amount. Boys take in this way from 50 cents to $1 out of their two weeks' pay. In a local **strike** in 1900, some fathers complained that the boys did not get the regular rate of wages. When shown that they were paid the standard wage the parents were mortified to learn that they were victims of the "knock-down" habit. The revelation **occasioned** considerable comment and when a company of men discussed the question, one of them said: "It's an old trick: we used to do it ourselves." No one contradicted him, and some fathers practice it still—they hide a bill in the **"bacca-box"** before they hand the pay over to the wife.

Many of the boys **patronize** the slot machine, while some of them follow with great **zeal** cock-fighting and stake 5 or 10 or 25 cents on the **main.** Most of the small boys, however, spend their money in luxuries, and to watch these boys on pay night in the candy shop is one of the most amusing sights imaginable. They compare their cash; they count their change; they boast how much ice cream, candy, peanuts and soda they consume. The small boy lays away his cigarette very **stealthily,** while the veteran puffs boldly into the air. The lad of 16 years is about to pass from the candy store, but still lingering where the younger boys are, he feels the dawn of independence, and smokes a cigar to the envy of the smaller lads. All the rivalry, the **cunning,** the **shrewdness,** the **vanity** and the **follies** of life are seen here as in a **microcosm.** It is the drama of life in its pleasures, anxieties and pains.

Boys from 12 to 14 years spend from $1 to $2 a month. Those limited to 50 cents or a $1 "blow it in" on pay-night. Those having $1.50 to $2 are **"flush"** the night after pay, but the evening following they are all **on a par**—every pocket is empty. The only time the economic vision of these boys is exercised is when the circus comes to town. Then close figuring is done. They come to the last 30 or 25 cents. That they stow away for the expected night, sacrificing the pleasures of the moment for the promise of a good show. Stores which give the boys **"tick"** soon get out of business. A boy that owes 25 cents steers clear of that bill. The small boy's trade can only be held on a strictly cash basis.

When the lad reaches 16 or 17 years he leaves the candy shop. He feels himself above the small boys that congregate there and he **hankers for** something other than the "soft stuff" sold in them. It is the turning point in the young man's career. From his early boyhood every pay-night meant **a dissipation** after the manner of boys. He still craves for that excitement and dissipation and, forsaking the candy store, he finds only one place of welcome—the saloon. Candy is no longer the basis of his dissipation. It is beer and tobacco. When this hour comes many are the boys in mining towns who **frequent** saloons, for there is no other place provided to meet their requirements.

Frequent: Often visit.

• • •

What happened next...

By 1914, most states had enacted child labor laws. Children were required to be at least twelve or fourteen years old to be employed, and work days were limited to ten hours. Both of these requirements were frequently ignored, and since there were few official inspections, there was really no way to enforce the law. In addition, many children's parents provided birth certificates in which the birth date had been falsified. So employers were hiring children they may have known were under the legal age limit, but they had official paperwork to protect them.

In 1904, the National Child Labor Committee (NCLC) formed. The NCLC worked tirelessly for child labor reform on the federal level. The first law of its kind was not passed until 1916, and it was in effect for only two years. That law prohibited the movement of goods across state lines if the manufacturers violated minimum age laws. Unfortunately, this law was almost impossible to enforce, and so it had little impact on the life and work conditions of child laborers.

It would be 1938 before the Fair Labor Standards Act was passed. That law regulated minimum wages of employment and work hours for children.

Did you know...

- Anthracite coal was once considered useless because it did not burn as easily as bituminous, or soft, coal. A handful of creative individuals redesigned furnaces and stoves, and anthracite coal became the most effective fuel for heating homes and businesses. It burns cleaner, longer, and with less waste than its softer counterpart.
- A payroll book from November 1918 revealed that miners usually worked eight to ten hours daily, but that sixteen-hour shifts were not uncommon. Weekly wages for unskilled laborers were $10.52 to $11.82, while skilled labor received an average of $15.77 weekly. Mine supervisors, or foremen, earned $140 a week.
- Miners used to send canaries down into the mines before descending themselves. If the canaries died, the level of methane gas

(a highly explosive gas) was dangerous. If the birds survived, miners knew oxygen levels were good and the air was safe to breathe.

- Rats were common in mines, and miners depended on them for their safety. If rats began scurrying across mine floors, that meant they were feeling the vibrations of an oncoming explosion. Miners recognized the warning and could sometimes escape injury or death by following the rats out of the mines.

Consider the following...

- What are the moral issues of child labor?
- Explain the relationship between poverty and child labor, and compare child labor as it exists in the twenty-first century with that in the Gilded Age and the Progressive Era.
- How might industrial America have been different without child labor?

For More Information

BOOKS

Bartoletti, Susan Campbell. *Kids on Strike!* Boston: Houghton Mifflin, 2003.

Kuchta, David. *Once a Man, Twice a Boy.* Nesquehoning, PA: Kiwi Publishing, 2002.

Leonard, Joseph W. *Anthracite Roots: Generations of Coal Mining in Schuylkill County, Pennsylvania.* Charleston, SC: History Press, 2005.

Poliniak, Louis. *When Coal Was King.* Lancaster, PA: Applied Arts Publishers, 1989. Reprint, 2004.

Richards, J. Stuart. *Early Coal Mining in the Anthracite Region.* Charleston, SC: Arcadia Publishing, 2002.

Roberts, Peter. *Anthracite Coal Communities: A Study of the Demography, the Social, Educational and Moral Life of the Anthracite Regions.* New York: Macmillan, 1904. Reprint, Westport, CT: Greenwood Press, 1970.

Williams, William G. *The Coal King's Slaves: A Coal Miner's Story.* Shippensburg, PA: Burd Street Press, 2002.

WEB SITES

Bache, Rene. "The Campaign to End Child Labor: Shrimps and Babies." *BoondocksNet.com.* http://www.boondocksnet.com/labor/cl_12_shrimps.html (accessed on August 12, 2006).

Bogan, Dallas. "Life of a Coal Miner; Its Slow Progress: Boy Begins in Breaker, Old Man Ends in Breaker." Originally published in the *LaFollette Press.* Reprinted on *Tennessee Genealogy and History.* http://www.tngenweb.org/campbell/hist-bogan/coalminer.html (accessed on August 12, 2006).

"The Campaign to End Child Labor: Newsboys in the Second Cities." *BoondocksNet.com.* http://www.boondocksnet.com/labor/cl_050408_newsboys.html (accessed on August 12, 2006).

Eckley Miner's Village. http://www.eckleyminers.org/about.html (accessed on August 12, 2006).

Hine, Lewis. "Child Labor in America 1908–1912: Photographs of Lewis W. Hine." *The History Place.* http://www.historyplace.com/unitedstates/childlabor/ (accessed on August 12, 2006).

Lauver, Fred. "A Walk Through the Rise and Fall of Anthracite Might." *Pennsylvania Historical and Museum Commission.* http://www.phmc.state.pa.us/ppet/miningmuseum/page1.asp?secid=31 (accessed on August 12, 2006).

Markham, Edward, Benjamin B. Lindsey, and George Creel. "The Campaign to End Child Labor: Children in Bondage." *BoondocksNet.com.* http://www.boondocksnet.com/editions/cib/(accessed on August 12, 2006).

Ohio State University, Department of History. "The Boys in the Breakers." *eHistory.com.* http://ehistory.osu.edu/osu/mmh/gildedage/content/breakerboys.cfm (accessed on August 13, 2006).

Van Kleeck, Mary. "The Campaign to End Child Labor: Child Labor in New York City Tenements." *BoondocksNet.com.* http://www.boondocksnet.com/labor/cl_080118_tenements.html (accessed on August 12, 2006).

U.S. Congress

American Antiquities Act of 1906; passed into law on June 8, 1906
Available on National Park Service *(Web site)*

"Keep it for your children and your children's children and all
who come after you."

— Theodore Roosevelt, on the Grand Canyon in 1903

In 1848, the American Association for the Advancement of Science
(AAAS) was established for the purpose of advancing science throughout the world by means of education and professional organization. As
the century progressed and as the United States expanded, it became obvious that some of the more valuable resources and archaeological sites,
ruins, and artifacts needed federal protection if they were to be preserved. Most of these sites were in the Southwest, remainders of once-
thriving Native American cultures.

The AAAS joined forces with the Archaeological Institute of America
(AIA) in 1899 and developed a bill that would allow for federal protection
of these sites. The bill was introduced to Congress by U.S. representative
Jonathan Prentiss Dolliver (1858–1910) of Iowa in 1900. His bill marked
the beginning of a six-year struggle to protect these valuable sites from private greed and exploitation (using something to one's own advantage). The
reason for the delay in passage of the bill was the scope of the proposal.
Some members of Congress felt a general bill protecting all archaeological
sites would be most beneficial. Other members believed only specifically
named sites and regions should be granted protection.

Throughout the course of debate regarding protection and preservation of archaeological sites, three individuals became key figures. Scholar
Edgar Lee Hewett (1865–1946) also possessed considerable political skills.
His talents allowed him to find the common ideas in the two approaches
to archaeological preservation and effectively communicate them to all

U.S. representative John F. Lacey of Iowa, who wrote the Yellowstone National Park Protection Act of 1894.
THE LIBRARY OF CONGRESS.

parties involved. His behind-the-scenes work was critical in the effort to pass the American Antiquities Act.

U.S. representative John F. Lacey (1841–1913) of Iowa was another major participant in this important conservation (preservation and protection) effort. The Republican congressman had been involved in several earlier conservation measures and was known for his concern for protection of both wilderness and wildlife. He wrote the Yellowstone National Park Protection Act of 1894, which turned the park into the first national wildlife refuge where hunting and trapping were outlawed. Lacey also wrote the first wildlife conservation law, the Bird and Game Act, which was passed in 1900.

President Theodore Roosevelt (1858–1919; served 1901–9) was considered, among other things, the first conservation president. Roosevelt's personal philosophy (see Chapter 5) that man is closely connected with the land directly affected his attitude toward preserving American lands and resources. No president before him had so aggressively used his power and authority to protect the country's natural resources and wildlife.

Lacey's commitment to conservation was obvious in his persistent support for and authoring of various protective bills and legislation. Roosevelt's appreciation for the wilderness and natural resources was directly related to his love of big game hunting. Hewett's commitment to the passage of the Antiquities Act developed more gradually and was an offshoot of another, more personal attachment to the Pajarito Plateau of New Mexico.

When doctors recommended that Hewett's wife spend more time in a drier climate that would not worsen her tuberculosis (a chronic lung disease, often fatal), the couple began spending summers in New Mexico. Soon, they became deeply attached to the natural beauty of the Pajarito region. Hewett had the idea that the entire region should be designated a national park so that the ancient Southwestern cultural ruins there would be preserved for scientific research. Although much of the land in that region was federally owned public land, some of it was privately owned. Hewett hoped that his efforts to make the area a national park would encourage these private owners to take protective measures of their own.

National Parks, Monuments, and Other Designations

There are many different kinds of national designations in America, and the differences between them can be confusing. Here is a brief explanation of each:

National parks: When Yellowstone became a national park in 1872, protected by federal law, a worldwide movement began to establish other parks. In the twenty-first century, more than one hundred nations have designated twelve hundred national parks or preserves. In the United States, national parks are available to the public for leisure activities such as hiking and camping. Only Congress can designate a national park.

National monuments: The 1906 Antiquities Act allowed U.S. presidents to designate specific areas, structures, or landmarks as monuments in order to preserve and protect them. National monuments are usually smaller than national parks and do not offer as many attractions or as large a variety of activities.

National preserves: Preserves are designated to protect a specific natural resource, such as a grove of trees. Certain activities like hunting or fishing may be allowed if they do not threaten the preserve. Many of these federally protected designations could qualify for national park status.

National reserves: Similar to preserves, but protection and management are provided at the state or local level.

National rivers and wild and scenic riverways: This designation provides protection to the land bordering free-flowing streams and rivers. These waterways cannot be dammed or altered in any way by humans. Activities allowed include hiking, canoeing, and hunting.

National lakeshores and seashores: These areas are federally protected to preserve their natural values but also provide water-oriented recreation. Some are developed, whereas others remain in their primitive states.

National scenic trails: These long-distance foot trails wind through scenic areas of great natural beauty. Similar to these are national historic trails, which mark routes taken throughout history by military, explorers, and migrant (traveling) groups. The Appalachian Trail is one well-known national scenic trail.

National historic site: Contains one historical feature that is directly related to its subject. An example would be the Springfield, Illinois, home of the late U.S. president Abraham Lincoln (1809–1865; served 1861–65). Most national historic sites have been authorized by acts of Congress.

National memorial: Used mostly for commemorative (remembrance) areas. These sites and structures do not necessarily have to be related to their subjects. For example, the Lincoln Memorial in Washington, D.C., is a national memorial.

National military parks, national battlefield parks, national battlefield sites, and national battlefields: Each of these titles is used to designate an area of specific importance to the U.S. military.

In 1898, Hewett began a five-year term as the first president of the Normal University at Las Vegas, New Mexico. Hewett's program of study included many courses in anthropology (the study of human beings and how they live), and he began taking students on summertime explorations in Pajarito. Having already established a friendship with Lacey, Hewett invited the congressman to join him on a trek through Pajarito in 1902. He hoped to convince him of the need to enact federal protection. Lacey did lend his support, but the bill that ultimately went to Congress was greatly altered, reducing the size of the proposed park by three-quarters. The name Pajarito Park was also changed to Cliff Dweller's National Park.

Although that bill would go through several more changes over the years, in 1916, the Bandelier National Monument at the southern end of the Pajarito Plateau was designated by President Woodrow Wilson (1856–1924; served 1913–21). Hewett, discouraged by his defeat in the battle for Pajarito Park, realized how much he had learned throughout the process of trying to get the bill passed. The experience gained during the long struggle for Pajarito made him a powerful partner in the fight for the Antiquities Act.

Realizing that his lack of success may have stemmed from not knowing as much as he should about archaeology, Hewett obtained formal training in the field. After studying abroad in Europe, he returned to America in 1904 and found that he was not alone in his desire to promote legal protection for valuable archaeological sites and regions. The entire archeological community, along with the Smithsonian Institution, the Department of Interior (created in 1849, the department of the federal government concerned with conservation), and concerned congressmen, joined forces in the battle to protect America's precious lands.

Although Hewett was still focused on Pajarito, he did not neglect the Antiquities bill. He worked closely with government and archaeological committees and revised the proposal several times. The Department of the Interior favored the national parks approach. Hewett and Lacey, however, loudly stressed the importance of specific legislation to protect archaeological sites specifically and as something separate from national parks. Congress did not appreciate the purpose of such legislation and did not act on the bill for years.

Hewett decided that the direct approach—asking the government for protection of these valuable sites—was not working. Rather than ask Congress to make the government responsible for protecting these

Cliff dwellings at Bandelier National Monument in Santa Fe National Forest, New Mexico. © CORBIS.

lands, Hewett worded the proposal in such a way that the protection was an indirect responsibility of the government. His draft stated that it would be illegal for any citizen to damage ruins on federal land. This particular issue of looting and damaging federal property was a major concern at the turn of the century. The public knew that vandalism on such a level was occurring with alarming frequency, and they wanted to see an end to it. Hewett's revision of the bill would allow the government to prevent such illegal activity directly (as stated in the provisions of the law) while at the same time indirectly (by preventing vandalism, the government was providing protection) require it to protect the lands.

After more debate about the amount of lands in the Southwest to be protected, Hewett's version of the bill finally passed Congress. On June 8, 1906, President Roosevelt signed into law the Act for the Preservation of American Antiquities (otherwise known as the American Antiquities Act). The law gave the president the authority to designate as national monuments specific landmarks, structures, and other objects of historic or scientific interest located on lands owned or controlled by the federal government. It also made vandalism of such federal grounds a crime, and authorized permits for legitimate archaeological explorations.

Things to remember while reading the American Antiquities Act of 1906:

- With the closing of the wilderness frontier as more and more settlers made their homes in the West and Southwest, many sites and geologic structures were just being discovered. People vandalized these valuable historic places for personal gain. For example, they would steal rocks from structures and sites and then sell them as souvenirs.

- Not everyone was in favor of federal protection of national monuments. Many native tribes in the Southwest considered these regions their own and felt the government had no right to intrude on their private grounds.

- The concept of conserving natural resources was completely new in the Progressive Era. Prior to the conservation movement, many, if not most, Americans believed there was an endless supply of natural resources. Society, including the government, had a basic mindset that protective measures were unnecessary.

• • •

American Antiquities Act of 1906

Be it enacted by the Senate and House of Representatives of the United States of America in Congress assembled, That any person who shall **appropriate, excavate,** injure, or destroy any historic or prehistoric ruin or monument, or any object of **antiquity,** situated on lands owned or controlled by the Government of the United States, without the permission of the Secretary of the Department of the Government having **jurisdiction** over the lands on which said antiquities are situated, shall, upon conviction, be fined in a sum of not more than five hundred dollars or be imprisoned for a period of not more than ninety days, or shall suffer both fine and imprisonment, in the **discretion** of the court.

Appropriate: Steal.

Excavate: Dig up.

Antiquity: The past.

Jurisdiction: Authority.

Discretion: Judgment.

Sec. 2. That the President of the United States is hereby authorized, in his discretion, to declare by public proclamation historic landmarks, historic and prehistoric structures, and other objects of historic or scientific interest that are situated upon the lands owned or controlled by the Government of the United States to be national monuments, and may reserve as a part thereof parcels of land, the limits of which in all cases shall be confined to the smallest area compatible with proper care and management of the objects to be protected: Provided, That when such objects are situated upon a tract covered by a **bona fied** [sic] unperfected claim or held in private ownership, the tract, or so much thereof as may be necessary for the proper care and management of the object, may be **relinquished** to the Government, and the Secretary of the Interior is hereby authorized to accept the relinquishment of such tracts in behalf of the Government of the United States.

Bona fide: Authentic, real.

Relinquished: Given.

Sec. 3. That permits for the examination of ruins, the excavation of archaeological sites, and the gathering of objects of antiquity upon the lands under their respective jurisdictions may be granted by the Secretaries of the Interior, Agriculture, and War to institutions which they may deem properly qualified to conduct such examination, excavation, or gathering, subject to such rules and regulation as they may prescribe: Provided, That the examinations, excavations, and gatherings are undertaken for the benefit of reputable museums, universities, colleges, or other recognized scientific or educational institutions, with a view to increasing the knowledge of such objects, and that the gatherings shall be made for permanent preservation in public museums.

Sec. 4. That the Secretaries of the Departments aforesaid shall make and publish from time to time uniform rules and regulations for the purpose of carrying out the provisions of this Act.

Approved, June 8, 1906.

• • •

What happened next...

President Roosevelt used his new power for the first time three months after the signing of the bill. Devil's Tower in Wyoming was the first national monument, quickly followed by the Petrified Forest in Arizona. Shortly after that, two cultural monuments were declared: El Morro, New Mexico (a 200-foot sandstone bluff used as a landmark for travelers in the desert), and Montezuma Castle in Arizona (a five-story, twenty-room cliff dwelling built by the Sinagua Indians).

Devil's Tower in Wyoming, the first national monument established following the signing of the American Antiquities Act of 1906, by President Theodore Roosevelt. © CORBIS.

Roosevelt loosely interpreted the guidelines of the Act, which specifically stated that objects must be of scientific interest. In 1908, he stretched that specification and proclaimed more than 800,000 acres (3,237 square kilometers) of the Grand Canyon as a national monument. President Woodrow Wilson went even further with Roosevelt's interpretation when he created Katmai National Monument in Alaska in 1918. That monument included more than one million acres (4,000 square kilometers) of land. It was later enlarged to almost 2.8 million acres (11,331 square kilometers) by other Antiquities Act proclamations and was the country's largest national park system. The Petrified Forest, the Grand Canyon, and Katmai were eventually converted to the status of national parks.

Congress did not oppose such relaxed use of the Antiquities Act until 1943. At that time, President Franklin D. Roosevelt (1882–1945; served 1933–45) declared Jackson Hole in Wyoming a national monument. He did this so that he could accept a land donation by John D. Rockefeller Jr. (1874–1960). This donation would be added to Grand Teton National Park in Wyoming. Earlier, Congress had denied authorization to expand the park. By making Jackson Hole a national monument, Roosevelt was able to expand the park despite Congress's wishes.

Although subsequent presidents used their authority under the Antiquities Act, none did so with such enthusiasm. It would be 1978 before a president would use his power in such a way. President Jimmy Carter (1924–; served 1977–81) proclaimed fifteen new national monuments in Alaska. In doing so, he doubled the acreage protected by law in that state.

It would be 1996 before another national monument was proclaimed. President Bill Clinton (1946–; served 1993–2001) established the Grand Staircase-Escalante National Monument in Utah that year. He also used the Act to enlarge existing national monuments, as did several presidents before him.

The ruins and archaeological sites in the Southwest spurred progressive thinkers and politicians into the conservation movement of the Progressive Era. Those same ruins and sites are, in the twenty-first century, under threat of collapse from natural erosion (wearing down of the soil and land) and the tourism industry. Throughout the twentieth century, the ruins consistently needed repair, and an organized group of craftsmen used mortar made from cement to repair the antiquities. Even though the craftsmen used all the skills and knowledge they had at that time, by the 1970s, it became clear that the mortar was not preserving the ruins but hastening their decay.

Throughout the 1980s, the threat to the ruins was largely ignored, as key personnel in the Park Service retired, the repair unit disbanded, and finances were scarce. Left unattended, the ruins were at the mercy of the weather and the unceasing visitation by tourists from all over the world. By the 1990s, the situation was worse than ever, causing a handful of park rangers to begin comparing notes of what they observed among the various ruins on these federally protected lands. The result was a program called "Vanishing Treasures."

The program attacked the problem from three different angles: by documenting the rate of deterioration; by repairing those ruins in the most immediate danger, while experimenting with and researching new materials and repair methods; and by training a new generation of craftsmen. The program remains active into the twenty-first century.

The Antiquities Act was an important piece of legislation when it passed Congress. Without it, commercial developers would have divided the Grand Canyon into parcels of land and sold it to businesses. This law saved countless natural and archaeologically important sites in America. Undeniably, the Act provided protection when congressional indifference prevented conservation bills from passing in a timely manner. The wording and protective measures of the Act remain virtually the same as they were when signed into law in 1906.

Did you know...

- California has more national monuments (thirteen) than any other state.
- Congress also has the power to declare national monuments, though that power does not come from the Antiquities Act. Whereas a president's declaration takes immediate effect, it can take Congress years to declare a national monument.
- Of the 105 national monuments proclaimed under the Antiquities Act, 46 have been larger than 5,000 acres (20 square kilometers); 28 have been larger than 50,000 acres (202 square kilometers).
- Nearly 25 percent of America's national parks were originally designated national monuments, including the Grand Canyon.

Consider the following...

- If you could visit just one national monument, which one would you choose and why?
- The Antiquities Act is still in effect in the twenty-first century. In what ways is it more important than it was in 1906? In what ways is it less important?
- Giving the U.S. president the sole power to declare something a national monument implies a certain level of trust and knowledge. Some presidents invoked that power more than twenty times, others none at all. Do you think someone else should have a say in deciding what will be a national monument, and if so, who?

For More Information

BOOKS

Butcher, Devereux. *Exploring Our National Parks and Monuments.* 9th ed. Lanham, MD: Roberts Rinehart Publishers, 1995.

Harmon, David, McManamon, Francis P., and Dwight T. Pitcaithley, eds. *The Antiquities Act: A Century of American Archaeology, Historic Preservation, and Nature Conservation.* Tucson: University of Arizona Press, 2006.

Place, Chuck. *Ancient Walls: Indian Ruins of the Southwest.* Golden, CO: Fulcrum Publishing, 1992.

WEB SITES

"Archeology Program: Antiquities Act 1906–2006." *National Park Service.* http://www.cr.nps.gov/archeology/sites/antiquities/ (accessed on August 13, 2006).

"Archeology Program: Edgar Lee Hewett and the Political Process." *National Park Service.* http://www.cr.nps.gov/archeology/pubs/antiq/antiq01.htm (accessed on August 13, 2006).

"Archeology Program: Vanishing Treasures." *National Park Service.* http://www.cr.nps.gov/archeology/vt/crisis.htm (accessed on August 13, 2006).

Library of Congress. "The Evolution of the Conservation Movement, 1850–1920." *American Memory.* http://memory.loc.gov/ammem/amrvhtml/conshome.html (accessed on August 13, 2006).

"A National Monument, Memorial, Park ... What's the Difference?" *National Atlas.* http://www.nationalatlas.gov/articles/government/a_nationalparks.html (accessed on August 13, 2006).

"U.S. National Monuments." *GORP.* http://gorp.away.com/gorp/resource/us_nm/main.htm (accessed on August 13, 2006).

14

Ida M. Tarbell

Excerpt from *The History of the Standard Oil Company*
   Originally published in 1904; available at Rochester History Resources *(Web site)*

"There were . . . twenty-six refineries in the town—some of them very large plants. All of them were feeling more or less the discouraging effects of the last three or four years of railroad discriminations in favour of the Standard Oil Company. To . . . these refineries Mr. Rockefeller . . . told them, 'this scheme is bound to work. It means an absolute control by us of the oil business. There is no chance for anyone outside. But we are going to give everybody a chance to come in. You are to turn over your refinery to my appraisers, and I will give you Standard Oil Company stock or cash, as you prefer, for the value we put upon it. I advise you to take the stock. It will be for your good.'"

As America entered the Gilded Age (approximately 1878–99), a new breed of businessmen appeared. These men gained unimaginable amounts of wealth at the expense of America's working class. They ran their companies without a sense of honesty and with an eye always on profit. It was common knowledge that these businessmen—called robber barons—were unethical and conducted their business in questionable and sometimes obviously illegal ways. The powerful robber baron became a symbol of America's Industrial Revolution (1877–1900), the era when America's economy came to depend upon industry rather than agriculture.

Only a handful of men were considered robber barons in the Gilded Age. Although their numbers were few, they gained and controlled the

Standard Oil magnate John D. Rockefeller. © HULTON ARCHIVE/GETTY IMAGES.

largest percentage of the country's wealth at that time. John D. Rockefeller (1839–1937) was not the first robber baron, but he is often considered the perfect example of one. Rockefeller established the Standard Oil Company and America's petroleum (gasoline) industry.

Rockefeller built his first oil refinery in 1863. By 1877, he controlled 90 percent of the American oil industry. His business became so large that he found it difficult to manage. Rockefeller's response was to form the first "trust" in 1882. A trust is an organization of several businesses in the same industry. By banding together, the trust can control production and distribution of a product or service, thereby limiting competition.

Trusts cause problems for several reasons. One reason is that a direct result of a trust is a monopoly in which one company or group of companies has control of an entire industry. Standard Oil had a monopoly in the oil industry. Monopolies bring their owners and top-level executives great profit and power, but they prohibit smaller businessmen and companies from making any money at all. Another problem stemming from trusts has to do with capitalism, an economy in which all businesses have an equal opportunity to thrive. Since the basis of capitalism is competition, a monopoly undermines the cornerstone of America's economy.

Although most people knew Rockefeller built his oil empire by exploiting (using to his own advantage) smaller companies and labor, the attitude throughout the Gilded Age was that government should not regulate business. To do so, many believed, would weaken the philosophy underlying capitalism, that competition leads to success for businesses and choices for consumers.

Rockefeller knew America depended on oil for its daily existence. Families and businesses used it to heat their homes and buildings; factories needed it to run their machines. By establishing his trust, Rockefeller forced consumers to pay whatever price he wanted to charge for his oil. America was growing weary of this situation.

Some Americans accepted the situation; others took action. At a time when corruption was infiltrating every aspect of life from politics to big business, a group of journalists made it their job to uncover and publicize that corruption. Pioneers of investigative journalism, these writers were called "muckrakers" (muckraking means digging up dirt). One of the most popular among them was Ida M. Tarbell (1857–1944). Tarbell wrote for the popular magazines of the day, including *McClure's,* a literary and political journal.

Tarbell began her investigation into the Standard Oil Company in 1902. Her findings and report were published in nineteen parts in *McClure's* from November 1902 to October 1904. In 1904, she published the entire account in book form under the title *The History of the Standard Oil Company.*

Tarbell's exposé focused on Rockefeller's involvement with the railroads. By the early 1870s, Cleveland, Ohio, was one of the nation's primary oil refining centers. It was also home to Standard Oil, which was the most profitable refinery in the city. Standard Oil, by nature of its size, had become one of the largest shippers of oil and kerosene, and it depended upon the railroads to move its products across the nation.

With so many new railroad lines, competition was fierce. In an effort to compete, railroads tried to undercut each other by charging lower and lower shipping rates. While this was good for companies that relied upon the railroads, it was devastating to the railroads themselves. Unable to make a profit, the railroads formed a monopoly to stabilize shipping rates. This monopoly was called the South Improvement Company.

The railroads knew they needed support if their monopoly was to work. Rockefeller, being the most wealthy and frequent shipper, was the obvious choice among customers. He agreed to support the South Improvement Company on the condition that he received preferential treatment. This meant he received hefty rebates (refunds) for each shipment he sent, but he was also given rebates for the shipment of competing products. So any other oil or kerosene other than that coming from the Standard refinery that the railroads shipped brought Rockefeller a rebate.

The Sherman Antitrust Act

U.S. senator John Sherman (1823–1900) of Ohio introduced the Sherman Antitrust Act in Congress. The Act declared it a federal crime to form trusts and monopolies both within states and when dealing with foreign trade.

The Sherman Act was passed on July 2, 1890. Under it, criminals had to pay just $5,000 and spend one year in prison for breaking the law. Considering that the wealthiest men in America formed the trusts and monopolies, this fine was not enough to keep them from breaking the law. In addition, the government was not inclined to enforce the Act because men like Rockefeller gave large sums of money to political campaigns. It would take the power of President Theodore Roosevelt (1858–1919; served 1901–9), known as the trust-busting president, to enforce the Sherman Act.

*Ida M. Tarbell, author of an
exposé on John Rockefeller and
the Standard Oil Company.*

The South Improvement Company announced a steep increase in freight charges, which incurred the wrath of business owners who depended upon the railroads. The protests that followed the announcement brought the situation into the public eye, and it was then that Tarbell discovered (through research and detective work) Rockefeller's involvement in the scheme.

Things to remember while reading the excerpt from *The History of the Standard Oil Company*

- Women writers of the early twentieth century wrote primarily about social events and domestic or household-related topics. Tarbell was a woman in a field dominated by men, and she was highly respected for her unwavering honesty and assessment. She was one of the highest-paid journalists of her day.

- The South Improvement Company lasted less than one year, but it brought to America's attention undeniable evidence of the corrupt relationship between big business and the railroad industry.

- Even those small businessmen who did not want to become part of the South Improvement Company often sold their business to Rockefeller. They realized that the only other option was to be run out of business entirely.

- Tarbell's father's oil business failed as a direct result of the corrupt business practices of Rockefeller.

- Standard Oil was the largest company in the world during its peak years, and Rockefeller was the wealthiest man in the world for years.

• • •

Excerpt from *The History of the Standard Oil Company*

Crude: Raw.

Refined: Processed to remove impurities.

Oil had risen to fourth place in the exports of the United States in the twelve years since its discovery, and every year larger quantities were consumed abroad, but it was **crude** oil, not **refined,** which the foreigners were beginning to demand; that is, they had found they could import crude, refine it at home, and sell it cheaper than they could buy American refined. France, to encourage her home refineries, had even put a tax on American refined.

In the fall of 1871, while Mr. Rockefeller and his friends were occupied with all these questions, certain Pennsylvania refiners, it is not too certain who, brought to them a remarkable scheme, the **gist** of which was to bring together secretly a large enough body of refiners and shippers to persuade all the railroads handling oil to give to the company formed **special rebates** on its oil, and **drawbacks on that of other people.** If they could get such rates it was evident that those outside of their combination could not compete with them long and that they would become eventually the only refiners. They could then limit their output to actual demand, and so keep up prices. This done, they could easily persuade the railroads to transport no crude for exportation, so that the foreigners would be forced to buy American refined. They believed that the price of oil thus exported could easily be advanced fifty per cent. The control of the refining interests would also enable them to fix their own price on crude. As they would be the only buyers and sellers, the **speculative** character of the business would be done away with. In short, the scheme they worked out put the entire oil business in their hands. It looked as simple to put into operation as it was dazzling in its results. Mr. [Henry Morrison] Flagler [a wealthy real estate and railroad developer] has sworn that neither he nor Mr. Rockefeller believed in this scheme. But when they found that their friend Peter H. Watson, and various Philadelphia and Pittsburg [sic] parties who felt as they did about the oil business, believed in it, they went in and began at once to work up a company—secretly. It was evident that a scheme which aimed at concentrating in the hands of one company the business now operated by scores, and which proposed to effect this **consolidation** through a practice of the railroads which was contrary to the spirit of their **charters,** although freely indulged in, must be worked with fine discretion if it ever were to be effective.

The first thing was to get a charter—quietly. At a meeting held in Philadelphia late in the fall of 1871 a friend of one of the gentlemen interested mentioned to him that a certain estate then in **liquidation** had a charter for sale which gave its owners the right to carry on any kind of business in any country and in any way; that it could be bought for what it would cost to get a charter under the general laws of the state, and that it would be a favour to the **heirs** to buy it. The opportunity was promptly taken. The name of the charter bought was the "Southern (usually written South) Improvement Company." For a beginning it was as good a name as another, since it said nothing.

Gist: Idea.

Special rebates: Monetary refunds.

Drawbacks on that of other people: Specific, per-barrel monetary refunds for oil shipped by other companies.

Speculative: Uncertain.

Consolidation: Combination.

Charters: Documents incorporating an institution and listing its rights.

Liquidation: The process of turning property and assets into money.

Heirs: Descendents of a deceased person.

With this charter in hand Mr. Rockefeller and Mr. Watson and their associates began to seek **converts.** In order that their great scheme might not be injured by premature public discussion they asked of each person whom they approached a pledge of secrecy. Two forms of the pledges required before anything was revealed were published later. The first of these, which appeared in the *New York Tribune*, read as follows:

> I, A. B., do faithfully promise upon my honour and faith as a gentleman that I will keep secret all transactions which I may have with the corporation known as the South Improvement Company; that, should I fail to complete any bargains with the said company, all the preliminary conversations shall be kept strictly private; and, finally, that I will not disclose the price for which I dispose of my product, or any other facts which may in any way bring to light the internal workings or organization of the company. All this I do freely promise. Signed [name]; Witnessed by [name]

A second, published in a history of the "Southern Improvement Company," ran:

> The undersigned pledge their solemn words of honour that they will not communicate to any one without permission of Z (name of director of Southern Improvement Company) any information that he may convey to them, or any of them, in relation to the Southern Improvement Company. Signed [name]; Witness [name]

The work of persuasion went on swiftly. By the 18th of January the president of the Pennsylvania road, J. Edgar Thompson, had put his signature to the contract, and soon after Mr. [Cornelius] Vanderbilt and Mr. Clark signed for the Central system, and Jay Gould and General [George] McClellan for the Erie. The contracts to which these gentlemen put their names fixed gross rates of freight from all common points, as the leading shipping points within the Oil Regions were called, to all the great refining and shipping centres—New York, Philadelphia, Baltimore, Pittsburg[h] and Cleveland. For example, the open rate on crude to New York was put at $2.56. On this price the South Improvement Company was allowed a rebate of $1.06 for its shipments; but it got not only this rebate, it was given in cash a like amount on each barrel of crude shipped by parties outside the combination.

The open rate from Cleveland to New York was two dollars, and fifty cents of this was turned over to the South Improvement Company, which at the same time received a rebate enabling it to ship for $1.50. Again, an independent refiner in Cleveland paid eighty cents a barrel to get his crude from the Oil Regions to his works, and the railroad sent forty cents of this money to the South Improvement Company. At the same time it cost the Cleveland refiner in the combination but forty cents to get his crude oil.

Like drawbacks and rebates were given for all points-Pittsburg[h], Philadelphia, Boston and Baltimore.

An interesting provision in the contracts was that full **waybills** of all petroleum shipped over the roads should each day be sent to the South Improvement Company. This, of course, gave them knowledge of just who was doing business outside of their company—of how much business he was doing, and with whom he was doing it. Not only were they to have full knowledge of the business of all shippers—they were to have access to all books of the railroads.

Waybills: Documents identifying the handling and accounting of the shipment of freight.

The parties to the contracts agreed that if anybody appeared in the business offering an equal amount of transportation, and having equal facilities for doing business with the South Improvement Company, the railroads might give them equal advantages in drawbacks and rebates, but to make such a miscarriage of the scheme doubly improbable each railroad was bound to co-operate as "far as it legally might to maintain the business of the South Improvement Company against injury by competition, and lower or raise the gross rates of transportation for such times and to such extent as might be necessary to overcome the competition. The rebates and drawbacks to be varied **pari passu** with the gross rates."

Pari passu: Equally.

The reason given by the railroads in the contract for granting these extraordinary privileges was that the "magnitude and extent of the business and operations" purposed to be carried on by the South Improvement Company would greatly promote the interest of the railroads and make it desirable for them to encourage their undertaking. The evident advantages received by the railroad were a regular amount of freight,—the Pennsylvania was to have forty-five per cent of the Eastbound shipments, the Erie and Central each 27 ½ per cent., while West-bound freight was to be divided equally between them—fixed rates, and freedom from the system of cutting which they had all found so harassing and disastrous. That is, the South Improvement Company, which was to include the entire refining capacity of the company, was to act as the **evener of the oil business**.

Evener of the oil business: The company that would ensure fairness.

It was on the second of January, 1872, that the organization of the South Improvement Company was completed. The day before the Standard Oil Company of Cleveland increased its capital from $1,000,000 to $2,500,000, "all the stockholders of the company being present and voting therefore." These stockholders were greater by five than in 1870, the names of O. B. Jennings, Benjamin Brewster, Truman P. Handy, Amasa Stone, and Stillman Witt having been added. The last three were officers and stockholders in one or more of the railroads centring [sic] in Cleveland. Three weeks after this increase of capital Mr. Rockefeller had the charter and contracts of the South Improvement Company in hand, and was ready to see what they would do in helping him carry out his idea of wholesale combination in Cleveland. There were at that time some twenty-six refineries in the town—some of them very large plants. All of them were feeling more or less the discouraging effects of the last three or four years of railroad discriminations in favour of the Standard Oil Company. To the owners of these refineries Mr. Rockefeller now went one by one, and explained the South Improvement Company. "You see," he told them, "this scheme is bound to work. It means an absolute control by us of the oil business. There is no chance for anyone outside. But we are going to give everybody a chance to come in. You are to turn over your refinery to my appraisers, and I will give you Standard Oil Company stock or cash, as you prefer, for the value we put upon it. I advise you to take the stock. It will be for your good." Certain refiners objected. They did not want to sell. They did want to keep and manage their business. Mr. Rockefeller was regretful, but firm. It was useless to resist, he told the hesitating; they would certainly be crushed if they did not accept his offer, and he pointed out in detail, and with gentleness, how beneficent the scheme really was—preventing the creek refiners from destroying Cleveland, ending competition, keeping up the price of refined oil, and eliminating speculation. Really a wonderful **contrivance** for the good of the oil business.

Contrivance: Deceitful scheme.

Under the combined threat and persuasion of the Standard, armed with the South Improvement Company scheme, almost the entire independent oil interest of Cleveland collapsed in three months' time. Of the twenty-six refineries, at least twenty-one sold out.

• • •

What happened next...

Although it came too late to help many of the smaller, independent oil businesses, Tarbell's exposé increased public pressure to put an end to Rockefeller's unethical behavior. The public had been aware of the robber baron's basic lack of honesty, but Tarbell's report gave concrete evidence as to Rockefeller's greed and willingness to exploit others. By 1906, anti-Rockefeller sentiment was at its highest, partially because President Roosevelt publicly attacked him as a criminal.

The federal government had seven lawsuits pending against Standard Oil by 1907, claiming it was twenty times bigger than its closest competitor. In 1908, the government launched its biggest suit against Standard Oil, determined to break up the oil trust. It would take three years, but on May 15, 1911, the government ordered Standard Oil to

A 1907 editorial cartoon shows President Theodore Roosevelt on a ship called the Teddysey *trying to be lured onto a rocky island inhabited by businessmen (clockwise from top) J. P. Morgan, Andrew Carnegie, and John D. Rockefeller. At the time, the federal government had several lawsuits pending against Rockefeller's Standard Oil Company.* © THE GRANGER COLLECTION, NEW YORK.

dismantle and separate into thirty-four smaller companies, each with its own board of directors. The trust was broken.

Tarbell continued her career in journalism. In 1999, the New York University Department of Journalism ranked her book on Standard Oil fifth on a list of the top one hundred works of journalism. A commemorative stamp with her photo on it was issued by the U.S. Post Office in 2002.

Did you know...

- By the time the Standard Oil Company was ordered to dismantle, John D. Rockefeller had already been retired for fourteen years.

- Rockefeller was seen as a contradiction. Although he was a dishonest and greedy businessman, he was a deeply religious man who donated millions of dollars to charitable causes.

- Antitrust legislation is still in effect in the twenty-first century. The largest antitrust lawsuit of the twentieth century was brought against the computer company Microsoft by the federal government. After two years of litigation, the company was found guilty of violating the Sherman Act. Eventually, Microsoft was ordered to share its computer interfaces with third-party companies (such as those who sell computers). The government appealed the settlement. As of 2006, no final decision had been made.

- Oil companies in the twenty-first century that grew out of Standard Oil include Mobil, Amoco, Conoco, and BP.

Consider the following...

- You are John D. Rockefeller's teenage child. You know that your father is dishonest and engages in criminal activity, but you live a life of luxury and privilege because of his money. You enjoy the wealth, but you are not comfortable with how your father makes his money. What would you do?

- What are some modern, powerful companies or business people whose success you know is the result of corruption?

- Can you name three instances in your lifetime when a major political or social scandal has been uncovered by investigative journalists?

For More Information

BOOKS

Coffey, Ellen Greenman. *John D. Rockefeller: Richest Man Ever*. San Diego: Blackbirch Press, 2001.

Segall, Grant. *John D. Rockefeller: Anointed with Oil*. New York: Oxford University Press, 2001.

Somervill, Barbara A. *Ida Tarbell: Pioneer Investigative Reporter*. Greensboro, NC: M. Reynolds, 2002.

Tarbell, Ida M. *The History of the Standard Oil Company*. New York: McClure, Phillips & and Co., 1904. Reprint, New York: Harper & Row, 1966. Also available online at *Rochester History Resources*. http://www.history.rochester.edu/fuels/tarbell/MAIN.HTM (accessed on August 14, 2006).

WEB SITES

"Standard Oil Trust." *U-S-History.com.* http://www.u-s-history.com/pages/ h1804.html (accessed on August 14, 2006).

Tarbell, Ida M. "John D. Rockefeller: A Character Study." *Allegheny College.* http://tarbell.allegheny.edu/archives/jdr.html (accessed on August 14, 2006).

"Whatever Happened to Standard Oil?" *U.S. Highways: From US 1 to (US 830).* http://www.us-highways.com/sohist.htm (accessed on August 14, 2006).

Upton Sinclair

Excerpt from *The Jungle*
Originally published in 1905; available at The Literature Network *(Web site)*

> "For it was the custom, as they found, whenever meat was so spoiled that it could not be used for anything else, either to can it or else to chop it up into sausage."

The Industrial Revolution (approximately 1877–1900) in America created hundreds of thousands of much-needed jobs in the last half of the nineteenth century. Native-born Americans as well as the millions of immigrants (people who leave their country to settle in a foreign land) who crossed the oceans to land at Ellis Island near New York City and Angel Island in San Francisco, California (immigration processing centers), filled those low-paying positions. Many of the jobs involved long hours and backbreaking work.

Working conditions in factories and industry were unsafe and heartless. Company owners and management were, in general, more concerned with making money than with their employees' safety and health. To these men, any money spent on employees—whether in terms of wages, benefits, or sanitary and safe working conditions—meant less money for their own pockets. The connection between healthy, happy workers and high levels of productivity was not obvious in the Gilded Age and the Progressive Era.

Working-class urban America had firsthand experience working in these miserable conditions. Most men of the upper class also were aware of the plight of industrial workers. After all, their families were living lives of luxury at the direct expense of the overworked employees. The rest of society was either unaware or simply did not understand the degree of suffering imposed upon workers.

This state of ignorance changed when a new breed of journalists—called muckrakers—began publishing articles, novels, and exposés on America's hidden exploitation (improper use of a person for someone else's gain) of its workers. Muckrakers were given their name by U.S. president Theodore Roosevelt (1858–1919; served 1901–9), who acknowledged the journalists' important role in exposing industrial greed and exploitation.

Muckraking was the result of two related phenomena in the early twentieth century. Journalists breaking into print at that time were formally educated, trained to write about issues with a focus on accuracy and truth. This education separated these "new" journalists from the "old" journalists, who tended to sensationalize (exaggerate facts and focus on the emotional aspects of) their stories to increase their appeal to readers. The atmosphere of America at the turn of the century was one of reform. Many major changes had occurred in the last half of the nineteenth century, largely due to industrialism; not all of the changes were good. Reform was necessary if progress was to continue. Muckrakers embodied the spirit of new journalism and reform. Through their writings, America received both an education in the working conditions of the time and its inspiration to change them.

In 1904, a young journalist named Upton Sinclair (1878–1968) was sent by his editors to Chicago, Illinois, to investigate and report on the lives of workers in the stockyards (enclosed yards where food animals are temporarily kept before going to slaughter). Sinclair spent seven weeks in the meatpacking plants, where he learned every detail of every step of the process of how a cow or a pig becomes meat for human consumption. He lived among and interviewed hundreds of workers and became familiar with both their work and home lives. The journalist left Chicago with a thorough understanding of the structure of the meatpacking business.

The result of Sinclair's research was *The Jungle,* a story that appeared serially (one chapter at a time) in *Appeal to Reason,* the newspaper for which Sinclair wrote. The writer had approached a handful of publishing companies in hopes of getting his work published, but he was told by all of them that his book was too shocking for America's reading tastes. Sinclair financed the first printing of *The Jungle* himself and announced in the newspaper that the story would be available in book form. In doing so, he received twelve thousand prepaid orders for the book. Finally, Doubleday, Page, & Company learned of the interest and took

Gustavus Swift: The Man Who Changed the Meat Industry

Chicago meatpacking pioneer Gustavus Swift.
© BETTMANN/CORBIS.

As the human population in the East was increasing, so were the number of cattle in the West. Herds of cattle were being driven to new railroad towns such as Abilene, Kansas. From there, they were sent to Chicago and on to other parts of the country. Shipping the cattle live, however, was not cost effective. The animals would get hurt in transit, which lowered their price and ability to be eaten.

The solution was to find a way to slaughter the cattle in Chicago and ship only the edible parts East. Swift began shipping beef in winter by rail, with the boxcar doors open. That was not an ideal situation. In 1878, Swift hired an engineer named Andrew Chase to develop an improved refrigerated train car. Although the refrigerated car had already been invented in 1868, it did not work well and so was not used. Chase was successful, and his refrigeration technology made Chicago the meatpacking center of America. At the same time, the meat business became Chicago's main industry.

Gustavus Swift (1839–1903) arrived in Chicago in 1875. He would become owner of one of the two largest companies in the meatpacking industry. (Philip Armour was the other; see box.) Swift began his career as a country butcher in Massachusetts. He began dealing in cattle and moved west with the business until he arrived in Chicago at the age of thirty-six. At that time, Chicago's meat business was in pork, not beef. Refrigeration technology did not yet exist, so in order to safely ship meat across the country, it had to be salted or smoked. This worked for pork, but Americans liked their beef fresh. So although cattle were moving through Chicago, they were not butchered there. Instead, the animals were sold and shipped live to regions where the demand for fresh beef was greatest: the ever-growing cities in the East.

Now that beef could safely be shipped to the East, Swift needed storage facilities, and he built them. The meat also had to be sold, so he hired a sales crew and established a distribution system in every major city. A massive advertising campaign convinced consumers that Swift meats were safe. Soon, the demand for his product required him to build five more packing plants.

Swift then organized stockyards to buy large quantities of cattle on a regular basis. When that proved successful, he branched out to manufacture and sell animal by-products (something produced in addition to a main product) such as glue, fertilizer, and soap. By controlling each step in the process of his business, Swift transformed into one of the first vertically integrated companies. Vertical integration is a business concept whereby one person or company controls each aspect or function of a process, allowing for the most profits. Vertical integration was a new idea in America, and Swift proved its effectiveness.

Philip Armour: Brutal Businessman, Generous Citizen

Chicago meatpacking businessman Philip Armour. THE LIBRARY OF CONGRESS.

Philip Armour (1833–1901) started a grain business in Chicago during the Civil War. Eventually, he and his brother opened a meatpacking business near the Union Stock Yards (a company that operated for 106 years and made Chicago the center of the nation's meatpacking industry). Armour took control of the operation when his brother became ill.

Armour's packinghouse process was based on a new idea. Instead of having one man butcher one hog, each worker was given one specific task. As the animals hung from a line and moved down the cutting line, each worker completed his task. By the end of the line, very little was left of the slaughtered animal.

Like Gustavus Swift, the other meatpacking king, Armour sold animal by-products such as oil, hairbrushes, and drugs. Even low-grade meats found a use in canned products such as pork and beans. This efficiency reduced the amount of pollution from Armour's factories, but the meat itself was not necessarily safe to eat. Before the Food and Drug Act of 1906, sausages included sawdust and dead rodents, and even spoiled meat was packed and sold.

As were many of his peers, Armour was more concerned about profit than his employees' well-being. A 1911 study confirmed that the average weekly wage for an Armour employee was $9.50. At the time, the living wage (the minimum amount that will cover bills and necessities) was $15.40. Workers went on strike (refused to work) at his factories three times, but Armour refused to negotiate. Despite these harsh decisions, Armour was praised in society for his charitable donations. His favorite charity was the Armour Mission, established by a brother. The mission offered a free kindergarten, a library, and medical care. He also donated money to the Armour Institute, which provided technical education for white and African American boys and training in the trades for girls.

over publication. The published version was highly censored because of the disturbing details of the treatment of animals and workers. The original manuscript was a full third longer than the version published in 1906.

Things to remember while reading the excerpt from *The Jungle:*

- Just prior to the publication of *The Jungle,* America was horrified to learn that the beef industry had been sending American soldiers in the Spanish-American War (1898) beef that had been preserved with embalming fluid (the liquid injected into the veins of corpses to keep them fresh looking). Soldiers became so ill from the meat that they could not fight. Some blamed the tainted meat for the deaths of countless soldiers. The event became a major scandal.

- Common food preservatives used at the turn of the century included borax (used in laundry detergents; acts as a disinfectant); formaldehyde (a toxic chemical that causes leukemia and brain cancer); salicylic acid (a chemical that removes the top layers of skin; also found in aspirin); and other dangerous compounds and chemicals.

- Although *The Jungle* was not the first piece of muckraking journalism, it is considered by many historians to be the greatest example of this style of writing because of its impact.

- The following excerpts from *The Jungle* are from chapters 9 and 14.

Upton Sinclair, author of The Jungle, *an exposé on the meatpacking industry.* © HULTON-DEUTSCH COLLECTION/CORBIS.

• • •

Excerpt from *The Jungle*

There were the men in the **pickle rooms,** for instance, where **old Antanas** had gotten his death; scarce a one of these that had not some **spot of horror** on his person. Let a man so much as scrape his finger pushing a truck in the pickle rooms, and he might have a sore that would **put him out of the world;** all the joints in his fingers might be eaten by the acid, one by one. Of the butchers and floorsmen, the beef-boners and trimmers, and all those who used knives, you could scarcely find a person who had the use of his thumb; time and time again the base of it had been slashed, till it was a mere lump of flesh against which the man pressed the knife to hold it. The hands of these men would be criss-crossed with cuts, until

Pickle rooms: Areas where meat was preserved in saltwater or vinegar.

Old Antanas: A worker at the packinghouse.

Spot of horror: Injury.

Put him out of the world: Kill him.

Tuberculosis: A contagious disease of the lungs.

Rheumatism: A painful, crippling disorder of the joints, muscles, and connective tissues.

Durham: Owner of the slaughterhouse.

Borax: A cleaning agent commonly found in laundry detergent.

Glycerine: A sweet, thick liquid found in fat and used to dissolve things.

Hoppers: Vats of boiling water and chemicals.

Made over again: Reformed to look new.

you could no longer pretend to count them or to trace them. They would have no nails,—they had worn them off pulling hides; their knuckles were swollen so that their fingers spread out like a fan. There were men who worked in the cooking rooms, in the midst of steam and sickening odors, by artificial light; in these rooms the germs of **tuberculosis** might live for two years, but the supply was renewed every hour. There were the beef-luggers, who carried two-hundred-pound quarters into the refrigerator-cars; a fearful kind of work, that began at four o'clock in the morning, and that wore out the most powerful men in a few years. There were those who worked in the chilling rooms, and whose special disease was **rheumatism;** the time limit that a man could work in the chilling rooms was said to be five years. There were the wool-pluckers, whose hands went to pieces even sooner than the hands of the pickle men; for the pelts of the sheep had to be painted with acid to loosen the wool, and then the pluckers had to pull out this wool with their bare hands, till the acid had eaten their fingers off. There were those who made the tins for the canned meat; and their hands, too, were a maze of cuts, and each cut represented a chance for blood poisoning. Some worked at the stamping machines, and it was very seldom that one could work long there at the pace that was set, and not give out and forget himself and have a part of his hand chopped off. There were the "hoisters," as they were called, whose task it was to press the lever which lifted the dead cattle off the floor. They ran along upon a rafter, peering down through the damp and the steam; and as old **Durham**'s architects had not built the killing room for the convenience of the hoisters, at every few feet they would have to stoop under a beam, say four feet above the one they ran on; which got them into the habit of stooping, so that in a few years they would be walking like chimpanzees. Worst of any, however, were the fertilizer men, and those who served in the cooking rooms. These people could not be shown to the visitor,—for the odor of a fertilizer man would scare any ordinary visitor at a hundred yards, and as for the other men, who worked in tank rooms full of steam, and in some of which there were open vats near the level of the floor, their peculiar trouble was that they fell into the vats; and when they were fished out, there was never enough of them left to be worth exhibiting,—sometimes they would be overlooked for days, till all but the bones of them had gone out to the world as Durham's Pure Leaf Lard!

There was never the least attention paid to what was cut up for sausage; there would come all the way back from Europe old sausage that had been rejected, and that was moldy and white—it would be dosed with **borax** and **glycerine,** and dumped into the **hoppers,** and **made over again** for home consumption. There would be meat that had tumbled out

Meatpacking workers split the backbones of hog carcasses at Swift & Company in 1906. © CORBIS.

on the floor, in the dirt and sawdust, where the workers had tramped and spit uncounted billions of **consumption** germs. There would be meat stored in great piles in rooms; and the water from leaky roofs would drip over it, and thousands of rats would race about on it. It was too dark in these

Consumption: Common term for tuberculosis.

Dung: Waste.

storage places to see well, but a man could run his hand over these piles of meat and sweep off handfuls of the dried **dung** of rats. These rats were nuisances, and the packers would put poisoned bread out for them; they would die, and then rats, bread, and meat would go into the hoppers together. This is no fairy story and no joke; the meat would be shoveled into carts, and the man who did the shoveling would not trouble to lift out a rat even when he saw one—there were things that went into the sausage in comparison with which a poisoned rat was a tidbit. There was no place for the men to wash their hands before they ate their dinner, and so they made a practice of washing them in the water that was to be ladled into the sausage. There were the butt-ends of smoked meat, and the scraps of corned beef, and all the odds and ends of the waste of the plants, that would be dumped into old barrels in the cellar and left there. Under the system of rigid economy which the packers enforced, there were some jobs that it only paid to do once in a long time, and among these was the cleaning out of the waste barrels. Every spring they did it; and in the barrels would be dirt and rust and old nails and stale water—and cartload after cartload of it would be taken up and dumped into the hoppers with fresh meat, and sent out to the public's breakfast. Some of it they would make into "smoked" sausage—but as the smoking took time, and was therefore expensive, they would call upon their chemistry department, and preserve it with borax and color it with **gelatine** to make it brown. All of their sausage came out of the same bowl, but when they came to wrap it they would stamp some of it "special," and for this they would charge two cents more a pound.

Gelatine: A mixture of proteins from animal bones, tissues, and other body parts.

• • •

What happened next...

The Jungle was an immediate success, not only in the United States but overseas as well. A copy was sent to President Roosevelt at the White House. Roosevelt, an avid reader who was known to read a book a day at times, was so moved and angered by the information in Sinclair's novel that he wired the author to come to the White House immediately to discuss the situation. Sinclair went from being a wage-earning newspaper reporter to a social activist seemingly overnight.

The Jungle was more than just a book about the exploitation of immigrants in Chicago's meatpacking industry. In one book, Sinclair exposed the brutality of the Chicago police force, corrupt politicians, hazardous working conditions in the steel mill industry, dishonest real estate developers, and more. More than anything, the book heightened public

Editorial cartoon from the Utica Saturday Globe *showing President Theodore Roosevelt taking control of the meatpacking scandal in the early 1900s.* © BETTMANN/CORBIS.

awareness of safety issues regarding food preparation. Public pressure forced Congress to consider a Pure Food and Drug bill in 1906. The bill would require the establishment of the Food and Drug Administration, which would be responsible for testing all food and drugs meant for human consumption. Certain drugs would require a written prescription from a licensed medical doctor before they could be purchased, and any habit-forming drugs would need a warning label.

Congress was in no hurry to pass the bill. Some of their biggest campaign contributors belonged to the powerful beef trust (several companies banding together to form an organization that limits competition by controlling the production and distribution of a product or service) and other wealthy and influential groups. Passage of the bill would certainly outrage these people. When it became apparent that the bill was in danger of not passing, President Roosevelt got involved and encouraged Congress to overcome its reluctance. The Pure Food and Drug Act was passed on June 30, 1906.

From the pages of *Puck*

One of the most important political magazines of the Progressive Era was called *Puck.* The periodical attacked the corruption of the beef trust even before Upton Sinclair's exposé was published. The following poem was published in the June 20, 1906, issue of *Puck,* and puts a humorous twist on the concerns the nation had about food safety at the time.

What to Eat

What shall I eat? I will no longer feed
On meat and cater to the packer's
  greed.
Let's see. There's fish—as fresh as e'er
  was seen—
Made fresh by rubbing it with Vaseline.

The market man "restores" and
  "touches up"
The somewhat faded fish on which
  I sup.
There's "full cream cheese" that's
  innocent of cream,
For things, you know, are seldom what
  they seem.

There's butter—more skimmed milk
  solidified
After a dosing with formaldehyde.
What shall I eat? Perhaps some tea and
  cake.

The cake is made with "bottled eggs,"
  "egg flake,"
Or other doctored product of the hen,
Laid long ago—I know not where or
  when:
The tea, touched up with graphite,
  comes—
Who know?—
From China or—more likely—from
  Cohoes.

There's raspberry jam, made up of
  equal parts
Of apple cores and glucose—nice on
  tarts.
But why continue the enumeration
Of substitution and adulteration.

Until the thought of eating makes one ill?
And yet I scan the café's dismal bill [of
  fare].
For I must eat. What shall I eat?
Ho, waiter!
Fetch me two boiled eggs and a baked
  'ptater.

SUZANNE WHITE JUNOD. "IN ROOSEVELT'S NAME
WE BUST TRUSTS: THE MEAT INSPECTION ACT OF
1906." U.S. FOOD AND DRUG ADMINISTRATION.
HTTP://WWW.FDA.GOV/OC/HISTORY/
2006CENTENNIAL/MEATINSPECTION. HTML

Accompanying that piece of legislation was another bill aimed specifically at the meatpacking industry. The Meat Inspection Act, signed by Roosevelt on the same day as the Pure Food and Drug Act, required all animals to be inspected by the U.S. Food and Drug Administration prior to slaughter. Any found with disease would be prohibited from becoming food for humans. All carcasses (bodies after death) were also inspected, as some disease was not obvious until the bodies were cut open. Finally, slaughterhouses and processing plants were now required to meet cleanliness standards. These standards would be enforced by regular inspection of facilities by U.S. Department of Agriculture officials.

On June 23, 2005, the Union Stock Yard Gate in Chicago was dedicated by the Friends of Libraries USA as a Literary Landmark. The landmark commemorated the one hundredth anniversary of the publishing of *The Jungle.* The Union Stock Yards closed in 1971 and only the gate remains as a National Historic Landmark.

Did you know...

- A common tactic in the twenty-first century for helping meat retain that juicy, red freshness is to pump the plastic-wrapped tray packaging with carbon monoxide, which keeps the flesh from turning brown. The carbon monoxide itself is not a problem—the amount added to packaging is low enough so that it is harmless; the concern, critics say, is that the gas's effect on the meat's color may cover up spoilage. Consumers often use color of meat as a gauge to freshness. Shoppers are urged to buy meat based on the freshness date stamped on packaging—not based on how red or brown the meat is.

- Most twenty-first-century food-processing plants continue to rely primarily on underpaid immigrants, refugees, and minorities for their employees.

- A mixture of used restaurant cooking grease and rendered animal fat (that which has been boiled off the animal carcass before slaughter) is a major component in most commercially produced pet foods.

- Five thousand animals a day were butchered in Chicago's Union Stockyards before the passage of the Food and Drug Act in 1906.

Consider the following...

- If you found out that the meat you eat was not safe for consumption, how difficult would it be for you to become a vegetarian, and how would you go about it?

- You are the manager of an early twentieth-century meatpacking plant. The owner has instructed you to keep production and profits up, even if it means your employees suffer. What are some ways you could help the workers without slowing down production?

- You are a worker in a meatpacking plant like the one Sinclair investigated. You know how filthy the plant is, how unsafe the meat is, and how the company cheats consumers. But you desperately need the work. What would you do?

For More Information

BOOKS

Arthur, Anthony. *Radical Innocent: Upton Sinclair*. New York: Random House, 2006.

Jensen, Carl. *Stories That Changed America: Muckrakers of the 20th Century*. New York: Seven Stories Press, 2000.

Mattson, Kevin. *Upton Sinclair and the Other American Century*. Hoboken, NJ: Wiley, 2006.

Poole, Steven. *Unspeak: How Words Become Weapons, How Weapons Become a Message, and How That Message Becomes Reality*. New York: Grove Press, 2006.

Sinclair, Upton. *The Jungle*. New York: Doubleday, Page & Co., 1906. Multiple reprints.

Weinberg, Arthur, ed., and Lila Shaffer Weinberg, ed. *The Muckrakers*. New York: Simon and Schuster, 1961. Reprint, Champaign: University of Illinois Press, 2001.

WEB SITES

"Gustavus Swift and the Refrigerator Car." *A Biography of America: Industrial Supremacy*. http://www.learner.org/biographyofamerica/prog14/transcript/page03.html (accessed on August 15, 2006).

"The Jungle." *The Literature Network*. http://www.online-literature.com/upton_sinclair/jungle (accessed on August 15, 2006).

"The Jungle." *SparkNotes*. http://www.sparknotes.com/lit/jungle/context.html (accessed on August 15, 2006).

Junod, Suzanne White. "In Roosevelt's Name We Bust Trusts: The Meat Inspection Act of 1906." *U.S. Food and Drug Administration*. http://www.fda.gov/oc/history/2006centennial/meatinspection.html (accessed on August 15, 2006).

Nichols, Rick. "Meat of the Issue: FDA on the Wrong Side." *PhiladelphiaInquirer.com*. http://www.philly.com/mld/inquirer/14051036.htm (accessed on August 15, 2006).

PBS. "Philip Danforth Armour (1833–1901)." *American Experience: Chicago, City of the Century*. http://www.pbs.org/wgbh/amex/chicago/peopleevents/p_armour.html (accessed on August 15, 2006).

"Swift and Company." *The Handbook of Texas Online*. http://www.tsha.utexas.edu/handbook/online/articles/SS/dis2.html (accessed on August 15, 2006).

Weiss, Rick. "FDA Is Urged to Ban Carbon-Monoxide-Treated Meat." *Washingtonpost.com*. http://www.washingtonpost.com/wp-dyn/content/article/2006/02/19/AR2006021901101.html (accessed on August 15, 2006).

16

Sears, Roebuck and Co.

Examples of mail-order homes offered through the Sears Modern Homes program, 1908–40

"$100 set of building plans free. Let us be your architect without cost to you."

In 1906, a Sears, Roebuck and Co. employee named Frank Kushel was manager of the china department. Recognized for his merchandising skills, Kushel was assigned the task of dismantling the catalog company's building materials department. Although Sears had been in the mail-order business for nearly twenty years, sales in that particular department were down. Inventory was stored in warehouses across the country. Something had to be done.

After giving the situation careful consideration, Kushel approached his boss, Richard Sears (1863–1914), with an idea. Instead of trying to unload the building materials on another company, Kushel wanted to develop a mail-order program in which customers could order entire home-building kits. Sears would publish a catalog that offered customers a choice of floor plans and building styles. One order would allow customers to buy everything they needed to build their own homes, from the nails and hinges to windows, paint, and woodwork. Sears already published a general merchandise catalog that offered everything needed to furnish a home. It was hoped that the sale of a home-building kit would increase the sales of the furnishings, too.

Sears recognized the genius of Kushel's plan, and in 1908, published the first catalog of the Sears Modern Homes program. The warehouses across the country were emptied of their contents so that all lumber and supplies were located in the same place. For the cost of one dollar, customers could choose a building style and floor plan and would receive a Bill of Materials List and full blueprints in the mail. Once a customer sent in his or her payment, that dollar was applied toward the balance. Within

Sears, Roebuck and Co. founder Richard W. Sears. Sears approved an idea a Sears employee had to create a mail-order home-building program. © AP IMAGES.

a few weeks, everything needed to build a home would arrive by train to the railroad depot nearest the customer's location. Thirty thousand pieces of lumber, screws, nails, and other supplies were in the shipment that most recipients considered to be proof of the fulfillment of the American Dream.

According to Rosemary Thornton, Sears homes historian, that first catalog, called the *Book of Modern Homes and Building Plans,* offered forty-four house designs for a flat fee ranging from $695 to $4,115. Response was immediate and enthusiastic, as America's middle class saw their dreams of owning a home become a reality. Sears was not the first company to offer mail-order homes. North American Construction Company of Michigan offered Aladdin Houses and Readi-Cuts (their brand names) starting in 1906. But Sears had already been in business for over twenty years when it began selling its homes. As a company, it had earned America's trust and established a solid reputation as a dependable, quality-conscious retailer. Montgomery Ward, Sears's main competitor in general merchandise, did not begin selling house plans from a catalog until 1910. This was one department in which Sears outsold its competitor.

The word "modern" had a particular meaning when applied to the Sears homes program. Buyers could be certain their kits would include all the materials necessary for centralized heating, electricity, and indoor plumbing. In many cases, the homes themselves were more modern than the communities in which they were being built. For example, if an area did not yet have a city-wide water program, consumers had no need for concern. For an extra $30, builders could purchase an outhouse. Homes without bathrooms were being offered by Sears well into the 1920s.

In 1911, Sears took the program one step further and began to offer mortgage loans to its customers who could not afford to purchase the do-it-yourself kits outright. The application for the loan contained just one question: What is your vocation (job)? Regardless of the answer, if an applicant had a job, he was guaranteed a loan. Most loans were given for a period of five to fifteen years at an annual interest rate of 6 percent. These terms were generous and allowed nearly anyone with a steady income the chance to become a homeowner.

A Study in Advertising

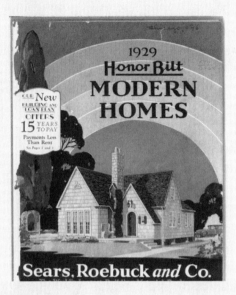

Title page of 1929 Sears, Roebuck and Co. "Honor Bilt Modern Homes" catalog. THE LIBRARY OF CONGRESS.

A look through the Sears Modern Homes catalogs offers a glimpse into the changes of advertising in the early twentieth century. The earliest catalog ads focus on consumer need and use terms like "economical" and "extremely low price." The point of the advertising is to reassure consumers that they will get the most from their money, no matter how small the amount.

As the second decade of the century progressed, the houses were being marketed to consumers who wanted their money to reflect their status. Terms such as "for better class workers" and "will please the man who is looking for something really different from the general run of buildings in any vicinity" spoke to each

individual's desire to have his or her peers recognize individual success. Sears's copywriters went so far as to claim that Modern Homes would improve the health, morals, and well-being of their occupants.

By the 1920s, the catalog was including a detailed list of all the items consumers would receive for their money. When possible, the ads would include endorsements of satisfied customers. As prices increased, so did the number of options available to consumers who wanted to customize their home to make it more fitting to their unique tastes and preferences.

The catalogs were printed in four-color press in the 1930s and featured monthly payment amounts rather than a flat fee. By incorporating and highlighting the lower dollar amount, advertisers appealed to a segment of society that would not have considered buying a home because the thousands of dollars required was beyond its means. Sears also changed its slogan to "America's New Low Cost Homes."

By 1939, the year before Sears discontinued its mail-order home program, black-and-white catalog pages offered very little information in terms of size, cost, and details of materials. Instead, the style of the catalog focused on the cleaner lines and images more popular during that time in history. One central figure was the exterior of the house, usually with one or two smaller illustrations of the interior layouts. Part of the reason for the return to black and white and the lack of important information was that Sears was no longer promoting their homes. Yet the neat, stylized ads remain evidence that even as the program was in its last years, the company still had a clear understanding of its modern customers.

Many Sears homes were a style known as a bungalow. Bungalows typically have low roofs with wide eaves (overhang of the lower edge of a roof). Outside, their porches usually have square columns, while inside, cabinets, shelves, and seating are often built into the walls. Bungalows are usually one to one-and-a-half stories tall. Often they have dormers (smaller windows projecting from the roof) and stone chimneys. These homes are known for their efficiency of space and simple lines. American bungalows tend to be simple, yet many families—then and now—have always found their layout and style to be attractive.

Things to remember while looking at images from the Sears Modern Homes catalogs:

- At the time of the development of the mail-order homes program, America's population was booming because of an increase in immigration (people moving to America from other countries) and the Industrial Revolution (approximately 1877–1900). Industrialization created more jobs, which in turn created a demand for affordable housing. At the same time, the strong economy increased the cost of labor, so new-home prices were at an all-time high. Workers who did not want to live in crowded urban areas needed single-family homes that could be built in suburbs. Most mail-order homes customers were middle-class Americans.
- Sears homes were designed by architects who were focused not on innovation, but on modification. They did not try to invent new designs or layouts. Instead, these men took what they knew to be popular among American consumers and used those features to make the homes attractive to potential buyers. And always, they offered options, such as the ability to increase the total square footage or to change the type of windows installed.
- In 1914, Sears improved its program by offering the "already cut and fitted" option. The lumber and materials for these homes were cut at the factory and arrived at the buyer's home completely ready to assemble. This eliminated the need for a carpenter or someone with construction know-how, as each piece of lumber was stamped with a letter and a number. The instruction book took the builder through the process step by step.
- Sears was able to sell its homes for less for several reasons. Manufacturing costs were lower because the company mass-produced

the materials. Lower manufacturing costs meant lower costs for customers. Precutting and fitting materials reduced construction time by up to 40 percent. In addition, all Sears homes used "balloon style" framing. This particular frame did not require a team of skilled carpenters to build, as did other methods. Balloon frames were built faster and usually needed only one person. The drawback to the balloon frames was that the layout was considered a fire hazard in some locations because it allowed a clear path for fire to travel throughout the house. Balloon frames were against building codes in some regions.

- The images on the following pages originally appeared in Sears Modern Homes catalogs, dating back to 1908. By paging through the images in chronological order, one can see the influence the changing times had on the homes and how Sears presented them to the consumer. For example, as architecture styles changed throughout the years, so did the styles of the homes offered. Often, they were older models that had sold well and were now available with options to make them look more modern. Such extras included a taller chimney or front porch columns. During the Great Depression years when money was scarce, Sears focused on value, and its advertising copy stressed getting the most out of one's dollar.

- As advertising techniques changed, so did the catalog. In its later years, ad styles were more tailored, with cleaner lines and less text. And as society became more credit-oriented, homes were advertised with an accompanying monthly payment rather than a full and final cost.

- At all times, the Sears Modern Homes catalog was a direct reflection of American culture and society. This awareness and understanding of its customers is the very reason Sears Modern Homes program was such a phenomenal success. By appealing to the public through emotion and an acknowledgement of necessity, Sears, Roebuck gave America shelter throughout the first half of the twentieth century.

• • •

Examples of mail-order homes offered through the Sears Modern Homes program

FOR LESS THAN $2,500.00 YOU CAN BUILD

THIS ELEGANT CONCRETE AND FRAME CONSTRUCTION NINE=ROOM $4,000.00 HOUSE

BY USING OUR PLANS, SPECIFICATIONS AND BILL OF MATERIALS WHICH YOU CAN GET FREE, AS EXPLAINED ON PAGE 2.

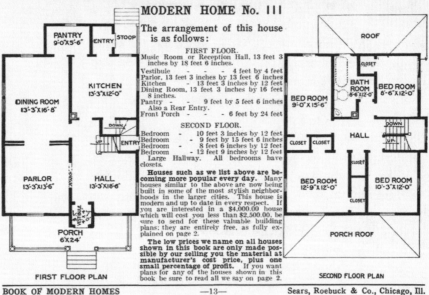

MODERN HOME No. 111

The arrangement of this house is as follows:

FIRST FLOOR.

Music Room or Reception Hall, 13 feet 3 inches by 18 feet 6 inches.
Vestibule - - - - 4 feet by 4 feet
Parlor, 13 feet 3 inches by 13 feet 6 inches
Kitchen - 13 feet 3 inches by 12 feet
Dining Room, 13 feet 3 inches by 16 feet 8 inches.
Pantry - - 9 feet by 5 feet 6 inches
Also a Rear Entry.
Front Porch - - - 6 feet by 24 feet

SECOND FLOOR.

Bedroom - 10 feet 3 inches by 12 feet
Bedroom - 9 feet by 15 feet 6 inches
Bedroom - 8 feet 6 inches by 12 feet
Bedroom - 12 feet 9 inches by 12 feet
Large Hallway. All bedrooms have closets.

Houses such as we list above are becoming more popular every day. Many houses similar to the above are now being built in some of the most stylish neighborhoods in the larger cities. This house is modern and up to date in every respect. If you are interested in a $4,000.00 house which will cost you less than $2,500.00, be sure to send for these valuable building plans; they are entirely free, as fully explained on page 2.

The low prices we name on all houses shown in this book are only made possible by our selling you the material at manufacturer's cost price, plus one small percentage of profit. If you want plans for any of the houses shown in this book be sure to read all we say on page 2.

PANTRY 9'-0"X5'-6" ENTRY STOOP
KITCHEN 13'-3"X12'-0"
DINING ROOM 13'-3"X16'-8"
DOWN
UP ENTRY
PARLOR 13'-3"X13'-6" HALL 13'-3"X18'-6"
VESTIBULE
PORCH 6'X24'

FIRST FLOOR PLAN

ROOF
CLOSET
BATH ROOM 6'-6"X12'-0" BED ROOM 8'-6"X12'-0"
BED ROOM 9'-0"X 15'-6"
CLOSET CLOSET HALL DOWN UP
CLOSET
BED ROOM 12'-9"X12'-0" BED ROOM 10'-3"X12'-0"
CLOSET
PORCH ROOF

SECOND FLOOR PLAN

BOOK OF MODERN HOMES   —13—   Sears, Roebuck & Co., Chicago, Ill.

Sears, Roebuck catalog page shows Modern Home Number 111, also known as the Chelsea, from 1908. The Chelsea was one of twenty-two styles ranging in base price from $650 to $2,500. The more popular models would be offered year after year, sometimes with small changes or options to the exterior and interior. SEARS®, ROEBUCK AND CO.

$1,995.00 and Our FREE BUILDING PLANS

WILL BUILD, PAINT AND COMPLETE, READY FOR OCCUPANCY, THIS MODERN NINE-ROOM $3,000.00 HOUSE

HOW TO GET ANY OF OUR PLANS FREE FULLY EXPLAINED ON PAGE 2.

MODERN HOME No. 52

Concrete Block Construction. On the opposite page we illustrate a few of the materials we specify on this our $1,995.00 house.

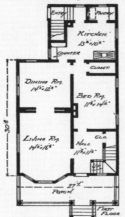

OUR $1,995.00 HOUSE

illustrated above, consists of nine good sized rooms and bathroom, as shown in these floor plans

FIRST FLOOR.

Kitchen - - - - - - 13 feet by 10 feet
Pantry.
Dining Room - - - - - 14 feet by 12 feet
Living Room - - 14 feet by 16 feet 6 inches
Reception Hall - 11 feet 6 inches by 11 feet
Bedroom - - - 11 feet 6 inches by 14 feet

SECOND FLOOR.

Bedroom - - - - - 12 feet by 12 feet
Bedroom - - - 9 feet 6 inches by 12 feet
Bedroom 10 feet 6 inches by 12 feet 6 inches
Bedroom - - - 11 feet 6 inches by 7 feet
Bathroom - - - 7 feet by 5 feet 9 inches
Linen closet and hall.   Bedrooms have closets.

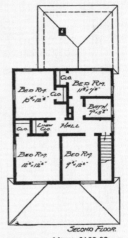

The Arrangement of Our Houses

is such that they can be well heated with very little expense. Our $1,995.00 house is but one of the many frame or concrete houses for which we are able to furnish our free building plans and specifications. No matter what price house you may want to build, remember we can save you from 25 to 50 per cent.
Size of Modern Home No. 52: Length, 47 feet 10 inches; width, 27 feet 4 inches, exclusive of porch.

DO NOT ATTEMPT BUILDING WITHOUT PLANS, don't pay an architect $100.00 or $150.00 for plans which in no way

compare in accuracy or detail with the plans we will furnish you free of charge on condition that you send us a small portion of your mill work order. If you were to attempt to build a house similar to the house illustrated above, it would cost you from $500.00 to $1,000.00 more.
See how you can get the plans for this house free on page 2.

Sears, Roebuck catalog page shows Modern Home Number 52, from 1909. SEARS®, ROEBUCK AND CO.

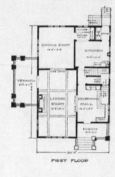

MODERN HOME No. 157

$1,766.00

For $1,766.00 we will furnish all the material to build this Eight-Room Residence, consisting of Mill Work, Ceiling, Siding, Flooring, Finishing Lumber, Building Paper, Pipe, Gutter, Sash Weights, Hardware, Mantel, Painting Material, Lumber, Lath and Shingles. NO EXTRAS, as we guarantee enough material at the above price to build this house according to our plans.

By allowing a fair price for labor, cement, brick and plaster, which we do not furnish, this house can be built for about $3,480.00, including all material and labor.

For Our Offer of Free Plans See Page 3.

A MODERN residence with exceptionally large living room 15 feet 6 inches by 26 feet 6 inches connected with the stair hall by means of a large cased opening and also connected with the dining room by a large cased opening. Every room is arranged to make the best use possible of all the available space. All the rooms on both first and second floors are large and well lighted and ventilated. The reception hall contains a Colonial combination wardrobe and closet with leaded art glass doors. Well proportioned open stairway. A long hall seat built in an L shape on two walls of the reception hall. The large living room on the first floor and the large chamber on the second floor each contains a mantel and fireplace.

Beauty doors for front and veranda entrances, veneered oak and glazed with bevel plate glass. The main rooms on the first floor are trimmed with clear oak casing, baseboard and molding and six-cross panel oak doors; oak paneled beam ceiling in the living room. Second floor is trimmed with cypress casing, baseboard and molding and five-cross panel clear cypress doors. Clear oak flooring for reception hall, living room and dining room; maple flooring for kitchen and pantry; clear yellow pine flooring for the second floor and porches.

Front porch, 12x6 feet; large veranda, 9 feet 6 inches by 18 feet 6 inches, connected directly with the living room by a pair of double doors. This could very easily be screened in and used as an outdoor sleeping porch. Built on a concrete foundation, frame construction, sided from the water table to window sills of the second story with narrow bevel edge cypress siding. The remainder of the house is finished with stonekote, more commonly known as cement plaster, and has cedar shingle roof on main house and porches.

Excavated basement under the entire house, 7 feet high from floor to joists. Rooms on the first floor are 9 feet from floor to ceiling; second floor, 8 feet 6 inches from floor to ceiling. Attic floored but not finished.

This house can be built on a lot 45 feet wide.

Complete Warm Air Heating Plant, for soft coal, extra	$132.57
Complete Warm Air Heating Plant, for hard coal, extra	135.03
Complete Hot Water Heating Plant, extra	288.20
Complete Steam Heating Plant, extra	225.75
Complete Plumbing Outfit, extra	156.31

SEARS, ROEBUCK AND CO. CHICAGO, ILLINOIS

—13—

Sears, Roebuck catalog page shows Modern Home Number 157, from 1911. This was the year Sears Modern Homes catalogs began showing the interior of some of their models as well. These illustrations provided a blueprint of the home's layout as well as suggestions for appliances and furniture—all sold by Sears—to furnish the homes. SEARS®, ROEBUCK AND CO.

MODERN HOME No. 161

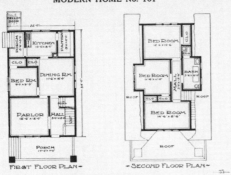

FIRST FLOOR PLAN

SECOND FLOOR PLAN

$788⁰⁰

For $788.00 we will furnish all the material to build this Seven-Room House, consisting of Mill Work, Ceiling, Siding, Flooring, Finishing Lumber, Building Paper, Pipe, Gutter, Sash Weights, Hardware, Painting Material, Lumber, Lath and Shingles.

By allowing a fair price for labor, cement, brick and plaster, which we do not furnish, this house can be built for about $1,870.00, including all material and labor.

For Our Free Offer of Plans See Page 1.

A COTTAGE that cannot help but please you if you are looking for an up to date, modern cottage. It has the appearance of a high priced house, both in exterior and interior. Large front porch, 17x7 feet, with square stonekote columns with panel tops.

Queen Anne windows. Birch Craftsman front door. Two-panel veneered birch interior doors throughout the house. Birch trim. Oak flooring for the first floor; clear yellow pine flooring for the second floor and porches. Birch open stairway in the reception hall with inside cellar stairs directly under the main stairs. Cased opening between the hall and parlor. Large pantry and two closets on the first floor. Three bedrooms, four closets and bathroom on the second floor.

Built on a concrete block foundation, frame construction, sided with narrow bevel edge cypress siding to the belt course and cedar shingles above the belt course. Gables sided with stonekote. Cedar shingle roof with the exception of the dormers, which are covered with galvanized steel roofing.

Painted two coats outside; your choice of color. Varnish and wood filler for interior finish.

Excavated basement under the entire house, 7 feet from floor to joists, with cement floor. Rooms on the first floor are 9 feet from floor to ceiling; second floor, 8 feet 6 inches from floor to ceiling.

This house can be built on a lot 30 feet wide.

Complete Hot Air Heating Plant, for soft coal, extra	$81.31
Complete Hot Air Heating Plant, for hard coal, extra	83.79
Complete Steam Heating Plant, extra	147.54
Complete Hot Water Heating Plant, extra	198.27
Complete Plumbing Outfit, extra	120.87

SEARS, ROEBUCK AND CO.   QUALITY GUARANTEED   CHICAGO, ILLINOIS

Sears, Roebuck catalog page shows Modern Home Number 161, also known as the Niota, from 1911. The Niota is an example of a cottage, which was designed for smaller families or for consumers on a tight budget. Cottages were often advertised as summer homes. SEARS®, ROEBUCK AND CO.

MODERN HOME No. 167

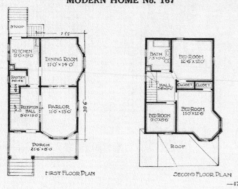

FIRST FLOOR PLAN
SECOND FLOOR PLAN
—47—

$753.00

For $753.00 we will furnish all the material to build this Eight-Room House, consisting of Mill Work, Flooring, Ceiling, Siding, Finishing Lumber, Building Paper, Pipe, Gutter, Sash Weights, Hardware, Painting Material, Lumber, Lath and Shingles. NO EXTRAS, as we guarantee enough material at the above price to build this house according to our plans.

By allowing a fair price for labor, cement, brick and plaster, which we do not furnish, this house can be built for about $1,573.00, including all material and labor.

For Our Offer of Free Plans See Page 3.

A WELL proportioned house which affords a great deal of room at a low cost. Large front porch, 21 feet 6 inches long by 8 feet wide, with Colonial columns. Bay window in the dining room and parlor. An octagon tower on the second floor, making it suitable for a corner lot. Crystal leaded front window in the parlor. Colored leaded art glass sash for the hall, with marginal light attic sash. Every room in the house is perfectly lighted and well ventilated by large windows. The reception hall contains an open staircase with a cased opening between it and the parlor, and another cased opening leading to the dining room. A door also opens from the reception hall directly into the kitchen. Inside cellar stairs directly under the main stairs and also an outside stairway under the rear porch. When reaching the second floor landing you are within a very few feet of the entrance to the three bedrooms or bathroom. By this you will notice there is no waste space whatever.

Dublin front door, 3x7 feet, glazed with bevel plate glass. Interior yellow pine doors for both first and second floor, with clear yellow pine trim, such as casing, baseboard and molding. Clear yellow pine flooring for both floors and porches.

Painted two coats outside; color to suit. Varnish and wood filler for two coats of interior finish.

Built on a concrete block foundation, frame construction, sided with narrow bevel cypress edge siding and has a cedar shingle roof.

Excavated basement under the entire house, 7 feet from floor to joists, with cement floor. First floor, 9 feet from floor to ceiling; second floor, 8 feet from floor to ceiling.

This house can be built on a lot 28 feet wide.

Complete Warm Air Heating Plant, for soft coal, extra	$ 78.05
Complete Warm Air Heating Plant, for hard coal, extra	80.54
Complete Steam Heating Plant, extra	173.49
Complete Hot Water Heating Plant, extra	205.72
Complete Plumbing Outfit, extra	117.27

SEARS, ROEBUCK AND CO. CHICAGO, ILLINOIS

Sears, Roebuck catalog page shows Modern Home Number 167, also known as the Maytown, from 1912. Although its design gave the impression that this house is more expensive and fancier than the Niota cottage, it was, in fact, offered at a lower base price and could be built on a smaller lot than the Niota. This is a good example of how architecture styles influenced appearance. SEARS®, ROEBUCK AND CO.

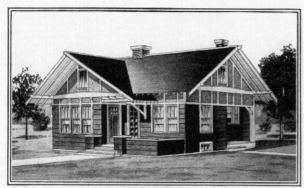

MODERN HOME No. 191

FLOOR PLAN

—28—

$892.00

For $892.00 we will furnish all the material to build this Five-Room Bungalow consisting of Lumber, Lath, Shingles, Mill Work, Flooring, Ceiling, Finishing Lumber, Building Paper, Pipe, Gutter, Sash Weights, Hardware and Painting Material. NO EXTRAS, as we guarantee enough material at the above price to build this house according to our plans.

By allowing a fair price for labor, cement, brick and plaster, which we do not furnish, this house can be built for about $1,800.00, including all material and labor.

For Our Offer of Free Plans See Page 3.

THIS California Bungalow has many points to recommend to the home builder who desires a real home, a dwelling that is something more than a place to exist.

The exterior leaves nothing to be desired. Sided with rough boards up to the height of 9 feet from the ground and stonekote or stucco under the wide overhanging eaves. There are two entrances to this bungalow from the front porch, one being a French door which opens into the dining room, the other a Craftsman door which opens into the living room. The living room with its beamed ceiling, rustic brick fireplace and built-in seat alongside of the fireplace, is a large airy apartment, having three large windows and two sash which admit an abundance of light and air. The dining room is also a good size room and has an attractive buffet of oak built in one side. There are two bedrooms and a bathroom, each of the two bedrooms having a good size clothes closet. The kitchen is just the right size, has a nice pantry in which is built a pantry case.

This house can be finished with siding instead of stonekote at about the same price for the complete house.

Front door is of oak, 1¾ inches thick and made in the Craftsman style. Dining room door is made of oak, 1¾ inches thick and is the French style of door, having small sash extending from bottom of the door entirely to the top. All inside doors are oak, made in the Craftsman style. The rear door is 1¾ inches thick, made of soft pine and glazed with the best quality double strength glass. Craftsman oak trim throughout the house. Oak floor in the living and dining rooms, and maple floor in the bedrooms and kitchen. Mosaic tile floor is furnished for the bathroom.

Built on a concrete foundation. Excavated under the entire house. We furnish cedar shingles and the best No. 1 quality framing timbers and siding.

Basement has a cement floor and is 7 feet from floor to joists. First floor is 9 feet from floor to ceiling.

Stain and paint for outside, varnish and wood filler for the interior finish.

This house, while it is only 28 feet wide, requires a lot at least 40 feet wide to set it off properly.

Complete Warm Air Heating Plant, for soft coal, extra	$ 56.44
Complete Warm Air Heating Plant, for hand coal, extra	59.72
Complete Steam Heating Plant, extra	126.70
Complete Hot Water Heating Plant, extra	155.81
Complete Plumbing Outfit, extra	119.00

SEARS, ROEBUCK AND CO. **CHICAGO, ILLINOIS**

Sears, Roebuck catalog page shows Modern Home Number 191, from 1913. This model represents the ever-popular bungalow, a smaller, one-story house with a wide front porch (called a veranda) and low, wide eaves. While this style of home was much smaller than the Niota or model Number 167, Sears suggested a larger lot (40 feet wide, as opposed to 28 or 30) to set it off properly. SEARS®, ROEBUCK AND CO.

$520.00

For $520.00 we will furnish all the material
build this Four-Room House with screened porc
consisting of Lumber, Lath and Shingles, Roofin
Mill Work, Ceiling, Siding, Flooring, Interior an
Exterior Trim, Finishing Lumber, Building Pape
Pipe, Gutter, Mantel and Painting Material. N
EXTRAS, as we guarantee enough material at t
above price to build this house according to o
plans.

Price does not include cement, brick or plaste

For Our Offer of Free Plans See Page 6.

THIS is a house planned and designed
United States Government architects aft
extensive investigation and at considerab
cost. We have added an additional door wi
porch on the front, the gable being sided wi
cedar shingles. Simple yet graceful in desig
its chief features are convenience in arrangeme
and economy in cost. Read the descriptions of t
rooms below and note how well the Governme
architects have planned to cut out all unnecessa
work on the part of the housewife and still pr
duce a house that can be made as comfortal
and enjoyable as a high priced residence.

This house has a double floor and is sheathed w
good wood sheathing, then covered with heavy buildi
paper, making it solid and warm.

Built on a concrete block foundation; No. 1 yell
pine frame construction; sided with clear cypress be
siding and for the roof Oriental Fire-Chief Shingle R
Roofing, 90 pounds per roll, guaranteed to last
fifteen years.

If estimates and specifications for plumbing,
water, steam or warm air heating systems are desi
write for them, mentioning Modern Home No. C248
No. C2003 in your request.

MACHINE MADE - CUT TO FIT

CORRECTLY MADE
EASY TO BUILD

Money, Time and Labor Saved.

Honor Bilt Modern Home { No. C2003 "Already Cut" and Fitted. Price, $570.00
{ No. C248 Not Cut and Fitted. Price, 520.00

Floor Plan.

32-0

BED ROOM
9-3 x 7-9

DINING
AND
LIVING
ROOM
11-6 x 19-0

KITCHEN
9-3 x 11-0

MANTEL   DUST TRAP

BED ROOM
9-3 x 7-9

SCREEN PORCH
9-3 x 7-6
CEMENT FLOOR

12-0

PORCH

Floor Plan.

The first thing you notice is a useful and enjoyable
spacious screened porch. By screening in Summer and
casing in with sash in Winter, this porch can be used as a
dining porch in hot weather, or a laundry room where
washing and ironing can be performed with comfort without filling the house with steam vapors, or as a sleeping
porch.

A pump can be located on this porch, making it unnecessary to go out of the house for a supply of water.

From the screened porch you can enter direct to the
combination dining room and living room without disturbing the women in the kitchen. Separate entrance to living
room from front of house.

The kitchen is lighted on three sides. Under the work
table is a fuel box which can be filled once a week. The
ashes drop from the stove through an iron pipe to a concrete ash bin beneath the floor. The sink, stove, cupboard
and work table are within easy reach of one another.

A door leads from the kitchen into the dining and living room. This
is the principal room in the house and extends the full depth, measuring
19 feet by 11 feet 6 inches. It has clear yellow pine trim of the very
latest design.

A five-cross panel yellow pine door leads into one of the bedrooms and
a cased opening leads into the other. Both bedrooms have closets and are
lighted from two sides.

Rooms are 9 feet from floor to ceiling.

QUALITY GUARANTEED

SEARS, ROEBUCK AND CO., CHICAGO, ILLINOIS

—24—

Sears, Roebuck catalog page shows Modern Home Numbers 248 and 2003, also known as the Wabash, from 1919. With World War I still fresh on the minds of Americans, Sears capitalized on sentiment by advertising this model as "Uncle Sam's Idea." According to the catalog text, the building was "planned and designed by United States Government architects." What the value of that was, the catalog did not say. But Sears paid a lot of money to have the government investigate building designs. SEARS®, ROEBUCK AND CO.

Sears, Roebuck catalog page shows Modern Home Numbers 208 and 2013, also known as the Elsmore, from 1921. By this time, Sears was printing its Modern Homes catalogs in color. This particular model is another example of the popular bungalow. Although not much different from the style of model Number 191 offered in 1913, the price was considerably higher. Sears, in an effort to keep up with more modern architecture, included some of the newer options, including a taller chimney and front porch columns. SEARS®, ROEBUCK AND CO.

FROM THE GOLDEN WEST

Honor Bilt

The Osborn
No. P12050A "Already Cut" and Fitted
$2,792.00

THE OSBORN is the most pleasing type of stucco and shingle sided bungalow in Spanish mission architecture. Where will you find its equal? Massive stucco porches and bulkheads, trimmed with red brick coping, give that needed touch of color, emphasizing its graceful lines. The timber columns resting on the large square piers or concrete columns, are in perfect harmony with the rest, and support the graceful roof with its wide verge boards and timber purlins. Here the architect has given careful study to every detail, and furnished a creation that is striking, yet restful. The shingle siding, the timber wood columns, corbels and purlins, can be painted or stained a rich brown, or dark brick red, with most pleasing effect, in contrast with the gray stucco porch walls and chimney.

The Osborn will appeal to the lover of nature because of its two open porches both sheltered by the main roof, and the sleeping porch in the rear. The side porch is private, size 13 feet by 8 feet 8 inches. The front porch is provided with steps and landing leading to the front entrance, and is 22 feet by 9 feet, which is of unusual size.

The Living Room. This spacious room extends the entire width of the house. Size, 23 feet 11 inches by 11 feet 11 inches. One is immediately impressed with the cozy brick mantel and fireplace which is at one end of the room. At each side of mantel is a bookcase with leaded glass doors, and a nine-light window above each bookcase. A window seat with hinged cover is at the other end of the room. The window seat has storage space for clothing, blankets, etc. At each side of the window seat is a coat closet. Ample wall space will accommodate a piano and pictures, while the large floor area provides a good setting for furniture, including davenport. Five windows furnish an abundance of light and ventilation.

The Dining Room. A cased opening with a bookcase on either side, leads from the living room to the dining room. Size, 13 feet 7 inches by 15 feet 1 inch. Walls are paneled according to the latest mode. Space accommodates a complete dining room set. French doors lead to private side porch. A cheerful atmosphere is assured with a flood of light and air from the windows and French doors.

The Kitchen. Directly back of the dining room is the kitchen. It is 8 feet 5 inches by 14 feet 3 inches. It has two large cupboards, a convenience that is appreciated by the busy housewife. Each cupboard is equipped with adjustable shelves. The large cupboard has a working surface that does away with the need of a table. Sink is placed underneath window. There is a space for the range and refrigerator or table. Three windows provide light and cross ventilation. A door leads to rear entry and steps to basement and grade.

The Bedrooms. From the dining room a door opens into the hall connecting with bedrooms, bathroom and hall coat closet. Each bedroom has a clothes closet, and is lighted and aired by two windows.

The Bathroom is located between bedrooms. It has a medicine cabinet. A window provides plenty of light and air.

Sleeping Porch. French doors connect the rear bedrooms with sleeping porch. There is a space for two beds and other suitable furnishings. One may sleep out-of-doors and still have all the comforts of an interior room.

The Basement. Lighted by cellar sash on three sides. Room for furnace, storage and laundry.

Height of Ceilings. Main floor, 9 feet from floor to ceiling. Basement, 7 feet from floor to joists. Basement has cement floor.

What Our Price Includes

At the price quoted we will furnish all the material to build this five-room and sleeping porch bungalow, consisting of:

Lumber; Lath;
Roofing, Best Grade Clear Red Cedar Shingles;
Siding, Best Grade Clear Red Cedar Shingles;
Framing Lumber, No. 1 Quality Douglas Fir or Pacific Coast Hemlock;
Flooring, Clear Maple for Kitchen and Bathroom. Clear Oak for Balance of Rooms;
Sleeping Porch Floor, Clear Edge Grain Fir;
Porch Ceiling, Clear Douglas Fir or Pacific Coast Hemlock;
Finishing Lumber;
High Grade Millwork (see pages 108 and 109);
Interior Doors, One-Panel Design of Douglas Fir;
Trim, Beautiful Grain Douglas Fir or Yellow Pine;
Windows, California Clear White Pine;
Screens for Sleeping Porch;
Medicine Case;
Kitchen Cabinet; **Kitchen Cupboard**;
Bookcase Colonnade; **Bookcases**;
Mantel; **Wall Safe**; **Window Seats**;
Eaves Trough and Down Spout;
40-Lb. Building Paper; **Sash Weights**;
Narcissus Design Hardware (see page 120);
Paint for Three Coats Outside Trim;
Stain, Two Brush Coats for Shingles on Walls;
Shellac and Varnish for Interior Trim and Doors;
Shellac, Paste Filler and Floor Varnish for Oak and Maple Floors.
Complete Plans and Specifications.

We guarantee enough material to build this house. Price does not include cement, brick or plaster.

See description of "Honor Bilt" Houses on pages 12 and 13.

For Our Easy Payment Plan See Page 146

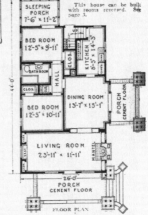

Can be built on a lot 42 feet wide

This house can be built with rooms reversed. See page 3.

FLOOR PLAN

SLEEPING PORCH 7'-6" x 11'-2"
BED ROOM 12'-5" x 9'-11"
KITCHEN 6'-5" x 14'-3"
BATHROOM
HALL
CLOS.
CLOS.
UP
DINING ROOM 13'-7" x 15'-1"
PORCH CEMENT FLOOR
BED ROOM 12'-5" x 10'-11"
LIVING ROOM 23'-11" x 11'-11"
44'-0"
26'-0" PORCH CEMENT FLOOR

OPTIONS

Sheet Plaster and Plaster Finish, to take the place of wood lath, $127.00 extra. See page 142.

Oriental Asphalt Shingles, guaranteed 17 years, instead of wood shingles, for the roof, $61.00 extra.

4-in-1 Style Oriental Asphalt Slate Surfaced Strip Shingles, guaranteed for seventeen years, instead of wood shingles for roof, $42.00 extra.

Oak Doors and Trim, for living room and dining room, $274.00 extra.

Storm Doors and Windows, $123.00 extra.
Screen Doors and Windows, galvanized wire, $55.00 extra.

For prices of Plumbing, Heating, Wiring, Electric Fixtures and Shades see pages 140 and 141.

Sears, Roebuck catalog page shows Modern Home Number 12050, also known as the Osborn, from 1925. The Osborn is an example of the Spanish Mission style of home, popular on the West Coast. Unlike most other kit homes, which were built using wood and brick, the Mission style used stucco, a cement-like finish. Because Sears offered this style of home, even homebuilders in the eastern states could enjoy living in the latest style. By 1925, Sears Modern Homes catalogs had changed their advertising to include a "What our price includes" section. SEARS®, ROEBUCK AND CO.

SIX ROOMS AND BATH
Monthly Payments as Low as $45 to $55
Built Complete on Your Lot

HonorBill

The Cedars
No. C3278 "Already Cut" and Fitted
$2,236.00

IT IS impossible to add a single feature that will improve the exterior appearance of this beautiful home. It would be hard to find a more attractive entrance than that which forms the main feature of the front of this house. The door is of 6-panel design, built of clear white pine, the balance of the entrance of clear cypress. While the sloping roof over the porch at the right and over the colonial gate at the left has a tendency to give this house the appearance of being large, by studying the floor plan you will note it is very compact and will give you a very practical and conveniently arranged home at low cost.

The material used to cover the exterior walls is Royal Red Cedar 24-inch Shingles, planned to be laid 10-inch face. All windows with the exception of those in the rear wall are equipped with shutters. We suggest staining the shingles a very light gray, with ivory or white trim, with dark shutters and roof.

Can be built on a lot 42 feet wide

FIRST FLOOR

The projection at the front of the house forms a passageway with a good size clothes closet on each side, which you will find convenient for outer wraps.

Upon entering the living room you immediately become impressed by the effect gained by the use of the plastered arch forming the opening between the living room and dining room, and also the arched opening which forms the entrance to the main stairway, which is given additional charm by the use of a small wrought iron railing on the exposed tread. A group of four sliding windows gives this room plenty of light. It is size 12 feet 5 inches wide by 21 feet 3 inches deep. A telephone stand is another convenient feature located on the stair landing.

To the right of the plan is devoted to the dining room and kitchen, the dining room being 10 feet 5 inches wide by 14 feet 5 inches deep, and contains four large windows and also a French door which forms the opening to the porch at the right which is 8 feet wide by 16 feet long. Both living room and dining room in this house are floored with clear oak flooring, while the flooring used for the kitchen is clear maple.

In the kitchen you will note that we have obtained a very attractive arrangement for all features, the left wall being arranged for kitchen table, and the right wall for kitchen cabinets and sink. The space underneath the main stairs is the opening to grade and cellar stairs which also forms a platform for refrigerator.

SECOND FLOOR

Every inch of floor space has been used to best advantage in the arrangement of the second floor of this home. By eliminating the usual large hall we have been able to obtain exceptionally large bedrooms, the two at the front being 12 feet 5 inches by 12 feet and 11 feet 5 inches by 13 feet. The rear bedroom is 11 feet 5 inches by 9 feet 1 inch. Each bedroom contains a good size closet, and linen closet with additional storage opens off the hall.

The bathroom will accommodate our fixtures as shown by specification No. 20, and also contains an attractive Venetian mirror medicine case.

Basement. The basement is planned to be excavated under the main part of the house only and contains space for laundry, heating plant, fuel and storage.

Height of Ceilings. Basement, 7 feet from floor to joists. First floor, 8 feet 6 inches. Second floor, 8 feet 6 inches.

What Our Price Includes

At the price quoted we will furnish all the material to build this six-room house, consisting of:

Lumber; Lath;
Roofing, Best Grade Clear Red Cedar Shingles;
Siding, Best Grade Extra Thick 24-Inch Clear Red Cedar Shingles;
Framing Lumber, No. 1 Quality Yellow Pine;
Flooring, 1¼x2¼-Inch Clear Oak, Living Room, Dining Room and Vestibule; ¹³⁄₁₆x2⅛-inch Clear Maple, Kitchen and Bathroom; ²⁵⁄₃₂x2¼-inch Yellow Pine, Balance of Rooms;
Porch Flooring, Clear Edge Grain Fir;
Porch Ceiling, Clear Yellow Pine;
Finishing Lumber;
High Grade Millwork (see pages 18, 19, 20 and 21);
Interior Doors, Two-Cross Panel Design of White Pine with Fir Panels;

Trim, Back Band Style, of Beautiful Grain Yellow Pine;
Windows of California Clear White Pine;
Medicine Case; Kitchen Cabinets; Colonial Shutters;
Flower Box; Wrought Iron Stair Rail;
Eaves Troughs and Down Spout;
Heavy Waterproof Building Paper; Sash Weights;
Narcissus Design Hardware (see page 101);
Paint for Three Coats Outside Trim;
Stain for Shingles on Walls for One Dip Coat;
Shellac and Two Coats of Varnish for Interior Doors and Trim;
Wood Filler and Two Coats Varnish for Oak Floors;
Two Coats Varnish for Maple and Yellow Pine Floors.
Complete Plans and Specifications.

Price does not include cement, brick or plaster. We guarantee enough material to build this house. See description of "Honor Bilt" houses on pages 12, 13, 14 and 15.

OPTIONS

Sheet Plaster and Plaster Finish, to take the place of wood lath, $158.00 extra.
Oriental Asphalt Shingles, guaranteed for 17 years, instead of wood shingles for roof, $45.00 extra.
4-In-1 Style Oriental Asphalt Slate Surfaced Strip Shingles, 12½ in. wide, guaranteed for 17 years, instead of wood shingles for roof, $60.00 extra.
Oak Doors and Trim in living room, dining room and vestibule; also oak stairs, $153.00 extra.
Storm Doors and Windows, $61.00 extra.
Screen Doors and Windows, galvanized wire, $40.00 extra.
Sealtite Blanket Insulation for Outside Walls and Over Ceiling Joists, $138.00 extra.

For prices of Plumbing, Heating, Wiring, Electric Fixtures and Shades see pages 121 and 122.

For Garages see pages 102 and 103.

For Our Easy Payment Plans See Pages 2 and 3—For Our Information Blanks See Pages 123 and 124

Sears, Roebuck catalog page shows Modern Home Number C3278, also known as the Cedars, from 1932. By this time, most Sears home kit customers were securing home loans through Sears. With that in mind, the company began advertising its models with two prices: the complete price if paid for upfront, and monthly payments. This Cedars was introduced in 1932, three years into the Great Depression. Knowing that money was tight, Sears advertised this model by saying that the roof made the home look larger than it really was. In doing so, Sears subtly told its customers that it knew they wanted value, but not at the expense of beauty or pleasing aesthetics. SEARS ®, ROEBUCK AND CO.

Gilded Age and Progressive Era: Primary Sources

189

THE BRENTWOOD . .

▲ FOUR ROOMS AND BATH

MODERN HOME
No. 13394C
ALREADY CUT AND FITTED
PRICE $869.00

At the price quoted above, we will guarantee to furnish all the material to build this beautiful little home consisting of lumber, lath, millwork, flooring, shingles, building paper, hardware, metal and painting materials; complete plans and instructions for erection.

FLOOR PLAN

THE attractive plan shown here, was recently illustrated by a large national magazine as an ideal low cost home. The floor plan is the same for both exteriors and consists of four livable rooms—living room, kitchen, two bedrooms and bath. Three closets, linen and broom storage are located where they can be used to best advantage.

Our famous labor saving method of furnishing all framing material cut to fit, enables considerable work to be done by the owner. Thousands of home builders have saved money by this method and our low cash prices and quantity guying.

The Brentwood No. 13394C is planned with clear bevel siding for exterior walls while the "D" plan is shown with wide shingles.

MODERN HOME
No. 13394D
ALREADY CUT AND FITTED
PRICE $923.00

These homes can be built on a 30 ft. lot. Height of ceilings 8 ft. 3 in. Cellar stairs lead to full basement providing space for furnace, fuel, fruit storage and laundry.

We will include with your order, complete heating, lighting and plumbing with all necessary plans for installation at our low cash optional prices.

Modern Homes Division

Sears, Roebuck catalog page shows Modern Home Numbers 13394C and 13394D, also known as the Brentwood, from 1933. This was the year Sears stopped offering home loans, as the program lost the company millions of dollars. Sears changed its advertising slogan to "America's New Low Cost Homes," though it was not printed on every catalog page. Advertising was more modern by this time, with simpler layout and sleeker lines. The Brentwood was considered an ideal low-cost home. SEARS®, ROEBUCK AND CO.

5 ROOM MODERN HOME

Croydon

The Croydon will give you and your family a spanking new outlook—fresh and inspiring as the spring of the year. It will prove to you that you can have a small house, absolutely modern, without a single trace of faddishness—and that it can be really inexpensive, too.

In the Croydon, there are no unnecessary details to raise the cost. There's a large, roomy living room that opens 'out to the side porch . . . and a miracle kitchen that will save you many steps.

BED ROOM 11'6" x 14'0"

BED ROOM 11'6" x 13'6"

SECOND FLOOR

PLAN No. 13718

KITCHEN 7'6" x 14'3"

LIVING ROOM 11'6" x 18'3"

DINING ROOM 11'6" x 10'4"

FIRST FLOOR

Page 20

Sears, Roebuck catalog page shows Modern Home Number 13718, also known as the Croydon, from 1939. Advertising now focused around illustration, and there was little text to supplement the ad. Clear evidence that Sears was no longer actively or enthusiastically promoting its home kits, the last catalog was published in 1940. SEARS®, ROEBUCK AND CO.

THE CRAFTON ..
▲ FOUR, FIVE AND SIX ROOMS WITH BATH

No. 3318A
ALREADY CUT
AND FITTED

No. 3318C
ALREADY CUT
AND FITTED

No. 3318D
ALREADY CUT
AND FITTED

JUST before this catalog went to press, we counted the number of home builders who have been made happy by building one of these attractive low cost American type bungalows. When over a thousand vote these plans their choice, there can be only one answer—they meet the requirements where four, five or six rooms are needed, at a minimum cost. No "gingerbread"—just attractive, livable space.

You have your choice of three plans. No. 3318A size 22 ft. wide by 30 ft. deep contains four rooms and bath. Plan No. 3318C size 24 ft. by 34 ft. 6 in. contains five rooms and bath, and plan No. 3318D size 26 ft. by 38 ft. contains six rooms and bath. All rooms well proportioned with good wall space and plenty of large windows.

Each plan has a large porch with baluster railing. The exterior walls are planned to be covered with No. 1 24-inch Cedar shingles, finished with one dip coat and one brush coat of super quality shingle stain.

The base price includes all necessary material according to specifications, plans and instructions for erection, to complete this home. All framing material cut to fit, reducing cost.

Fill out attached form for complete delivered price and details about optional equipment.

PLAN No. 3318X

Plan No. 3318X is the same as No. 3318D, but roof is raised and attic stairs are furnished over cellar stairs. This will make ideal storage. Write for details about this plan.

FLOOR PLAN 3318A

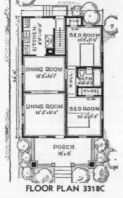

FLOOR PLAN 3318C

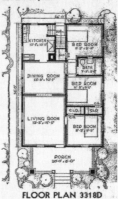

FLOOR PLAN 3318D

Sears, Roebuck and Co.

641   ▶ Page 25 ◀

A Sears, Roebuck bungalow home known as "The Crafton," a best-selling model during the Great Depression. SEARS®, ROEBUCK AND CO.

• • •

What happened next...

The end of World War I (1914–18) brought American soldiers home. Those who had started families before the war or who were ready to live on their own needed housing. Analysts estimated that one to two million homes were needed immediately. This sudden increase of potential homebuyers caused Sears home sales to skyrocket in the 1920s. During this time, Sears published its largest Modern Homes catalogs. The largest was 144 pages and offered more than ninety house designs plus garages, outhouses, and chicken coops. Home sales peaked at $12 million in 1929.

Those all-time-high home sales were directly followed by a serious decline in sales due to the Great Depression (1929–41). With an economic slump that resulted in the highest unemployment rates the country had ever experienced, few people were able to buy homes. Those who did buy Sears homes bought the more modest styles. The best-selling model was the Crafton, a 600- to 800-square-foot residence with four optional floor plans. The house sold for between $911 and $1,165.

Beginning in 1932, Sears Modern Homes program began operating at a loss. The company reported that sales of mail-order homes had dropped 40 percent in one year. Within two years, the company liquidated (accepted as a permanent financial loss) $11 million in mortgage loans. The depression caused thousands of businesses to close, and although the Modern Homes program closed in 1934, it reopened in 1935. At that point, it offered only houses, no financing or construction, which it had done from 1929 to 1933. The financing aspect of the program had become a major problem with the mortgage liquidation in 1934, and Sears was glad to be free of that part of the operation.

Although the company no longer actively promoted its mail-order homes program, customers continued to send in their forms and buy the kits. Sears published its last Modern Homes catalog in 1940 and ended the program that same year. More than one hundred thousand homes had been sold to Americans throughout the thirty-two years of the program. Since the sales records were destroyed, there is no way to know the location of those Sears homes. Historians do know that Syracuse, New York; Akron, Ohio; and much of Illinois have high concentrations of Sears homes, primarily because of industry. In 1918, Sears made its largest single sale to the Standard Oil Company, which bought

156 homes in eight different styles for a cost of $1 million. The homes were sold to the company's mineworkers in Carlinville, Illinois, for a $100 down payment and $40 a month until the selling price of $3,000 for a five-room house (or $4,000 for a six-room home) was reached. According to Thornton, 152 of those homes remain standing in the twenty-first century (three burned to the ground and one was moved to a rural location). Only six have their original siding.

Historians and others with an interest in twentieth-century architecture are among those who travel hundreds of miles in search of original Sears Modern Homes. One Sears home in Maryland sold for $816,000 in 2001. Determining if a home is actually a Modern Home is not always easy. The simplest way to identify one is to look for stamped lumber in the basement, but this is true only of models built after 1920. Prior to that year, the lumber was not precut and fitted. With earlier models, identification comes usually by comparing the home to an actual Sears Modern Homes catalog. However, because Sears was willing to customize its house models, it is not always possible to find a picture of a true Sears home. Some have been built using the top floor of one model and the bottom floor of another. There are no pictures in existence to represent those homes.

Did you know...

- Although many immigrants lived in tenement homes (inexpensive, overcrowded housing similar to apartment buildings) in the cities, testimonials from Sears homeowners indicate that a fair percentage of customers were immigrants with last names such as Kaczmasek, Von Lehmen, Schlag, Lichtenwalter, and Olpp.
- Sears offered three qualities of homes throughout its thirty-two-year program. Honor Bilt was the highest quality and most expensive. Standard Bilt (also known as Lighter Built) was meant for regions in the warmer climates that did not require much insulation. Simplex, or Econo Built, were two-room buildings most often used as summer cottages or hunting shacks. Although the quality of each level varied, all the homes were sturdy and built to last.
- Each kit contained thirty thousand pieces, including 750 pounds (340.5 kg) of nails, 27 gallons (102.2 liters) of paint, and a 75-page instruction booklet.
- Sears sold about 370 different styles of homes throughout the course of the program.

- Only approximately 10 percent of the Sears homes built have been discovered.

Consider the following ...

- Imagine you are a working-class immigrant in America in the early twentieth century. You have the opportunity to purchase a Sears Modern Home. What specific features would you look for in the layout and plan, and why?
- If a company sold mail-order homes in the twenty-first century, would you consider buying one? Why or why not?
- What aspects of buying a home out of a catalog would concern you as a homeowner?

For More Information

BOOKS

Sears, Roebuck Home Builder's Catalog: The Complete Illustrated 1910 Edition. New York: Dover Publications, 1990.

Stevenson, Katherine Cole, and H. Ward Jandl. *Houses by Mail: A Guide to Houses from Sears, Roebuck and Company.* Washington, DC: Preservation Press, 1986. Reprint, 1996.

Thornton, Rosemary. *The Houses That Sears Built.* 2nd ed. Alton, IL: Gentle Beam Publications, 2004.

WEB SITES

"History of Sears Modern Homes." *Sears Archives.* http://www.searsarchives. com/homes/history.htm (accessed on August 11, 2006).

Maxwell, Shirley, and James C. Massey. "The Story on Sears: Houses by Rail and Mail." *Old House Journal Online.* http://www.oldhousejournal.com/magazine/ 2002/july/sears.shtml (accessed on August 11, 2006).

Thornton, Rosemary. "Mail-Order Houses." *Christian Science Monitor.* http:// www.csmonitor.com/2002/0612/p11s02-lihc.html (accessed on August 11, 2006).

Thornton, Rosemary. "Windows on the Past." *The Old House Web.* http:// www.oldhouseweb.com/stories/Detailed/10102.shtml (accessed on August 11, 2006).

"What Is a Sears Modern Home?" *Sears Archives.* http://www.searsarchives. com/homes/ (accessed on August 11, 2006).

17

Triangle Shirtwaist Company Fire

"Thrilling Incidents in Gotham Holocaust That Wiped Out One Hundred and Fifty Lives"
Originally published in the Chicago Sunday Tribune, *March 26, 1911; available at*
The Triangle Factory Fire *(Web site)*

> "A 13 year old girl hung for three minutes by her finger tips to the sill of a tenth floor window. A tongue of flame licked at her fingers and she dropped into a life net held by firemen."

The Manhattan building owned by Max Blanck and Isaac Harris at 23–29 Washington Place in New York City was also known as the Asch building. The Asch building was the equivalent of a twenty-first century office building. The owners rented floors of the ten-story building to various businesses. These businesses, in turn, hired workers to make whatever products the companies sold.

One of the businesses housed in the Asch building was the Triangle Shirtwaist Company (also sometimes referred to as the Triangle Waist Company). Shirtwaist referred to a type of blouse worn by women in the late nineteenth and early twentieth centuries. It was white, with a tight waist, buttons down the front, and puffy sleeves. Although there were about five hundred shirtwaist factories in New York alone, the Triangle Company was the largest. The company employed around five hundred workers, most of them Italian and European Jewish girls and women. All five hundred employees were stuffed onto three floors: the eighth, ninth, and tenth. Blanck and Harris were the principal owners of the Triangle Company.

Although wages and working conditions were less than decent, the Triangle workers—mostly immigrants—were glad to have a job. The work day began at 7:30 AM and lasted until 9 o'clock in the evening during busy season. Normal work days ended around 4:45 PM. There was no such thing as overtime pay, and employees were not given any money to buy themselves dinner. Wages ranged from $1.50 a week for simpler work to $22 (an astronomical amount) a week for cutters, the men who actually cut the patterns used to make all the shirtwaists. The average weekly pay was $6–7.

The Asch building was a perfect example of the hundreds of other sweatshops (factories that provided inhumane working conditions and employee treatment) found throughout America's industrial regions during the turn of the century. In order to fit the greatest number of people into the building, machinery and equipment were placed in such a way that movement throughout the rooms or floors was dangerously limited. Ventilation (fresh air) in those buildings was poor. The overcrowded conditions made working not only difficult but unsafe.

In addition to the unsafe working conditions and low wages, the Triangle Shirtwaist Company mistreated its workers. One young worker, Pauline Newman, described her experience in the shop in the book *American Mosaic: The Immigrant Experience in the Words of Those Who Lived It*:

> They were the kind of employers who didn't recognize anyone working for them as a human being. You were not allowed to sing. Operators would like to have sung, because they, too, had the same thing to do, and weren't allowed to sing. You were not allowed to talk to each other. Oh, no! They would sneak up behind you, and if you were found talking to your next colleague you were admonished [scolded]. If you'd keep on, you'd be fired. If you went to the toilet, and you were there more than the forelady or foreman thought you should be, you were threatened to be laid off for a half a day, and sent home, and that meant, of course, no pay, you know? You were not allowed to use the passenger elevator, only a freight elevator. And ah, you were watched every minute of the day by the foreman, forelady. Employers would sneak behind your back. And you were not allowed to have your lunch on the fire escape in the summertime. And that door was locked.

In 1909, shirtwaist factory workers throughout New York gathered in protest of the poor working conditions and treatment as well as the unfair wages paid by their employers. Another of their demands was the recognition of a labor union (a formal organization that protects the rights of workers). Although many factories negotiated with workers to reach an agreement, the Triangle Shirtwaist Company did not, and workers were forced to return to the same dismal conditions against which they protested. If they chose not to return, someone else would

Labor Unions and the Garment Industry

The strike (when workers refuse to do their jobs until their demands for better conditions are met) in 1909 was called the "Uprising of the 20,000." Although working conditions in factories of any industry were pitiful, the shirtwaist industry proved particularly bad. Companies in that industry hired workers on an as-needed basis, so when the busy season passed, many lost their jobs. There was no job security. On top of that, workers were forced to buy their own equipment, and sewing machinery was expensive. Paychecks, too, as small as they were, were often short (less than they should have been).

In 1909, 150 women employees of the Triangle Shirtwaist Company were fired because they were members of the International Ladies' Garment Workers Union, the Women's Trade Union League, or both. These unions provided protection for female workers and, when necessary, fought on their behalf for more favorable wages and working conditions. Most factory owners hated labor unions because they forced the owners to pay decent wages and provide safer working conditions, which in turn took away from owners' profits. To join a labor union at the turn of the century was a good idea on the one hand but rather dangerous on the other, since no laws prohibited employers from firing workers for joining unions.

The "Uprising of the 20,000" was the first major labor strike in America led by women for women. Although 339 shops settled with the unions, the terms they agreed to were not nearly as good as the workers had hoped they would be. The strike was still considered a victory for the unions. It proved women to be as capable as men in the role of trade unionists.

Union leaders of the 1909 strike noted that Jewish women were often more committed to the movement than were their Italian counterparts, perhaps largely due to events in Russia within the past thirty years. By the time of the strike, Russian Jews were New York's largest immigrant group. They fled Russia beginning in 1882, when the czar (ruler) passed anti-Semitic (anti-Jew) laws and authorized pogroms (organized violence against Jews). Those who did not leave revolted in 1905, but the revolution failed.

These events led to a surge in immigration of Russian Jews with socialist beliefs. Socialism is the belief that everything should be publicly owned and distributed so that everyone gets the same amount of wealth in the form of products and services. In theory, poverty would not exist under socialism. In reality, that has not historically been true, as seen in Communist Russia. But a fundamental belief of socialism is in the power of the people who work together for a cause. As a result, Jewish workers were more likely to join labor unions than other immigrant groups. They understood that they had more power in numbers than if they worked alone.

quickly take over their jobs. By 1900, three-fourths of the 236,000 jobs in New York's garment industry were occupied by Jews, and 60 percent of the Jewish population was employed in the garment industry.

One of the victories claimed by the 339 shops that settled the strike was the 54-hour workweek. Since the Triangle Shirtwaist Company had not agreed to that new ruling, the employees of the shop were the only workers in the Asch building at 4:45 PM on Saturday, March 25, 1911. A fire broke out in a bin of rags belonging to a cutter on the eighth floor of the shop. Within moments, the entire floor was ablaze, and manager Samuel Bernstein attempted to extinguish the flames with buckets of water. His efforts would prove useless, since there were only twenty-seven buckets of water on hand, and the fire spread quickly due to the amount of fabric, sewing pattern papers, and other explosive flammables in the shop. Within minutes, the wood floor and ceiling were engulfed in deadly flames.

A clerk dragged a water hose into the shop, but when the faucet was turned on, no water came out. The owners of the building had it shut off to save money. Most employees on the eighth floor escaped the blaze by crawling out the window to the fire escape or by taking the passenger elevator. The elevator quit working almost immediately, thus leaving those employees on the ninth and tenth floor without a passage to safety.

Those workers on the tenth floor were able to reach the rooftop despite the panic and chaos. Professor Frank Sommer was teaching his class at the New York University Law School in the building next door when he saw dozens of workers from the Triangle Company running around on the rooftop fifteen feet below. The professor and his students found ladders and placed them so that the escaping workers could crawl to safety on the school roof. Approximately seventy workers had been trapped on that tenth floor, and all but one survived.

Ninth-floor workers were not so lucky. Without a fire escape or a door to lead them to safety, these victims had two choices: perish in the blaze, or jump out the window.

Things to remember while reading the *Chicago Sunday Tribune* article:

- Very few of the Triangle Shirtwaist Company employees could speak English.
- The building itself was fireproof and built to legal standards of the day.
- Working women were viewed as a threat by working men, who believed women stole jobs from them. They were also seen as inferior by middle-class women, who believed a woman's place was

Fire fighters struggle to extinguish a fire at the Asch building in New York City on March 25, 1911. Nearly 150 employees of the Triangle Shirtwaist Company died.
© UNDERWOOD & UNDERWOOD/CORBIS.

in the home. They had to struggle for acceptance by nearly every other social group in America in the early 1900s.

• • •

Chicago Sunday Tribune article reporting on the Triangle Shirtwaist Company Fire

Scores: Large numbers.

In the office buildings across Washington place **scores** of men detained beyond office hours worked at their desks. One of them saw a girl rush to a window and throw up the **sash.** Behind her dashed a **seething** curtain of yellow flame.

Sash: Window frame.

Seething: Violently moving.

She climbed to the sill, stood in black outline against the light, hesitating, then, with a last touch of **futile thrift,** slipped her **chatelaine bag** over her wrist and jumped. Her body went whirling downward through the woven wire glass of a **canopy** to the **flagging** below.

Futile thrift: Useless caution.

Chatelaine bag: A bag worn at the waist, similar to a purse.

Her sisters who followed, flamed through the air like rockets. Their path could be followed but hardly heard.

Canopy: Protective, rooflike covering mounted on a frame over a walkway.

It was eighty-five feet from the eighth floor to the ground, about ninety-five feet from ninth floor, 113 feet from the **cornice** of the roof, and the upward rush of a **draft** and the crackle of the flames drowned their cries.

Flagging: Pavement.

"Jimmy" Lehan, a traffic squad policeman, dashed up eight flights of stairs when the fire was at its height, braced his shoulders against a barred door, and burst it in. He found a score of girls made with fright. He ordered them down the smoke filled stairways, but they **balked.** He used his club, and **beat them down** to safety. Not one of the number **perished.**

Cornice: Molding that frames the edge of a roof and hangs over the sides of a building.

A boy who jumped from one of the upper floors was caught by a policeman who braced himself and held the youngster, practically uninjured, although both fell to the street.

Draft: Sudden current of air.

Balked: Refused.

Six girls fought their way to a window on the ninth floor over the bodies of fallen fellow workers and crawled out in a single file to an eight inch stone ledge running the length of the building.

Beat them down: Cleared a path.

Perished: Died.

More than a hundred feet above the sidewalk they crept along their **perilous** pathway to a swinging electric feed wire spanning Washington place.

Perilous: Dangerous.

The leaders paused for their companions to catch up at the end of the ledge and the six grabbed the wire **simultaneously.** It snapped like rotten **whipcord** and they crashed down to death.

Simultaneously: At the same time.

Whipcord: Strong, braided cord.

A 13 year old girl hung for three minutes by her finger tips to the sill of a tenth floor window. A tongue of flame licked at her fingers and she dropped into a life net held by firemen. Two women fell into the net at almost the same moment. The strands parted and the two were added to the death list.

A girl threw her pocketbook, then her hat, then her furs from a tenth floor window. A moment later her body came whirling after them to death.

At a ninth floor window a man and a woman appeared. The man embraced the woman and kissed her. Then he hurled her to the street and jumped. Both were killed.

Five girls smashed a pane of glass, dropped in a struggling tangle and were crushed into a shapeless mass.

A girl on the eighth floor leaped for a firemen's ladder which reached only to the sixth floor. She missed, struck the edge of a life net, and was picked up with her back broken.

From one window a girl of about 13 years, a woman, a man, and two women with their arms about one another threw themselves to the ground in **rapid succession.** The little girl was whirled to the New York hospital in an automobile.

Rapid succession: Quickly, one after the other.

She screamed as the driver and policeman lifted her into the hallway. A surgeon came out, gave one look at her face and touched her wrist. "She is dead," he said.

One girl jumped into a horse blanket held by the firemen and the policemen. The blanket ripped like **cheesecloth** and her body was mangled almost beyond recognition.

Cheesecloth: Loosely woven cotton gauze.

Another dropped into a **tarpaulin** held by three men. Her weight tore it from their grasp and she struck the street, breaking almost every bone in her body.

Tarpaulin: Waterproof canvas.

Almost at the same time a man somersaulted down upon the shoulder of a policeman holding the tarpaulin. He **glanced** off, struck the sidewalk, and was picked up dead.

Glanced: Bounced.

Within the building a man on the eighth floor stationed himself at the door of one of the elevators and with a club kept back the girls who had stampeded to the wire cages. Thirty were admitted to the car at a time. They were rushed down as fast as possible.

The call for ambulances was followed by successive appeals for police until 500 patrolmen arrived to cope with a crowd numbering tens of thousands [in] a mixture of the **morbidly** curious and of half crazed relatives and friends of the victims. A hundred mounted policemen had to charge the crowd repeatedly to keep it back.

Morbidly: Gruesomely.

Led by Fire Chief [Edward] Croker, a squad of firemen stormed the stairways and gained access to the building at 7 o'clock. Two searchlights from buildings opposite lighted the way of the fire fighters as they ascended to the top floors.

Oilcloth: Fabric treated with oil to make it waterproof.

Morgue: A place where bodies of the dead are kept until identified.

Slocum horror: A 1904 tragedy in which a steamboat called *General Slocum* burst into flames on New York City's East River, killing around one thousand people, mostly women and children.

Hypodermic injections: Shots given just below the skin.

Fifty roasted bodies were found on the ninth floor. They lay in every possible posture, some so charred that recognition was impossible. A half dozen were nude, with the flesh hanging in shreds to the bones.

Women with their hair burned away, with here and there a limb burned entirely off, and the charred stump visible, were lifted tenderly from the debris, wrapped in **oilcloth,** and lowered by pulleys to the street.

Across the street there rested on the sidewalk a hundred pine coffins, into which were placed the bodies. As fast as this was done the coffins were carried away in a kind of vehicle that could be pressed into service to the **morgue** at Bellevue hospital and to the Charities Pier morgue, opened for the first time since the **Slocum horror.**

One of the first physicians on the scene was Dr. Ralph A. Froelich, 119 Waverley Place. He saw most of the girls jump to the street and as each one fell he rushed to her side and administered **hypodermic injections** to deaden the pain. He treated twelve of the victims, whom he found still breathing, but each died within a short time.

• • •

What happened next...

The Triangle fire was brought under control in just eighteen minutes, and within ten more, it was completely put out. But by that time, 146 of the company's 500 employees had died either in the blaze or by jumping out of the ninth-floor windows. Although there are many eyewitness reports of girls willingly, if not reluctantly, jumping off window ledges, the fact remains that in the initial panic that ensued as the announcement of "Fire!" reached the ninth floor, a large portion of those jumpers were actually pushed to their deaths by frightened workers trapped in the room behind them.

When firefighters searched the fire-damaged floors of the Asch building in hopes of finding survivors, what they found instead were more bodies. One survivor was eventually found, trapped in the elevator shaft, hovering above a pile of about twenty-five corpses. Fifty more bodies were found lying on the floor of the eighth story alone.

Pine coffins were delivered to the scene of the fire so that bodies could be removed from the pavement. About one-third of the victims were identified by the end of the night; the rest would be identified, where possible, within the next couple days. For those bodies burned beyond recognition, loved ones used other means of identification: a piece

Friends and relatives file by open coffins in an attempt to identify the victims of the Triangle Shirtwaist fire. © HULTON ARCHIVE/GETTY IMAGES.

of jewelry, a hair comb, a repair in a shoe. One mother identified her daughter by a stocking that had recently been repaired. She recognized the stitching and the location of the mending.

Concern was growing about health and safety in factories and other urban buildings in the early twentieth century. Within weeks of the Triangle fire, union members and concerned citizens alike joined together in protest, demanding that someone be held accountable for the deadliest disaster to strike since the Industrial Revolution began. Additionally, they wanted factory conditions to change. Some of the wealthiest women in the world came to the aid of the strikers and the families of the victims who wanted justice. They offered money, time, and something the other concerned citizens did not have—connections to powerful people. They brought to the cause a level of publicity and public interest it otherwise would have lacked. The two women's unions organized a funeral march on April 5, and an estimated 120,000 people joined in the march.

The ruins of one of the floors hit by the Triangle Shirtwaist Company fire in New York City's Asch building in March 1911.
© BETTMANN/CORBIS.

Within two days of the fire, city officials began offering early con-clusions as to the reasons for the tragedy. The fire marshal believed the fire began when a lighted match was thrown into a bin of rags under cutting table Number Two on the eighth floor. Fire investigators found many cigarette cases near the spot of the fire's origin despite the company's no-smoking policy in the factory. Workers reported that smoking in the building was common, especially among the cutters, who were highly skilled and allowed to do most anything they wanted in an effort to keep them happy on the job. Fire Chief Edward Croker announced that the doors leading into the factory workplace had indeed been locked, even though workers were still inside. This was a common practice at the Triangle Company. Blanck and Harris insisted the precautionary measure was necessary to keep from being robbed by their employees.

Although the building itself had been built to legal standards at the time of its construction, eleven years had passed and it had not been inspected since. Building officials claimed their department was understaffed and underfunded and was not able to keep up with any inspections of buildings other than those being built.

The public's anger was mostly directed at company and building owners Blanck and Harris. Called the "shirtwaist kings," the two men got the most out of their employees, crowding 240 sewing machines onto one floor alone. Two weeks after the fire, the men were indicted on charges of manslaughter (accidental but unlawful killing of others).

The prosecutor (lawyer filing the charges) brought 103 witnesses to the stand. They all testified that it was company policy to keep doors locked for various reasons, but mostly, to keep employees from stealing shirtwaists. The defense countered with 52 witnesses, mostly salesmen, painters, and others who had cause to go onto the ninth floor. These witnesses claimed the doors were always open, although none of them had been there at the time of the fire.

After two hours of discussion, the jury found the building owners not guilty. Although the jurors believed the doors had likely been locked at the time of the fire, there was no way to prove the owners knew they were locked.

Three years after the fire, on March 11, 1914, twenty-three individual civil suits (lawsuits seeking damages under the laws established by a state or a country) against Blanck and Harris were settled. They paid an average of $75 for each life lost to those twenty-three families. The public was furious, and the general outrage led to the creation of the Factory Investigating Commission. The Commission's job was to thoroughly examine New York factories for safety and working conditions. Their findings led to the passage of more legislation than ever before known to the labor industry. Between 1911 and 1914, thirty-six reform factory codes were passed. Some of the new requirements were sprinkler systems, outward-opening doors, fire drills, and regular building inspections. Furthermore, the tragedy helped America understand and appreciate the role of labor unions. Labor union organizing in factories became increasingly successful.

Did you know...

- The water from the fire hoses that ran into the gutters was red with the blood of Triangle victims.
- Three men made a human chain that bridged the gap between the rooftop of the Asch building and another next door. Many survivors climbed across that chain to safety before the weight of the human burden broke the back of one of the men and several would-be survivors fell to their deaths below.
- The fire was the beginning of the end of business for partners Blanck and Harris. Blanck would continue to run a garment factory on his own. Years later, he would again be accused of locking employees into the factory during work hours. He would be found guilty this time and fined $20. The judge who delivered the sentence apologized for having to fine him at all.

Consider the following...

- Imagine you are a fifteen-year-old immigrant caught in the fire. You do not speak or understand much English. What would be your first move upon learning of the fire?
- You are the brother or the sister of a victim of the fire. What is your reaction upon learning the owners of the building go free, but that the tragedy results in the passage of major industrial reform?
- You happened to be on the street as the first women jumped through the windows. What would you do?

For More Information

BOOKS

Auch, Mary Jane. *Ashes of Roses*. New York: H. Holt, 2002.

DeAngelis, Gina. *The Triangle Shirtwaist Company Fire of 1911*. New York: Chelsea House Publishers, 2001.

Landau, Elaine. *The Triangle Shirtwaist Factory Fire*. New York: Children's Press, 2005.

Morrison, Joan, and Charlotte Fox Zabusky. *American Mosaic: The Immigrant Experience in the Words of Those Who Lived It*. New York: Dutton, 1980. Reprint, Pittsburgh: University of Pittsburgh Press, 1993.

Stein, Leon. *The Triangle Fire*. Philadelphia: Lippincott, 1962. Reprint, Ithaca, NY: Cornell University Press, 2001.

Von Drehle, David. *Triangle: The Fire That Changed America.* New York: Atlantic Monthly Press, 2003.

NEWSPAPERS

"Thrilling Incidents in Gotham Holocaust That Wiped Out One Hundred and Fifty Lives" *Chicago Sunday Tribune,* March 28, 1911, p. 2.

WEB SITES

"Big Apple History: The Triangle Tragedy." *PBSKids.org.* http://pbskids.org/ bigapplehistory/life/topic13.html (accessed on August 15, 2006).

Cornell University, ILR School. *The Triangle Factory Fire.* http://www.ilr.cornell. edu/trianglefire/ (accessed on August 16, 2006).

Leung, Alison. "Photos from the Triangle Factory Fire." *University of Sydney.* http://teaching.arts.usyd.edu.au/history/hsty3080/3rdYr3080/triangleweb site/index.html (accessed on August 15, 2006).

Library of Congress. "American Jewish Women." *American Memory: American Women.* http://memory.loc.gov/ammem/awhhtml/awas12/jewish.html (accessed on August 15, 2006).

Linder, Douglas. "The Triangle Shirtwaist Fire Trial, 1911." *University of Missouri-Kansas City School of Law.* http://www.law.umkc.edu/faculty/projects/ftrials/ triangle/trianglefire.html (accessed on August 15, 2006).

Newman, Pauline, and Joan Morrison. "Working for the Triangle Shirtwaist Company." *History Matters.* http://historymatters.gmu.edu/d/178/ (accessed on August 15, 2006).

"A Perfect Fit: The Garment Industry and American Jewry, 1860–1960." *Yeshiva University Museum.* http://www.yumuseum.org/APerfectFit/highlights.html (accessed on August 15, 2006).

18

Ruth Dodge

"Dr. Dodge's Wife Tells Story of *Titanic* Wreck"
Originally published in The Bulletin, *April 30, 1912; available at* The Virtual Museum
of the City of San Francisco *(Web site)*

"The most terrible part of the experience was that awful crying after the ship went down. We were a mile away, but we heard it—oh, how we heard it. It seemed to last about an hour, although it may have been only a short time, for some say a man could not have lived in that water over fifteen minutes. At last it died down."

By its very definition, the Gilded Age was one of great wealth, at least in terms of appearances, if not quality of character. The word "gilded" means "rich and superior in quality." Another meaning is "deceptively pleasing." Both definitions describe Gilded Age society.

For those fortunate members of the upper class, the Gilded Age was a time of glorious parties, lavish lifestyles, and carefree spending. Little thought was given to life outside their ornate (highly decorated) architecture and breathtaking interiors.

But much as it is today, great wealth was unevenly distributed in that era. The "haves" were few; the "have-nots" were many. Inspired architecture of the wealthy greatly contrasted with the rundown tenement housing of the poor. Expansive lawns became extinct, to be replaced with dirty sidewalks and littered alleys. None of the latest fashion in colorful silks clothed poor women. They were considered lucky if the soles of their shoes had not been replaced with cardboard.

Although the Progressive Era ushered in many needed social reforms, the issue of class distinction remained virtually unconsidered.

The wealthy were used to ignoring the poor; the poor were accustomed to being ignored. The attitude of many citizens of wealth was that they enjoyed their riches because God felt they deserved them. The lower classes were considered lazy or savage. To the privileged few, the poor got what they deserved. Out of a sense of necessity, those who lived in poverty gave up the hope of something better. To wish for more—more food, more money, more living space—only brought disappointment.

So on the surface, society looked grand. But to the perceptive eye, it was obvious that for every privileged life there existed many, many dark and difficult lives. Two opposing lifestyles were led side by side.

The *Titanic* was symbolic of everything the Gilded Age stood for. The pride of the White Star Line, the *Titanic* was the largest ship built to date. Like all companies, the White Star Line was always looking for ways to outperform the competition. The main competition at the time was Cunard, the company that manufactured the doomed *Lusitania* (sunk by the Germans in 1917) and the *Mauritania*. Both ships were impressive in terms of speed. Their engines were state of the art, the finest produced at that time. White Star Line's president, J. Bruce Ismay (1862–1937), was confident, however, that he could produce a vessel that would be bigger, heavier, and more luxurious than any ship anyone had ever seen.

And so came the *Titanic*. At 883 feet (269.1 meters, or $\frac{1}{6}$ mile) long, 92 feet (28 meters) wide, and 104 feet (31.7 meters) tall, it put all other sailing vessels to shame. It boasted 46,328 tons (42,019.5 metric tons) of steel and was said to be "practically unsinkable" by Ismay. After the sinking of the ship, everyone would forget the "practically" part of his claim and label Ismay a greedy scoundrel and a liar.

The *Titanic* cost $7.5 million to build (the equivalent of around $400 million today). Passengers who could afford a first-class passage enjoyed use of the on-deck heated swimming pool (the first of its kind), four electric elevators, and a fully equipped gymnasium. They could eat in the elegant dining hall (seating capacity of 554), or pay extra to enjoy their food served on fine china and glassware in a more private setting. At any time of day, these passengers could borrow books from the magnificent library, then stroll to one of the decks to read while basking in the sun. Those in need of a haircut visited one of two barbershops. Life was good on the *Titanic*. For some.

Beneath the grandeur of first and even second class was the steerage section of the ship. Steerage was in stark contrast to the opulence (luxury) of the top floors. No dining rooms or dancing for these passengers: They slept in small, windowless rooms the size of closets, in beds made up

with rough, inferior-quality sheets and blankets. Compared with the $4,350 one-way ticket for a first-class parlor passage, the $40 steerage passage got its buyers little else than transportation across the ocean.

Many passengers in third class were women and children. Unlike most of the White Star Line crew who worked in third class, these passengers spoke languages other than English. Communication between the two groups was strained at best. Unlike their first- and second-class shipmates, those in third class were not given the required lifeboat drill. It would prove to be a costly omission.

The *Titanic* set out on its maiden (first) voyage on April 10, 1912. It departed from Southampton, England, for a six-day voyage to New York. Through the years, the number of people onboard the *Titanic* has been disputed. It is generally accepted that on the day the ship hit the iceberg, 329 passengers were in first class, 285 were in second class, and 710 were in third class. There were 899 crew members onboard as well.

On the evening of April 14, 1912, the captain and crew received more than one warning of ice in the area. Despite those warnings, the *Titanic* forged ahead. At 11:40 PM, the ship hit an iceberg. It was about 400 miles off the coast of Newfoundland, Canada. The ship that had taken three years to build took fewer than three hours to sink. Of the more than 2,000 people onboard, only 705 survived.

Things to remember while reading "Dr. Dodge's Wife Tells Story of *Titanic* Wreck":

- The woman interviewed in the newspaper story, Ruth Dodge, and her husband, Dr. Washington Dodge, hailed from the San Francisco area. Dr. Dodge was a prominent banker; he and his wife were active in their community and generally well liked. This was the second marriage for both of them; each had a child from their previous marriages. Together, they had one son, Washington Dodge Jr., who accompanied them onboard the *Titanic*.

- When Ruth Dodge says the order was given for all women to gather on the port (left) side of the vessel, she actually means all upper-class women who held first-class tickets. Those women booked in third class are still in the steerage of the ship, many behind locked gates and doors.

- During the Progressive Era, actors, musicians, and athletes were not regarded as highly as they are today. Instead, the wealthy

An illustration showing the Titanic *hitting a giant iceberg on April 14, 1912, which led to its sinking.* © BETTMANN/CORBIS.

and the aristocrats (upper-class) of society fascinated the public and the media. The combined wealth of those celebrities onboard the *Titanic* was over $500 million.

- The *Titanic* had enough room for forty-eight lifeboats to be kept onboard. Management was concerned that the appearance of too many boats would affect the beauty of the ship. Only twenty lifeboats were made available to passengers and crew.

- The "awful crying" Ruth Dodge recalls came primarily from the third-class passengers. Although there were more third-class passengers than there were first- and second-class, only 25 percent of third-class passengers were saved. This compares with 53 percent of first- and second-class passengers saved.

• • •

"Dr. Dodge's Wife Tells Story of *Titanic* Wreck"

Was it cold? You can imagine how cold it was when I tell you that we passed fifty-six miles of icebergs after we got on the *Carpathia*. The baby had nothing on but his pajamas and a life preserver.

I think it is foolish to speak of the heroism displayed. There was none that I witnessed. It was merely a matter of waiting your turn for a lifeboat, and there was no keen anxiety to enter the boats because everybody had such confidence in that wretched ship. The officers told us that they had wireless communication with seven vessels, which were on the way to relieve us, and the men believed themselves as safe onboard as in the boats. It seemed the vaguest possibility that the ship might sink before one of the seven vessels arrived.

Of course, I left the *Titanic* before it began to settle into the water. The **steerage** passengers had not come on deck. In fact, there were few on the deck from which we left and more men than women.

TOOK SECOND BOAT.

It happened this way. There seems to have been an order issued that all women should **congregate** on the **port** side of the vessel. The vessel was injured on the **starboard** side, and even when I left the ship there was a slight **list** to starboard. We did not hear this order. I was in my stateroom, had **retired** again after the accident when the doctor came saying he had met our steward and had been told to get into a life preserver. I slipped on my fur coat over my night robe and preserver, put on my shoes without stockings; I did not stop to button them.

We had made a practice of sitting on the starboard side of the deck, the gymnasium was there, and naturally when we went above we turned to starboard. They were lowering boats. I entered the second boat with my baby. This boat had an officer in command, and enough officers to man the oars. Several women entered with me and as we **commenced** to lower the boat the women's husbands jumped in with them. I called to the doctor to come, but he refused because there were still a few women on deck. Every woman in that second boat with the exception of myself, had her husband with her.

BOATS HALF FILLED.

I supposed all the women were congregated on the port side because it would naturally be the highest side, and the safest because [it would be] the last to go down. We had no idea then that there would not be enough boats to go around. In fact, the first boats were only half filled.

Steerage: Lowest deck of a ship.

Congregate: Gather.

Port: When facing forward, the left side of a ship.

Starboard: When facing forward, the right side of a ship.

List: Lean.

Retired: Gone to bed.

Commenced: Began.

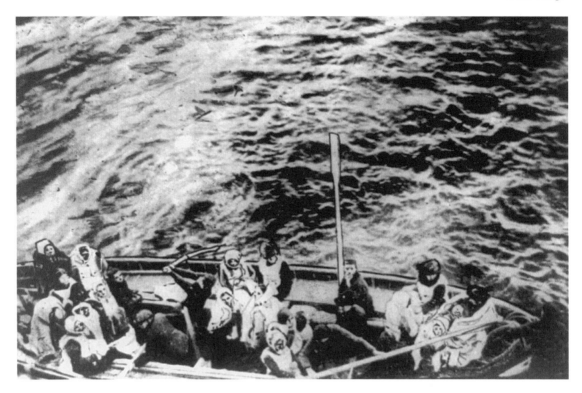

A group of survivors of the Titanic *wait in their lifeboat for the rescue ship* Carpathia. THE LIBRARY OF CONGRESS.

There must have been some confusion in orders, else I do not see why some of the women were not sent from port to starboard to enter those boats being lowered there. My husband got into the thirteenth boat. At that time there were no women on the starboard side. There was not one women [sic] in the boat he entered, and no member of the crew.

[White Star Line president] Bruce Ismay entered the fifteenth boat from starboard. It was being lowered at the same time, and the doctor says he remembers this because there was some fear that the boats might swing into each other as they were lowered down the side of the vessel.

CRYING OF THE DOOMED.

The most terrible part of the experience was that awful crying after the ship went down. We were a mile away, but we heard it—oh, how we heard it. It seemed to last about an hour, although it may have been only a short time, for some say a man could not have lived in that water over fifteen minutes. At last it died down.

Our officer and the members of the crew wanted to go back and pick up those whom they could, but the women in the boat would not left [sic] them. They told them if they attempted to turn back their husbands would

The Unsinkable Molly Brown

Titanic *survivor Molly Brown.* © BETTMANN/CORBIS.

Margaret Tobin was born on July 18, 1867, in Hannibal, Missouri. Born into a family of Irish immigrants, young Margaret moved to the mining town of Leadville, Colorado, while still in her teens. There, she worked in a general store. Margaret Tobin married James Joseph Brown in 1886. The couple moved to a nearby town, where the new Mrs. Brown opened a soup kitchen (a place that serves free soup to the needy).

Around the same time, Brown became active in women's rights, especially the right to vote. When her husband became wealthy working for a mining company, the Browns moved to Denver. There, they quickly joined the ranks of high society. Brown helped establish the Denver Woman's Club, a national network designed to help improve living conditions for women and children. She is also credited with playing a key role in the development of the first juvenile court. Prior to

take the oars from them, and the other men outnumbered the crew. I told them I could not see how they could forbid turning back in the face of those awful cries. I will remember it until I die, as it is. I told them: "How do I know, you have your husbands with you, but my husband may be one of those who are crying."

They argued that if we got back where the people were struggling, some of the steerage passengers, crazed with fear and the cold, might capsize the boat struggling to get it, or might force the officers to overload so we would all go down.

WOMEN HYSTERICAL.

After the crying died down, two or three of the women became hysterical—about what I don't know; they were missing none of their people. I was trying to keep baby from realization of what was happening, but when these women shrieked he would begin crying and asking, "Where's papa?"

"Finally I did what everyone thinks a strange thing. I changed lifeboats in midocean. We overtook the first boat. It was hardly half filled. They

her efforts, children accused of crimes were held accountable and tried in the adult court system. The social reformist attended Denver's Carnegie Institute in 1901 to study literature and language.

In 1912, Brown and her daughter Helen were on vacation in Europe when they received word that Brown's grandson was very sick. Brown cut her trip short and booked passage back to America on the luxurious *Titanic*. Brown joined a number of other members of high society on that tragic voyage. Her first-class stateroom cost $4,350 for the 6-day trip.

Brown was reading in her room when the *Titanic* struck an iceberg just before midnight on April 14, 1912. The collision hurled her out of bed, so she picked herself up and joined several gentlemen standing in the hall. At that point, no one thought anything serious had happened, but they all knew something was not quite right.

By the time the passengers and crew realized the grave danger they were in, Brown was resolved

not to let fear get the best of her. She had been traveling across the ocean for years; she was not concerned for her safety. Instead, Brown helped fellow passengers off the *Titanic* and into lifeboats. Even at that point, she believed the ship was unsinkable. Soon she was ordered into a lifeboat and told to row. She and another woman rowed the lifeboat away from the sinking *Titanic*. As the screams of children and the barking of dogs faded, the sounds of the exploding boilers filled the air. Brown watched in horror as the hissing ship disappeared into the murky water.

When Brown finally docked in New York, reporters surrounded her and asked why she thought she survived. Her response was, "Typical Brown luck. We're unsinkable." Upon returning to Denver, Brown found herself a hero. For her efforts that night on the *Titanic*, she was awarded the French Legion of Honour in 1932.

And though she had never been called Molly in her lifetime, she became famous as "The Unsinkable Molly Brown" thanks to a 1960s musical by the same name.

---

offered to take any of us aboard, and to get away from the hysteria of the others. I changed.

ON THE *CARPATHIA*.

The most pathetic thing was the scene on board the *Carpathia* during the rescue. As each boat drew up the survivors would peer over, straining to see the face of someone they had left behind. They were the young brides—everybody on board, of course, had known they were brides, and they had watched them laughing and **promenading** with their husbands.

Promenading: Leisurely walking.

The moans of anxiety and disappointment as each boat failed to bring up those that they were looking for were awful and finally that awful despair which fell over everyone when we knew there were no more boats to pick up.

Still they would not give up hope. "Are you missing anyone?" the passengers would ask each other, never "Have you lost anyone?"

KINDNESS OF PASSENGERS.

Too much cannot be said of the kindness of the *Carpathia*'s passengers. They gave up staterooms, they took the very clothing off their bodies for us.

I left the *Carpathia* wearing garments given me by a women whose name I do not know and will never know.

Bloomer: Baggy.

She exhibited the **bloomer** trousers she had cut for Baby Dodge from a blanket given her by a sailor.

I am sorry that I knew the names of so few passengers. There were two men aboard particularly, who every day used to come on the sun deck to play with the baby, and we often fell into conversation. Those men were not among the survivors. I do wish I had known their names that I might tell their wives some of the beautiful things they had said to me of their home life, casually, in these conversation[s].

• • •

What happened next...

Although the captain and crew knew the *Titanic* had hit an iceberg, passengers were at first unaware of any real danger. The noise and the sudden jolt woke those who had been asleep. Those still awake knew something had happened but had no idea how serious their situation was.

The exact size of the iceberg that sunk the *Titanic* will never be known for certain. Newspapers reported it as being 50 to 100 feet (15.2 to 30.5 meters) high and 200 to 400 feet (61 to 121.9 meters) long. The chief steward of another ship photographed the suspected iceberg on April 15, 1912. This man had not yet heard of the disaster. He was intrigued by the smear of red paint he noticed along the base of the iceberg. So he snapped a photo.

The *Titanic* crew member on lookout saw the iceberg before the collision. He rang the warning bell three times. He phoned the bridge with the warning, but by then it was too late. Thirty-seven seconds later, the *Titanic* hit the iceberg. Distress signals were immediately sent to other ships in the area to let them know the *Titanic* needed help. The *Carpathia* was nearest, but even so, was 58 miles (93 kilometers) away.

At 12:25 AM, the order was given to get women and children into the lifeboats. Twenty minutes later, the first boat was lowered into the water. Even though it could seat 65 people, only 19 of the seats were filled. This underusage happened with all but two of the lifeboats (in each of those two, capacity was overflowing with seventy passengers) and would be a source of criticism in the investigation that followed.

The suspected iceberg that sank the Titanic; *this photograph was taken shortly after the accident.* © BETTMANN/CORBIS.

Those unfortunate passengers riding in steerage were all but forgotten. In the mass confusion above deck, no one is sure if orders were ever given to evacuate passengers from the lower decks. Some of the gates to the upper deck were locked. Some passengers who did manage to reach an open gate for escape were turned back by crew members. Other crew allowed only women and children from third class to ascend the stairs to rescue.

By the time third-class passengers were able to get to the upper decks, most of the lifeboats were either rowing toward the *Carpathia* or had already made it to the rescue ship. It would later be revealed that, had the lifeboats been filled to capacity, another 473 passengers could have made their way to safety. All the women and children lost in the disaster could have been saved.

At 2:20 AM on April 15, 1912, the *Titanic* disappeared beneath the sea. By May, 328 corpses were recovered. In all, 705 passengers died in the sinking of the *Titanic*. Of first-class passengers, 60 percent survived. Forty-four percent of second-class passengers survived, as did

A painting by Willy Stoewer entitled Titanic Sinking. © BETTMANN/CORBIS.

25 percent of third-class. Twenty-four percent of the crew survived. (Although official reports of these numbers vary one or two percent, depending on the source and the time of the report, these figures are generally accepted as accurate.)

An investigation was conducted by British officials from May 2 to July 3, 1912. Crew members and survivors testified during the inquiry. Accounts of what happened that fateful night varied greatly, as they tend to do when mass confusion sets in. Some eyewitnesses reported that crew members were out to save themselves at the expense of passengers' lives. Some insisted that certain crew members actually shot some passengers during the chaos, either to keep order or to get themselves a spot on the lifeboats.

Whatever may have happened that night, the first International Convention for Safety of Life at Sea was called in London, England, in 1913.

Rules and regulations were established. Every ship would be required to have enough lifeboat space for each passenger onboard. A law now required lifeboat drills for all passengers during each voyage. Ships also would need to maintain a 24-hour radio watch. Another direct result of the tragedy was the formation of the International Ice Patrol. This organization would warn ships of icebergs in the North Atlantic shipping lanes.

The sinking of the *Titanic* forever left its mark on Washington Dodge. He was found dead of a suicidal gunshot wound to the head in 1919. Some modern experts believe he suffered from Post Traumatic Stress Disorder (a condition in which one suffers from anxiety and stress brought on by a tragic event), while others believe he felt stigmatized as a coward, having survived the disaster while many women and children died. Still others who knew him claim his health was not good even as he sailed the ship.

Ruth Dodge lived a full life and died of natural causes in July 1950. She was seventy-two years old. Washington Dodge Jr. suffered from exposure to the cold weather the night of the sinking, but recovered. He died of a heart attack in 1974 at the age of sixty-two.

The wreck of the *Titanic* was discovered on September 1, 1985, by Robert Ballard (1942–), a member of a joint U.S.-France expedition. An oceanographer and marine biologist with the Woods Hole Oceanographic Institution, Ballard found the ship lying in two pieces on the ocean floor about 13,000 feet (4,000 meters) down and 2,000 feet (609.6 meters) apart. At one time, scientists had believed that the ship must have sustained one long gash that ripped through the hull. They now learned that the collision produced many thin gashes and ruptured the seams of the hull plates.

Almost immediately, a debate began over who owned the wreck and what should be done with it. Ballard and many Americans did not believe the remains of the *Titanic* should be disturbed. They considered the wreckage—and the artifacts (objects) inside, such as coffee cups, mirrors, and jewelry—a memorial to the people who had died. But the French wanted to excavate the ship and everything that went with it. The French Research Institute for Exploitation of the Sea (IFREMER, from the French translation) determined the salvation of the ship was not only possible but worth the $200 million such an undertaking would cost.

The remains of the *Titanic* were salvaged over a fifty-four-day period. The French institute agreed to perform the excavation on the condition

The Making of a Blockbuster

American director James Cameron was certain the public's fascination with the 1912 tragedy of the *Titanic* was still strong enough that they would pay to see a movie about it in 1997. He hired Leonardo DiCaprio (1974–) and Kate Winslet (1975–) to play the main characters.

DiCaprio plays Jack Dawson, a nineteen-year-old orphan who won his passage on the *Titanic* in a poker game. Onboard, he meets the wealthy and beautiful Rose DeWitt Bukater (played by Winslet). Rose is engaged to a man whose fortune was made in steel, but she falls in love with Jack. It would have been a forbidden love even had Rose not been engaged to be married. Jack was a poor man who never knew where he would find his next meal. Women of Rose's class were not supposed to speak to men like Jack, let alone fall in love with them. Jack returns Rose's love. When the ship sinks, he gives his life so that Rose can survive. In typical movie symbolism, the "bad" guy is punished while the "good" guy is rewarded.

The film was scheduled to be released in July 1997. When Cameron announced his epic was not yet finished, the studios panicked. The film had already become the most expensive movie ever made at a reported $200 million. When he finally finished filming, *Titanic* was over three hours long. Hollywood doubted anyone would sit through it.

The movie opened on December 19, 1997. That first weekend saw only $28 million in ticket sales. By New Year's Day, however, the movie had brought in $100 million and was the talk of the nation. For almost four months, the film held the number one spot at the box office. It became the highest grossing film of all time with more than $1.8 billion in ticket sales throughout the world. It continues to hold that record in 2006.

It won eleven Academy Awards in March 1998, including Best Picture of 1997. Cameron won the Best Director award.

The film has been criticized for its historical inaccuracies. Historians claim Jack and Rose would never have had the chance to meet, much less get to know one another. Classes

that the artifacts and ship never be sold at private auction but instead be put on display for the public. Many artifacts are on display in the Maritime Museum in Southampton, England, the city from which the fateful voyage embarked.

Did you know...

- A first-class ticket for a parlor suite on the *Titanic* cost $4,350. That translates to $50,000 today.
- The *Titanic* took three years to build. That is about how long it took to make the 1997 movie of the same name.

were kept completely segregated (separated) from one another except during church services on Sunday. Other critics contend that the film portrayed the British crew members as unethical while American members were heroic. Still others claim that third-class passengers were not fenced in below decks. However, other accounts report that doors and gates were locked in steerage, prohibiting those passengers from getting to the lifeboats.

Kate Winslet and Leonardo DiCaprio in the 1997 film Titanic. THE KOBAL COLLECTION.

- The *Titanic* was the largest sailing vessel when it took to the sea in April. But that record was broken just five weeks later with the launch of Hamburg-America's *Imperator* in May 1912.
- On its maiden (and only) voyage, the *Titanic* used 14,000 gallons of drinking water each day.
- There was just one black family onboard the *Titanic*. The parents and two daughters were initially to leave England on another boat. But that ship's policy forbid children in the dining room. Not wanting to be separated from their children, the parents exchanged their tickets for second-class passage on the *Titanic*. The father did not survive.

- The last American survivor from the *Titanic* incident, Lillian Gertrud Asplund, died on May 7, 2006. She was ninety-nine years old.

Consider the following...

- Ruth Dodge speaks first of heroism and then mentions that those in the lifeboats did not want to return to the *Titanic* because third-class passengers might be crazed from the cold and fear. What standards did people use to decide a person's value and worth?
- Why do people remain fascinated with the sinking of the *Titanic*?
- Imagine being a third-class passenger in steerage when you realize the ship is sinking. You find a way out but are met by a steward who refuses to let you pass. You cannot speak English. What would you do?

For More Information

BOOKS

Ballard, Robert, and Michael Sweeney. *Return to Titanic: A New Look at the World's Most Famous Lost Ship*. Washington, DC: National Geographic, 2004.

Brewster, Hugh. *882½ Amazing Answers to Your Questions About the Titanic*. New York: Scholastic Paperbacks, 1998.

White, Ellen Emerson. *Voyage on the Great Titanic: The Diary of Margaret Ann Brady, R.M.S. Titanic, 1912*. New York: Scholastic, 1998.

WEB SITES

"Dr. Dodge's Wife Tells Story of Titanic Wreck." *The Virtual Museum of the City of San Francisco*. http://www.sfmuseum.org/hist5/dodge3.html (accessed on August 16, 2006).

"The Grave of the Titanic." *Gulf of Maine Research Institute*. http://octopus.gma.org/space1/titanic.html (accessed on August 15, 2006).

The Molly Brown House Museum. http://mollybrown.org/ (accessed on August 15, 2006).

Molly Brown's Resources for Students. http://mollybrown.org/forstudents/index.asp (accessed on August 15, 2006).

"Titanic." *Encyclopaedia Britannica*. http://search.eb.com/titanic/01_01.html (accessed on August 15, 2006).

"Titanic: The Exhibition." *Museum of Science and Industry*. http://www.msichicago.org/scrapbook/scrapbook_exhibits/titanic1/titanic_artifacts.html (accessed on August 15, 2006).

Titanic Historical Society. http://www.titanichistoricalsociety.org (accessed on August 15, 2006).

Where to Learn More

The following list focuses on works written for readers of middle school and high school age. Books aimed at adult readers have been included when they are especially important in providing information or analysis that would otherwise be unavailable.

Books

Aaseng, Nathan. *Plessy v. Ferguson: Separate but Equal.* San Diego: Lucent Books, 2003.

Andrist, Ralph K. *The Long Death: The Last Days of the Plains Indians.* New York: Macmillan, 1964. Reprint, Norman: University of Oklahoma Press, 2001.

Ballard, Robert, and Michael Sweeney. *Return to Titanic: A New Look at the World's Most Famous Lost Ship.* Washington, DC: National Geographic, 2004.

Bartoletti, Susan Campbell. *Kids on Strike!* Boston: Houghton Mifflin, 2003.

Bausum, Ann. *With Courage and Cloth: Winning the Fight for a Woman's Right to Vote.* Washington, DC: National Geographic Children's Books, 2004.

Blaisdell, Bob, ed. *Great Speeches by Native Americans.* Mineola, NY: Dover Publications, 2000.

Bolotin, Norman, and Christine Laing. *The World's Columbian Exposition: The Chicago World's Fair of 1893.* Washington, DC: Preservation Press, 1992. Reprint, Champaign: University of Illinois Press, 2002.

Brewster, Hugh. *882½ Amazing Answers to Your Questions About the Titanic.* New York: Scholastic Paperbacks, 1998.

Butcher, Devereux. *Exploring Our National Parks and Monuments.* 9th ed. Lanham, MD: Roberts Rinehart Publishers, 1995.

Carnegie, Andrew, and David Nasaw. *The Gospel of Wealth and Other Writings.* New York: Penguin Classics, 2006.

Chang, Iris. *The Chinese in America: A Narrative History.* New York: Viking, 2003.

Coffey, Ellen Greenman. *John D. Rockefeller: Richest Man Ever.* San Diego: Blackbirch Press, 2001.

Creelman, James. *On the Great Highway: The Wanderings and Adventures of a Special Correspondent.* Boston: Lothrop, 1901.

Daniels, Roger. *American Immigration: A Student Companion.* New York: Oxford University Press, 2001.

DeAngelis, Gina. *The Triangle Shirtwaist Company Fire of 1911.* New York: Chelsea House Publishers, 2001.

Edge, Laura B. *Andrew Carnegie: Industrial Philanthropist.* Minneapolis: Lerner, 2004.

Fireside, Harvey. *Plessy v. Ferguson: Separate But Equal?* Springfield, NJ: Enslow Publishers, 1997.

Freedman, Russell. *Kids at Work: Lewis Hine and the Crusade Against Child Labor.* New York: Clarion, 1998.

Frost-Knappman, Elizabeth, and Kathryn Cullen-Dupont. *Women's Suffrage in America.* Rev. ed. New York: Facts on File, 2005.

Gibson, Charles Dana. *The Gibson Girl and Her America: The Best Drawings.* New York: Dover Publications, 1969.

Greenwood, Janette Thomas. "The New South." In *The Gilded Age: A History in Documents.* New York: Oxford University Press, 2000.

Harmon, David, McManamon, Francis P., and Dwight T. Pitcaithley, eds. *The Antiquities Act: A Century of American Archaeology, Historic Preservation, and Nature Conservation.* Tucson: University of Arizona Press, 2006.

Hill, Jeff. *Women's Suffrage.* Detroit: Omnigraphics, 2006.

Jensen, Carl. *Stories That Changed America: Muckrakers of the 20th Century.* New York: Seven Stories Press, 2000.

Kraft, Betsy Harvey. *Theodore Roosevelt: Champion of the American Spirit.* New York: Clarion Books, 2003.

Landau, Elaine. *The Triangle Shirtwaist Factory Fire.* New York: Children's Press, 2005.

Leonard, Joseph W. *Anthracite Roots: Generations of Coal Mining in Schuylkill County, Pennsylvania.* Charleston, SC: History Press, 2005.

Lingen, Marissa K. *Chinese Immigration.* Philadelphia: Mason Crest Publishers, 2004.

Marrin, Albert. *Sitting Bull and His World.* New York: Dutton Children's Books, 2000.

Mattson, Kevin. *Upton Sinclair and the Other American Century.* Hoboken, NJ: Wiley, 2006.

McClain, Charles J. *In Search of Equality: The Chinese Struggle Against Discrimination in Nineteenth-Century America.* Berkeley: University of California Press, 1996.

McNeese, Tim. *Plessy v. Ferguson.* New York: Chelsea House, 2006.

Merriam, Eve. *Emma Lazarus Rediscovered.* New York: Biblio Press, 1998.

Miscevic, Dusanka, and Peter Kwong. *Chinese Americans: The Immigrant Experience.* Westport, CT: Hugh Lauter Levin Associates, 2000.

Moore, H. S. *Liberty's Poet: Emma Lazarus.* Austin, TX: TurnKey Press, 2005.

Morrison, Joan, and Charlotte Fox Zabusky. *American Mosaic: The Immigrant Experience in the Words of Those Who Lived It.* New York: Dutton, 1980. Reprint, Pittsburgh: University of Pittsburgh Press, 1993.

Muccigrosso, Robert. *Celebrating the New World: Chicago's Columbian Exposition of 1893*. Chicago: Ivan R. Dee, 1993.

O'Neill, Terry, ed. *The Indian Reservation System*. San Diego: Greenhaven Press, 2002.

Pascal, Janet. *Jacob Riis: Reporter and Reformer*. New York: Oxford University Press, 2005.

Peffer, George Anthony. *If They Don't Bring Their Women Here: Chinese Female Immigration Before Exclusion*. Champaign: University of Illinois Press, 1999.

Rau, Dana Meachen. *Andrew Carnegie: Captain of Industry*. Minneapolis: Compass Point Books, 2006.

Richards, J. Stuart. *Early Coal Mining in the Anthracite Region*. Charleston, SC: Arcadia Publishing, 2002.

Riis, Jacob. *How the Other Half Lives: Studies among the Tenements of New York*. New York: Charles Scribner's Sons, 1890. Multiple reprints.

Riis, Jacob. *The Making of an American*. New York: Macmillan, 1901. Multiple reprints.

Roberts, Peter. *Anthracite Coal Communities: A Study of the Demography, the Social, Educational and Moral Life of the Anthracite Regions*. New York: Macmillan, 1904. Reprint, Westport, CT: Greenwood Press, 1970.

Roop, Connie, and Peter Roop. *Sitting Bull*. New York: Scholastic Paperbacks, 2002.

Roosevelt, Theodore. *Ranch Life and the Hunting-Trail*. New York: The Century Co., 1888. Multiple reprints.

Royster, Jacqueline Jones, ed. *Southern Horrors and Other Writings: The Anti-Lynching Campaign of Ida B. Wells, 1892–1900*. Boston: Bedford Books, 1997.

Sandler, Martin W. *Island of Hope: The Story of Ellis Island and the Journey to America*. New York: Scholastic, 2004.

Schraff, Anne E. *Booker T. Washington: "Character Is Power."* Berkeley Heights, NJ: Enslow Publishers, 2005.

Sears, Roebuck Home Builder's Catalog: The Complete Illustrated 1910 Edition. New York: Dover Publications, 1990.

Segall, Grant. *John D. Rockefeller: Anointed with Oil*. New York: Oxford University Press, 2001.

Sinclair, Upton. *The Jungle*. New York: Doubleday, Page & Co., 1906. Multiple reprints.

Somervill, Barbara A. *Ida Tarbell: Pioneer Investigative Reporter*. Greensboro, NC: M. Reynolds, 2002.

Stein, Leon. *The Triangle Fire*. Philadelphia: Lippincott, 1962. Reprint, Ithaca, NY: Cornell University Press, 2001.

Stevenson, Katherine Cole, and H. Ward Jandl. *Houses by Mail: A Guide to Houses from Sears, Roebuck and Company*. Washington, DC: Preservation Press, 1986. Reprint, 1996.

Tarbell, Ida M. *The History of the Standard Oil Company*. New York: McClure, Phillips & and Co., 1904. Reprint, New York: Harper & Row, 1966. Also available at *Rochester History Resources*. http://www.history.rochester.edu/ fuels/tarbell/MAIN.HTM (accessed on August 14, 2006).

Thornton, Rosemary. *The Houses That Sears Built*. 2nd ed. Alton, IL: Gentle Beam Publications, 2004.

Von Drehle, David. *Triangle: The Fire That Changed America*. New York: Atlantic Monthly Press, 2003.

Weinberg, Arthur, ed., and Lila Shaffer Weinberg, ed. *The Muckrakers*. New York: Simon and Schuster, 1961. Reprint, Champaign: University of Illinois Press, 2001.

Wells, Ida B., et al. *The Reason Why the Colored American Is Not in the World's Columbian Exposition*. Chicago, 1893. Reprint, Urbana: University of Illinois Press, 1999.

White, Ellen Emerson. *Voyage on the Great Titanic: The Diary of Margaret Ann Brady, R.M.S. Titanic, 1912*. New York: Scholastic, 1998.

Williams, William G. *The Coal King's Slaves: A Coal Miner's Story*. Shippensburg, PA: Burd Street Press, 2002.

Yin. *Coolies*. New York: Philomel Books, 2001.

Web sites

"Archeology Program: Antiquities Act 1906–2006." *National Park Service*. http:// www.cr.nps.gov/archeology/sites/antiquities/ (accessed on August 13, 2006).

"Big Apple History: The Triangle Tragedy." *PBSKids.org*. http://pbskids.org/ bigapplehistory/life/topic13.html (accessed on August 15, 2006).

"Booker T. Washington Delivers the 1895 Atlanta Compromise Speech." *History Matters*. http://historymatters.gmu.edu/d/39/ (accessed on August 14, 2006).

Boydston, Jeanne. "Cult of True Womanhood." *PBS: Not for Ourselves Alone*. http://www.pbs.org/stantonanthony/resources/index.html?body=culthood. html (accessed on August 10, 2006).

Carnegie, Andrew. "The Gospel of Wealth." *North American Review*. June 1889. Reprinted at *American Studies at the University of Virginia*. http://xroads. virginia.edu/~DRBR/wealth.html (accessed on July 25, 2006).

"A Charles Dana Gibson 'LIFE Magazine' Gallery." *The Herald Square Hotel*. http://www.heraldsquarehotel.com/CharlesDGibson_cvrs.htm (accessed on August 14, 2006).

Chernow, Rob. "Blessed Barons." *Time.com*. http://www.time.com/time/ time100/builder/other/barons.html (accessed on July 25, 2006).

"Chief Sitting Bull." *The History Channel*. http://www.historychannel.com/ exhibits/sioux/sittingbull.html (accessed on July 17, 2006).

"Chief Sitting Bull." *SittingBull.org*. http://www.sittingbull.org/ (accessed on August 9, 2006).

"Chinese Exclusion Act." *Digital History*. http://www.digitalhistory.uh.edu/ database/article_display.cfm?HHID=419 (accessed on July 14, 2006).

Cornell University, ILR School. *The Triangle Factory Fire.* http://www.ilr.cornell. edu/ trianglefire/ (accessed on August 16, 2006).

Crozier, William, Clarke Chambers, Patrick Costello, Chad Gaffield, and Beverly Stadium, eds. "On the Lower East Side: Observations of Life in Lower Manhattan at the Turn of the Century." *Tenant Net.* http://tenant.net/ Community/LES/contents.html (accessed on August 9, 2006).

Davis, Kay. "Documenting 'The Other Half': The Social Reform Photography of Jacob Riis & Lewis Hine." *University of Virginia.* http://xroads.virginia. edu/~MA01/Davis/photography/reform/reform.html (accessed on August 9, 2006).

"The Dawes Act." *NebraskaStudies.org.* http://www.nebraskastudies.org/0600/ stories/0601_0200.html (accessed on July 20, 2006).

"Dawes Severalty Act." *University of Denver: Sturm College of Law* http://www. law.du.edu/russell/lh/alh/docs/dawesact.html (accessed on August 11, 2006).

"Dr. Dodge's Wife Tells Story of Titanic Wreck." *The Virtual Museum of the City of San Francisco.* http://www.sfmuseum.org/hist5/dodge3.html (accessed on August 16, 2006).

Eckley Miner's Village. http://www.eckleyminers.org/about.html (accessed on August 12, 2006).

"Exhibits." *History Channel: Woman's Suffrage.* http://www.historychannel.com/ exhibits/woman/herstory.html (accessed on August 10, 2006).

"The Gibson Girl: The Ideal Woman of the Early 1900s." *Eyewitness to History.* http://www.eyewitnesstohistory.com/gibson.htm (accessed on August 14, 2006).

Gibson-Girls. http://www.gibson-girls.com/ (accessed on August 14, 2006).

"The Grave of the Titanic." *Gulf of Maine Research Institute.* http://octopus. gma.org/space1/titanic.html (accessed on August 15, 2006).

Harmon, Alexandra. "American Indians and Land Monopolies in the Gilded Age." *The Journal of American History.* http://www.historycooperative.org/ journals/jah/90.1/harmon.html (accessed on July 20, 2006).

Hine, Lewis. "Child Labor in America 1908–1912: Photographs of Lewis W. Hine." *The History Place.* http://www.historyplace.com/unitedstates/ childlabor/ (accessed on August 12, 2006).

"History of Allotment, Part 2." *Indian Land Tenure Foundation.* http://www. indianlandtenure.org/ILTFallotment/introduction/introII.htm (accessed on July 20, 2006).

"History of Sears Modern Homes." *Sears Archives.* http://www.searsarchives. com/homes/history.htm (accessed on August 11, 2006).

"Immigration, the Journey to America: The Chinese." *Thinkquest.org.* http:// library.thinkquest.org/20619/Chinese.html (accessed on July 14, 2006).

Junod, Suzanne White. "In Roosevelt's Name We Bust Trusts: The Meat Inspection Act of 1906." *U.S. Food and Drug Administration.* http://www. fda.gov/oc/history/2006centennial/meatinspection.html (accessed on August 15, 2006).

Lauver, Fred. "A Walk Through the Rise and Fall of Anthracite Might." *Pennsylvania Historical and Museum Commission.* http://www.phmc.state. pa.us/ppet/miningmuseum/page1.asp?secid=31 (accessed on August 12, 2006).

Leung, Alison. "Photos from the Triangle Factory Fire." *University of Sydney.* http://teaching.arts.usyd.edu.au/history/hsty3080/3rdYr3080/trianglewebsite/ index.html (accessed on August 15, 2006).

Library of Congress. "Address of Frances E. Willard, President of the Woman's National Council of the United States . . . at its First Triennial Meeting, Albaugh's Opera House, Washington, D.C., February 22–25, 1891." *American Memory: Votes for Women.* http://lcweb2.loc.gov/cgi-bin/query/ r?ammem/naw:@field(DOCID+@lit(rbnawsan4556div3)): (accessed on August 10, 2006).

Library of Congress. "The Evolution of the Conservation Movement, 1850–1920." *American Memory.* http://memory.loc.gov/ammem/amrvhtml/conshome. html (accessed on August 13, 2006).

Library of Congress. "Immigration: Native Americans." *American Memory.* http://memory.loc.gov/learn/features/immig/native_american.html (accessed on July 20, 2006).

Library of Congress. "Mark Twain's Observations About Chinese Immigrants in California." *American Memory: Rise of Industrial America, 1876–1900: Chinese Immigration to the United States, 1851–1900.* http://memory.loc.gov/learn/ features/timeline/riseind/chinimms/twain.html (accessed on July 14, 2006).

Library of Congress. "Votes for Women." *American Memory.* http://memory.loc. gov/ammem/naw/ (accessed on August 10, 2006).

Library of Congress. "Women's Suffrage in the Progressive Era." *American Memory.* http://memory.loc.gov/learn/features/timeline/progress/suffrage/ suffrage.html (accessed on August 10, 2006).

"The Light of Liberty." *National Geographic Kids.* http://www.nationalgeographic. com/ngkids/9907/liberty/liberty.html (accessed on July 18, 2006).

Linder, Douglas. "The Triangle Shirtwaist Fire Trial, 1911." *University of Missouri-Kansas City School of Law.* http://www.law.umkc.edu/faculty/projects/ ftrials/triangle/trianglefire.html (accessed on August 15, 2006).

"Links." *The Wisconsin Mosaic: People's Voices—Frances Willard.* http://www.scils. rutgers.edu/~dalbello/FLVA/voices/839/voices/willard/links.html (accessed on August 10, 2006).

Lower East Side Tenement Museum. http://www.tenement.org/ (accessed on August 9, 2006).

Lum, Lydia. "Angel Island: Journeys Remembered by Chinese Houstonians." *HoustonChronicle.com.* http://www.chron.com/content/chronicle/special/ angelisland/intro.html (accessed on July 14, 2006).

"Lynching." *Spartacus.* http://www.spartacus.schoolnet.co.uk/USAlynching.htm (accessed on August 11, 2006).

Markham, Edward, Benjamin B. Lindsey, and George Creel. "The Campaign to End Child Labor: Children in Bondage." *BoondocksNet.com.* http://www. boondocksnet.com/editions/cib/(accessed on August 12, 2006).

Martin, Faith. "Frances Willard: America's Forgotten Feminist." *Spring Valley Press.* http://www.geocities.com/~svpress/articles/fwillard.html (accessed on August 10, 2006).

Maxwell, Shirley, and James C. Massey. "The Story on Sears: Houses by Rail and Mail." *Old House Journal Online.* http://www.oldhousejournal.com/magazine/2002/july/sears.shtml (accessed on August 11, 2006).

The Molly Brown House Museum. http://mollybrown.org/ (accessed on August 15, 2006).

Molly Brown's Resources for Students. http://mollybrown.org/forstudents/index.asp (accessed on August 15, 2006).

"A National Monument, Memorial, Park...What's the Difference?" *National Atlas.* http://www.nationalatlas.gov/articles/government/a_nationalparks.html (accessed on August 13, 2006).

"Native Americans: Indian Wars Time Table." *U-S-History.com.* http://www.u-s-history.com/pages/h1008.html (accessed on July 17, 2006).

Newman, Pauline, and Joan Morrison. "Working for the Triangle Shirtwaist Company." *History Matters.* http://historymatters.gmu.edu/d/178/ (accessed on August 15, 2006).

Ohio State University, Department of History. "The Boys in the Breakers." *eHistory.com.* http://ehistory.osu.edu/osu/mmh/gildedage/content/breakerboys.cfm (accessed on August 13, 2006).

PBS. "Philip Danforth Armour (1833–1901). *American Experience: Chicago, City of the Century.* http://www.pbs.org/wgbh/amex/chicago/peopleevents/p_armour.html (accessed on August 15, 2006).

PBS. "The Richest Man in the World: Andrew Carnegie." *American Experience.* http://www.pbs.org/wgbh/amex/carnegie/index.html (accessed on July 25, 2006).

PBS. "Sitting Bull." *New Perspectives on the West.* http://www.pbs.org/weta/thewest/people/s_z/sittingbull.htm (accessed on July 17, 2006).

PBS. "Theodore Roosevelt." *New Perspectives on the West.* http://www.pbs.org/weta/thewest/people/i_r/roosevelt.htm (accessed on July 25, 2006).

PBS. "Transcontinental Railroad: Native Americans." *American Experience.* http://www.pbs.org/wgbh/amex/tcrr/sfeature/sf_interview.html#c (accessed on July 17, 2006).

"A Perfect Fit: The Garment Industry and American Jewry, 1860–1960." *Yeshiva University Museum.* http://www.yumuseum.org/APerfectFit/highlights.html (accessed on August 15, 2006).

"Plessy v. Ferguson." *Landmark Supreme Court Cases.* http://www.landmarkcases.org/plessy/home.html (accessed on August 14, 2006).

"Progress Made Visible: World's Columbian Exposition, Chicago, 1893." *University of Delaware Library.* http://www.lib.udel.edu/ud/spec/exhibits/fairs/colum.htm (accessed on August 11, 2006).

"Ranch Life and the Hunting-Trail." *Bartleby.com.* http://www.bartleby.com/54/ (accessed on July 20, 2006).

Riis, Jacob A. "How the Other Half Lives." *Yale University: American Studies Program.* http://www.yale.edu/amstud/inforev/riis/title.html (accessed on August 15, 2006).

"Standard Oil Trust." *U-S-History.com.* http://www.u-s-history.com/pages/h1804.html (accessed on August 14, 2006).

The Statue of Liberty–Ellis Island Foundation, Inc. http://www.ellisisland.org/ (accessed on July 18, 2006).

"Swift and Company." *The Handbook of Texas Online.* http://www.tsha.utexas.edu/handbook/online/articles/SS/dis2.html (accessed on August 15, 2006).

Tarbell, Ida M. "John D. Rockefeller: A Character Study." *Allegheny College.* http://tarbell.allegheny.edu/archives/jdr.html (accessed on August 14, 2006).

Thornton, Rosemary. "Mail-Order Houses." *Christian Science Monitor.* http://www.csmonitor.com/2002/0612/p11s02-lihc.html (accessed on August 11, 2006).

Thornton, Rosemary. "Windows on the Past." *The Old House Web.* http://www.oldhouseweb.com/stories/Detailed/10102.shtml (accessed on August 11, 2006).

"Titanic: The Exhibition." *Museum of Science and Industry.* http://www.msichicago.org/scrapbook/scrapbook_exhibits/titanic1/titanic_artifacts.html (accessed on August 15, 2006).

Titanic Historical Society. http://www.titanichistoricalsociety.org (accessed on August 15, 2006).

"Transcript of Chinese Exclusion Act (1882)." *OurDocuments.gov.* http://www.ourdocuments.gov/doc.php?doc=47=transcript (accessed on July 14, 2006).

"U.S. National Monuments." *GORP.* http://gorp.away.com/gorp/resource/us_nm/main.htm (accessed on August 13, 2006).

Van Kleeck, Mary. "The Campaign to End Child Labor: Child Labor in New York City Tenements." *BoondocksNet.com.* http://www.boondocksnet.com/labor/cl_080118_tenements.html (accessed on August 12, 2006).

"What Is a Sears Modern Home?" *Sears Archives.* http://www.searsarchives.com/homes/ (accessed on August 11, 2006).

"Whatever Happened to Standard Oil?" *U.S. Highways: From US 1 to (US 830).* http://www.us-highways.com/sohist.htm (accessed on August 14, 2006).

"Women of Valor: Emma Lazarus." *Jewish Women's Archive.* http://www.jwa.org/exhibits/wov/lazarus/el1.html (accessed on July 18, 2006).

World's Columbian Exposition: A Vision of the Future, A Reflection of Its Present. http://mason.gmu.edu/~ssaltzgi/Worlds_Fair/world_fair_essay.htm (accessed on August 11, 2006).

"The World's Columbian Exposition: Idea, Experience, Aftermath." *American Studies at the University of Virginia.* http://xroads.virginia.edu/~ma96/WCE/title.html (accessed on August 11, 2006).

Wormser, Richard. "Jim Crow Stories: The Fourteenth Amendment Ratified." *PBS: The Rise and Fall of Jim Crow.* http://www.pbs.org/wnet/jimcrow/stories_events_14th.html (accessed on August 14, 2006).

Wormser, Richard. "Jim Crow Stories: Plessy v. Ferguson." *PBS: The Rise and Fall of Jim Crow.* http://www.pbs.org/wnet/jimcrow/stories_events_plessy.html (accessed on August 14, 2006).

Index

Illustrations are marked by (ill.)

N

O

P